The Daily Telegraph
ATLAS OF THE
WORLD TODAY

Published by The Daily Telegraph
135 Fleet Street, London EC4P 4BL
First Published 1987

© Ilex Publishers Limited 1987

Paperback ISBN 0-86367-107-1

Conditions of Sale:
This book is sold subject to the conditions that it shall not,
by way of trade or otherwise, be lent, re-sold, hired out or
otherwise circulated without the copyright holder's prior
consent in any form of binding or cover other than that in which it is published.

Atlas of the World Today
Created and Produced by Ilex Publishers Limited
29/31 George Street, Oxford OX1 2AJ

Designed by Designers & Partners Limited, Oxford, UK

Additional research by Jenny Saville

Colour separations by Trilogy, Italy

Maps by Engineering Surveys Reproduction Limited, UK

Printed in Italy

Typeset by Dentset, Oxford, UK

The Daily Telegraph
ATLAS OF THE
WORLD TODAY

by Neil Grant
and Nick Middleton

The Daily Telegraph

CONTENTS

Introduction	7
Nations of the World	8
Shape of the Land	12
World Vegetation	16
World Climate	
Climate Zones	20
Mean Temperatures and Wind Patterns — January	22
Mean Temperatures and Wind Patterns — July	24
Rainfall	26
Environment	30
Population Density	34
World Population Growth	38
Gross National Product	42
GNP Growth Rate	46
Religions of the World	50
Languages of the World	54
World Food Production	58
World Grain Trade	62
World Food Consumption	66
World Health	70
World Disease	74

Foreign Aid	78
Mineral Wealth	82
World Tourism	86
World Energy Production	90
World Energy Consumption	94
World Manufacturing	98
International Trade	102
Foreign Investment	106
Exchange Rates	110
World Road and Rail Transport	114
World Air and Sea Transport	118
World Communications	122
Literacy and Learning	126
World Development	130
Governments in Power	134
Alliances and Associations	138
Nations in Turmoil	142
Military Expenditure	146
Military Might	150
Sources	154
Index	157

INTRODUCTION

Popular interest in worldwide current affairs is not new, but has been dramatically intensified in the last decade. Now that international travel is commonplace and communications networks can link continents in seconds, public concern can focus as easily and as swiftly on a starving Ethiopian child as on a Moscow summit.

In spite of huge advances in science and technology, threats to national and worldwide security now loom larger and more tangible than ever. We may have wiped out the smallpox virus and be making strides towards an effective cure for cancer, but at the same time we are developing weapons capable of decimating the human race at one stroke.

At least as a result of the phenomenal technological advances, a greater proportion of the population than ever can now be made aware of current affairs worldwide. There is the opportunity for more people to understand in greater depth the political and social framework on which modern society is built.

Research on an international scale has developed to the extent that commerce and industry can plan detailed sales strategies across continents: sometimes supply appears almost to anticipate demand.

Thanks to the United Nations and other international organizations, a vast array of international statistics on practically every conceivable subject is now available to anyone who wants to know. At the touch of a button we can study the gross export earnings of Japan, or ponder the average six-year-old's daily sweet intake.

Of course, statistics are only as reliable as the statisticians who compile them. As all governments — to a greater or lesser extent — present information in its most favourable light, statistics compiled by government officials can sometimes be subject to cosmetic treatment before they are published. Some countries will also have less information available on their internal affairs than others — this may not only be because they have a policy of discretion in certain areas, but also they often lack the physical resources to collect and interpret data meaningfully.

Thus the energy crisis in the industrial world can be accurately measured in terms of stocks of fossil fuels, but the no less serious fuel crisis in large parts of the Third World — the shortage of firewood — can be only roughly estimated.

The world picture as it appears in this book is a broad one. This is a small canvas for such a large subject. But it should help put into focus the state of human society and its physical environment in the 1980s, highlighting those aspects which are of special concern to us today.

NATIONS OF THE WORLD

NATIONS OF THE WORLD

On 10th January, 1946, 51 countries attended the first meeting of the General Assembly of the United Nations. Subsequently, the number of member states has steadily risen incorporating former possessions of European colonial powers that have gained independence, as the map indicates. In 1985, 159 countries were members of the UN General Assembly.

The map shows most countries and certain non-sovereign territories; some independent islands are too small to be depicted. The 59 non-sovereign territories of the world are shown in ALLIANCES AND ASSOCIATIONS. Countries are listed below in alphabetical order with their population (1985 estimates) and land area. Familiar or abbreviated names of certain countries have been used in preference to the sometimes lengthy official ones, for example "China" rather than "The People's Republic of China".

COUNTRY	CAPITAL	POPULATION (millions)	AREA (thousands of square miles)
Afghanistan	Kabul	16.5	250
Albania	Tirane	3.1	11
Algeria	Algiers	21.7	920
Angola	Luanda	8.8	481
Argentina	Buenos Aires	30.6	1,068
Australia	Canberra	15.7	2,968
Austria	Vienna	7.5	32
Bangladesh	Dacca	101.2	56
Belgium	Brussels	9.9	12
Belize	Belmopan	0.2	9
Benin	Porto Novo	4.1	43
Bhutan	Thimphu	1.4	18
Bolivia	Sucre	6.4	424
Botswana	Gaborone	1.1	232
Brazil	Brasilia	135.6	3,286
Brunei	Bandar Seri Begawan	2.4	2
Bulgaria	Sofia	9.1	43
Burkina Faso	Ouagadougou	6.9	106
Burma	Rangoon	37.2	262
Burundi	Bujumbura	4.7	11
Cameroon	Yaoundé	9.9	184
Canada	Ottawa	25.4	3,852
Central African Rep	Bangui	2.6	241
Chad	N'djamena	5.0	496
Chile	Santiago	12.0	292
China	Beijing	1,059.5	3,705
Colombia	Bogotá	28.7	440
Congo	Brazzaville	1.7	132
Costa Rica	San José	2.6	20
Cuba	Havana	10.0	44
Cyprus	Nicosia	0.7	4
Czechoslovakia	Prague	15.7	49
Denmark	Copenhagen	5.1	17
Djibouti	Djibouti	0.4	8
Dominican Rep.	Santo Domingo	6.2	19
Ecuador	Quito	9.4	109
Egypt	Cairo	47.0	387
Eire	Dublin	3.6	27
El Salvador	San Salvador	5.6	8
Equatorial Guinea	Malabo	0.4	11
Ethiopia	Addis Ababa	44.6	472
Fiji	Suva	0.7	7
Finland	Helsinki	4.9	130
France	Paris	54.6	211
Gabon	Libreville	1.2	103
Gambia	Banjul	0.6	4
Germany, East	East Berlin	16.8	42
Germany, West	Bonn	60.9	96

*Greenland is an overseas territory of Denmark
New Caledonia is an overseas territory of France

COUNTRY	CAPITAL	POPULATION (millions)	AREA (thousands of square miles)	COUNTRY	CAPITAL	POPULATION (millions)	AREA (thousands of square miles)
Ghana	Accra	13.6	92	Nigeria	Lagos	95.2	357
Greece	Athens	9.9	51	Norway	Oslo	4.1	125
Greenland	Godthaab	0.1	840	Oman	Muscat	1.2	82
Guatemala	Guatemala City	8.0	42	Pakistan	Islamabad	100.4	310
Guinea	Conakry	6.1	95	Panama	Panama City	2.2	29
Guinea-Bissau	Bissau	0.9	14	Papua New Guinea	Port Moresby	3.5	178
Guyana	Georgetown	1.0	83	Paraguay	Asunción	3.7	157
Haiti	Port-au-Prince	6.6	11	Peru	Lima	19.7	496
Honduras	Tegucigalpa	4.4	43	Philippines	Manila	54.5	116
Hungary	Budapest	10.7	36	Poland	Warsaw	37.2	121
Iceland	Reykjavik	0.3	40	Portugal	Lisbon	10.1	36
India	New Delhi	758.9	1,267	Qatar	Doha	0.3	4
Indonesia	Jakarta	167.0	735	Romania	Bucharest	23.0	92
Iran	Tehran	44.6	636	Rwanda	Kigali	6.1	10
Iraq	Baghdad	15.9	168	Saudi Arabia	Riyadh	11.5	830
Israel	Jerusalem	4.3	8	Senegal	Dakar	6.4	76
Italy	Rome	57.3	116	Sierra Leone	Freetown	3.6	28
Ivory Coast	Abidjan	9.8	125	South Africa	Pretoria	32.4	471
Jamaica	Kingston	2.3	4	Soviet Union	Moscow	275.1	8,649
Japan	Tokyo	120.7	144	Spain	Madrid	38.5	195
Jordan	Amman	3.5	38	Sri Lanka	Colombo	16.2	25
Kampuchea	Phnom Pehn	7.3	70	Sudan	Khartoum	21.5	967
Kenya	Nairobi	20.6	225	Surinam	Paramaribo	0.4	63
Korea, North	Pyongyang	20.4	47	Swaziland	Mbabane	0.7	7
Korea, South	Seoul	41.3	38	Sweden	Stockholm	8.4	174
Kuwait	Kuwait	1.8	7	Switzerland	Bern	6.4	16
Laos	Vientiane	4.1	91	Syria	Damascus	10.5	71
Lebanon	Beirut	2.7	4	Taiwan	Taipei	18.5	12
Lesotho	Maseru	1.5	12	Tanzania	Dar es Salaam	22.5	365
Liberia	Monrovia	2.2	43	Thailand	Bangkok	51.4	198
Libya	Tripoli	3.6	679	Togo	Lome	3.0	22
Luxembourg	Luxembourg	0.4	1	Tunisia	Tunis	7.1	63
Madagascar	Tananarive	10.0	227	Turkey	Ankara	49.3	301
Malawi	Lilongwe	6.9	46	Uganda	Kampala	15.5	91
Malaysia	Kuala Lumpur	15.6	127	United Arab Emirates	Abu Dhabi	1.3	32
Mali	Bamako	8.0	479	United Kingdom	London	56.1	94
Mauritania	Nouakchott	1.9	398	United States	Washington DC	238.0	3,615
Mexico	Mexico City	79.0	762	Uruguay	Montevideo	3.0	68
Mongolia	Ulan Bator	1.9	604	Venezuela	Caracas	17.3	352
Morocco	Rabat	22.0	172	Vietnam	Hanoi	59.7	128
Mozambique	Maputo	14.0	309	Yemen, South	Aden	2.1	129
Namibia	Windhoek	1.5	318	Yemen Arab Rep. (N)	Sana	6.8	75
Nepal	Katmandu	16.5	54	Yugoslavia	Belgrade	23.1	99
Netherlands	Amsterdam	14.4	16	Zaire	Kinshasa	30.0	906
New Caledonia	Nouméa	1.5	9	Zambia	Lusaka	6.7	291
New Zealand	Wellington	3.3	104	Zimbabwe	Harare	8.4	151
Nicaragua	Managua	3.3	50				
Niger	Niamey	6.1	489				

SHAPE OF THE LAND

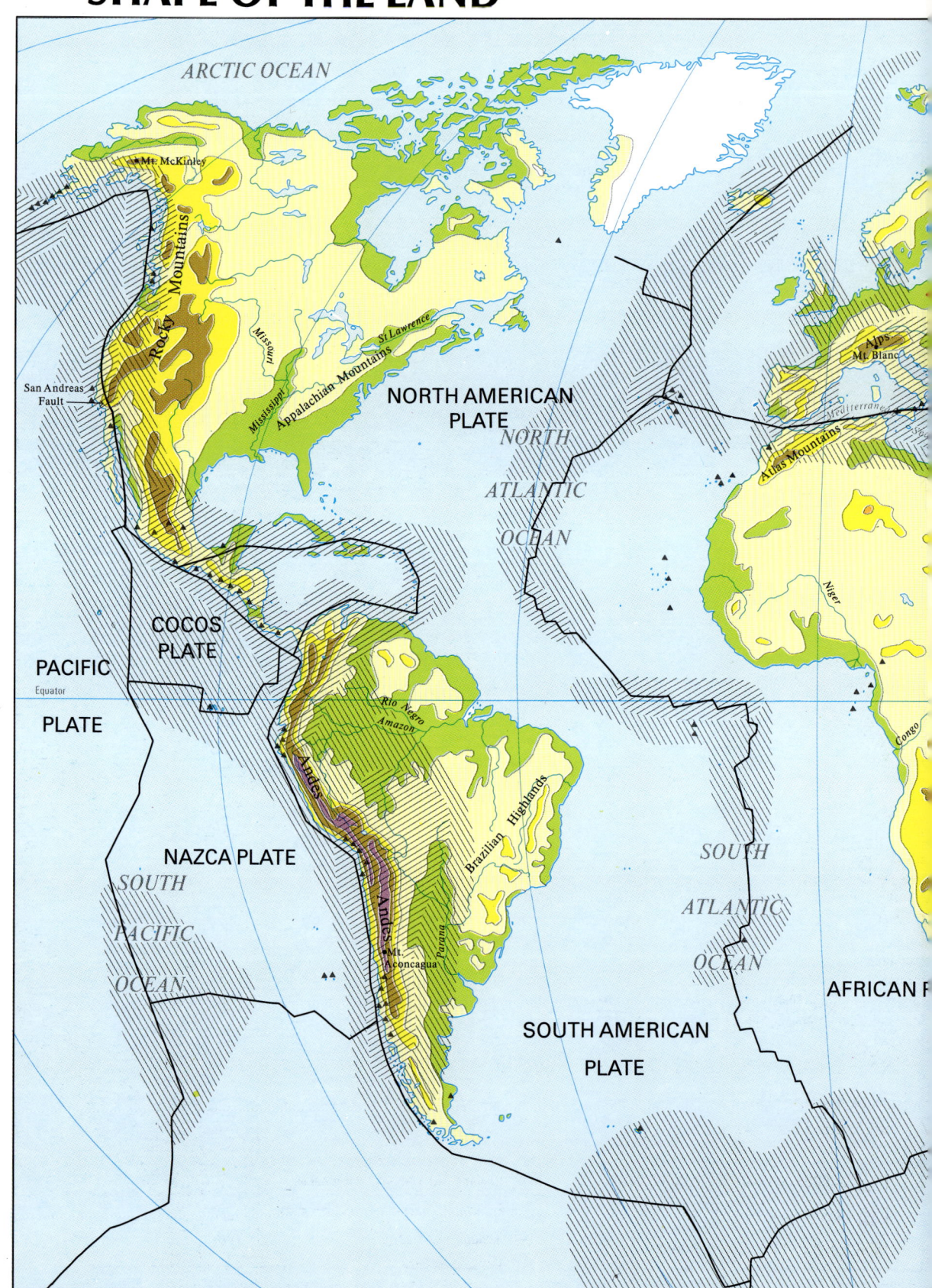

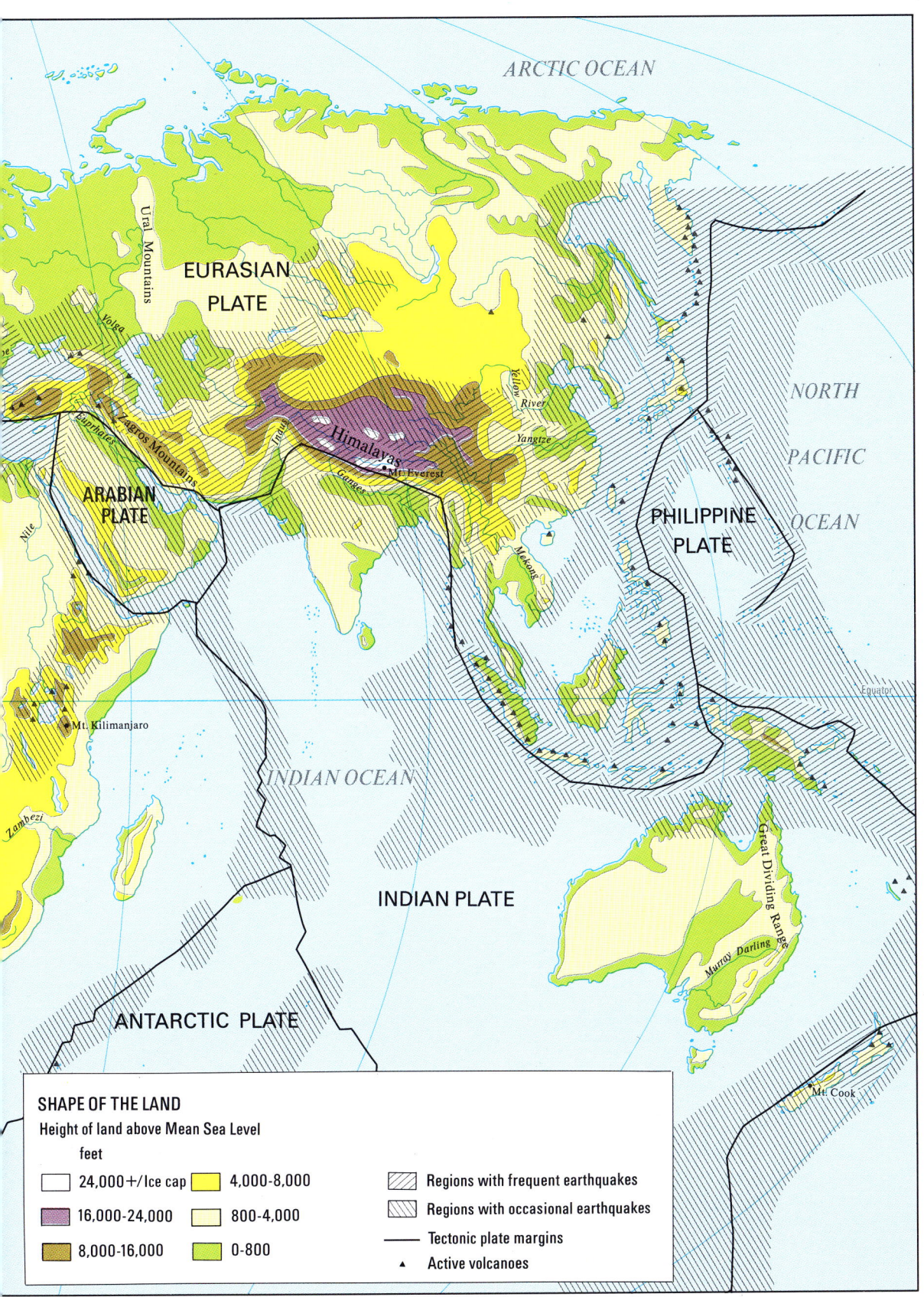

SHAPE OF THE LAND

Seen from space the Earth looks like a vast jigsaw puzzle in which the pieces have become separated. The western bulge of Africa, for instance, fits neatly into the recess of the Caribbean, and it takes no great effort of imagination to see how the continents were once a single, huge, integrated landmass which, over the geological ages, split up and drifted slowly apart. The theory of continental drift was first put forward as long ago as 1858, but not until very recent times was it widely accepted, largely as a result of new understanding of the nature of the Earth's crust — the thin, solid layer overlying the partly molten rocks of the mantle.

We now know that the crust is based on eight vast regions (plus some smaller ones) known as "plates", which shift in relation to each other. Movement of these plates can be used to explain not only continental drift but also major physical features of the Earth's crust such as mountain ranges and oceanic trenches. Typically, a trench is created when one plate moves underneath another, and arcs of islands such as Japan or Indonesia are probably the results of such movements. Island arcs are invariably areas of high seismic activity (earthquakes and volcanoes), and Japan and Indonesia lie on the "ring of fire" which roughly surrounds the Pacific Ocean and marks the borders of the plate underneath that ocean.

The San Andreas fault which caused the San Francisco earthquake in 1906 (and will one day cause another) marks a line where two plates meet and move at an angle to each other. The existence of the fault can be easily seen from the air, marked by the abrupt termination of features such as ridges and gulleys.

Far beneath our feet, far, that is, in relation to a mine shaft, not so far in relation to the Earth's diameter, things are in terrible turmoil at

Pangaea
The Earth's protocontinent, as it was about two million years ago.

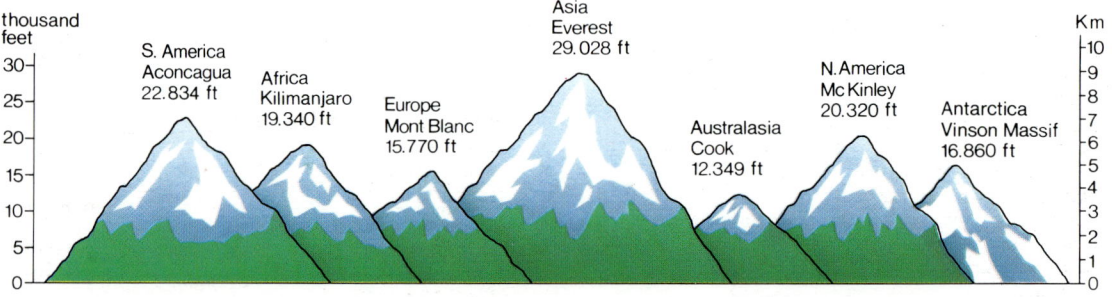

temperatures so high that rock flows like honey. Immense pressures build up which cause folds in the Earth's crust manifest as mountain ranges. Fortunately, most of these geological changes occur very slowly, over millions of years. Occasionally, however, we are made aware of vast, ungovernable forces below by volcanoes and earthquakes. (They actually occur at the rate of dozens a day, but most are insignificant.)

A volcano is a hole from which molten rock, or lava, ash and gas are violently ejected, and in this way mountains may be formed very quickly. Earthquakes have similar origins in the internal frictions of the

Highest mountains of each continent
The greatest mountain range in the world is largely invisible. It runs under the oceans from roughly the Red Sea to the coast of California, passing south of Australia. The average height above the ocean floor is about 8,000 feet.

Discounting such submarine intrusions, the highest mountain in the world is Mount Everest in the Himalayas, the greatest mountain range, which contains about 90 of the world's 100 highest peaks.

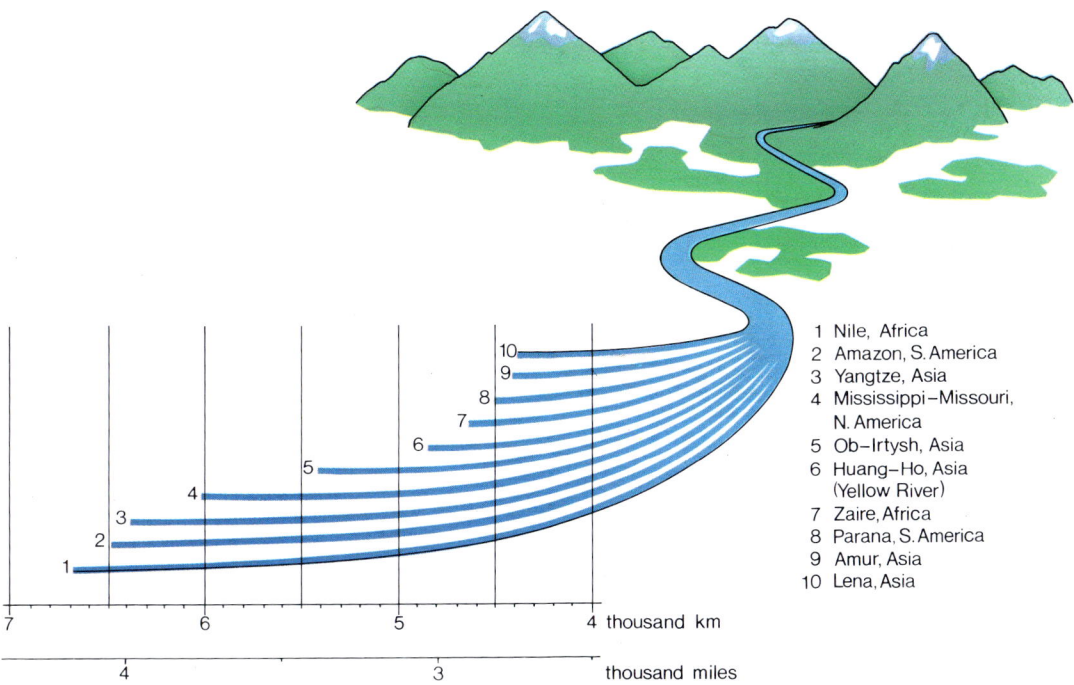

1 Nile, Africa
2 Amazon, S. America
3 Yangtze, Asia
4 Mississippi–Missouri, N. America
5 Ob–Irtysh, Asia
6 Huang–Ho, Asia (Yellow River)
7 Zaire, Africa
8 Parana, S. America
9 Amur, Asia
10 Lena, Asia

World's longest rivers

The question "How long is a river?" is often as hard to answer as "How long is a piece of string?". It may be virtually impossible to locate the precise, original source, or to define a legitimate tributary. Moreover, rivers constantly change their course (or have it changed for them). The Nile is probably shorter than the latest official figure because loops, or meanders, are constantly being cut off. The Amazon, much the largest river in terms of volume of water, can be regarded as also longer than the Nile if, when nearing the mouth, you choose to turn south around the Ilha de Marajo. However, you then emerge from the estuary of the River Para, a tributary of the Tocantins, not the Amazon, so this is generally regarded as cheating.

crust, and often occur in the same regions as volcanoes. The worst volcanoes and earthquakes are associated with areas near the edges of the plates that make up the crust, though not all. Hawaii, thousands of miles from the edge of the Pacific plate, is located on a weak point in the crust, a "hot spot", and thus often suffers volcanic eruptions.

World's worst natural disasters

Disaster	Location and date	Deaths
Circular Storm	Ganges Delta Islands, Bangladesh. November 1970	1,000,000
Flood	Huang-Ho, China October 1887	900,000
Earthquake	Shensi Province, China. January 1556	830,000
Landslide	Kansu Province, China December 1920	180,000
Volcanic Eruption	Tambora Sumbawa, Indonesia. April 1815	92,000
Avalanches	Yungay, Huascarán, Peru May 1970	18,000

WORLD VEGETATION

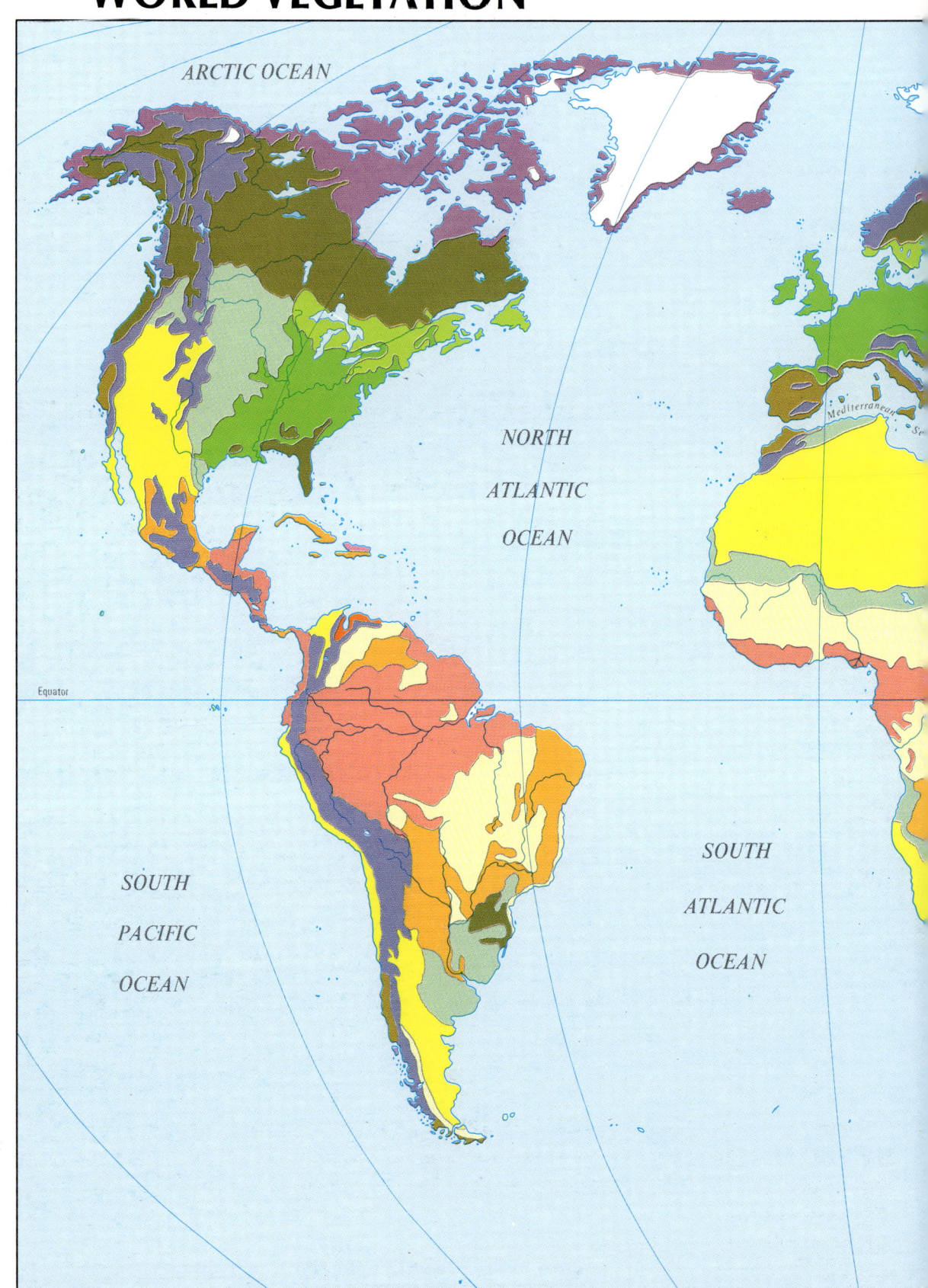

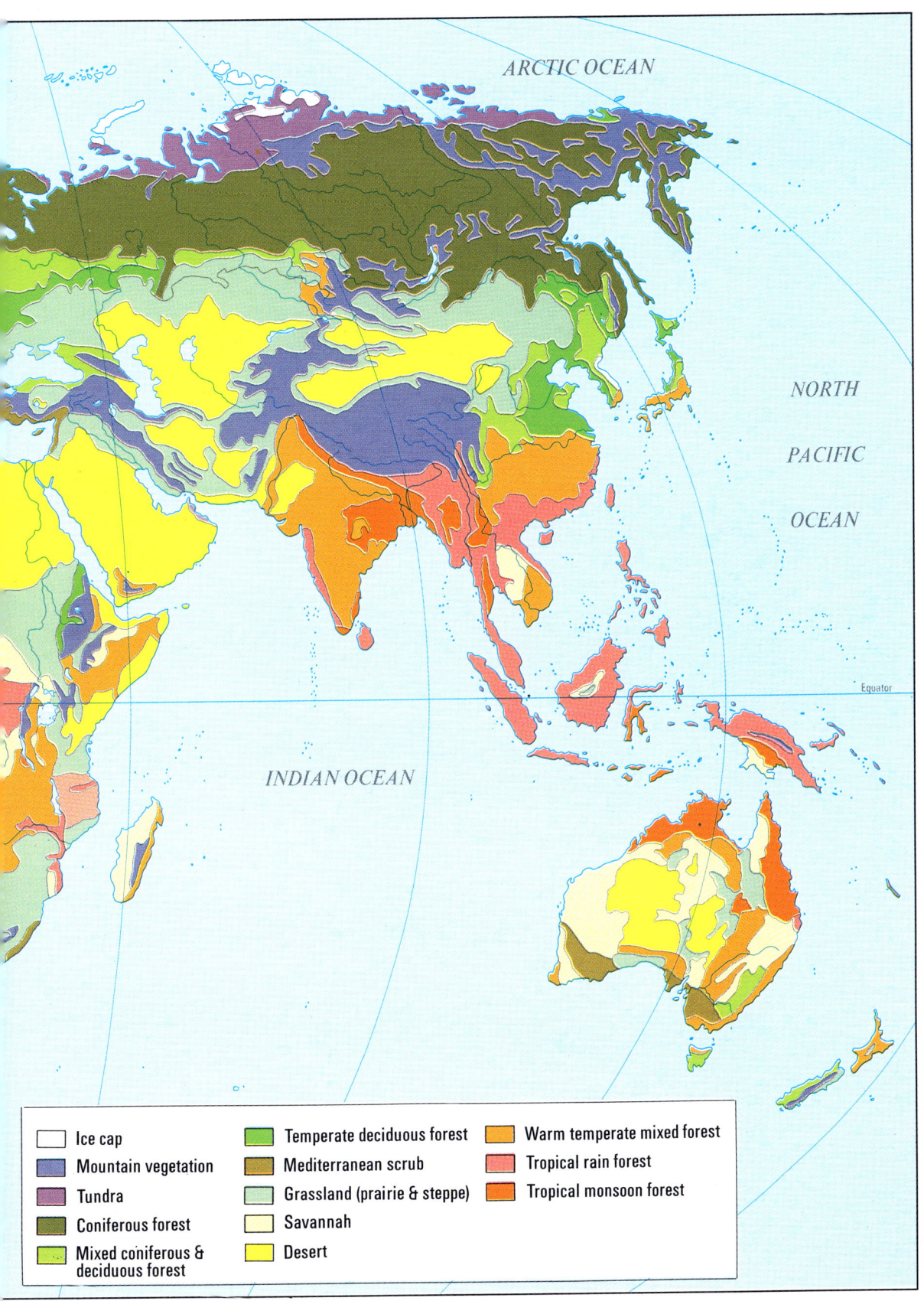

WORLD VEGETATION

Except for regions near the poles which are permanently covered by ice, virtually the whole of the land surface of the Earth bears some kind of plant life, of which there are nearly half a million different species. However, there is considerable variation between different environments. Less than one quarter of the total area, for instance, is estimated to be capable of being cultivated and even that is more than double the proportion cultivated at present.

Beginning at the top, the first of the Earth's main zones of vegetation is tundra, or "cold desert", which merges into the northern coniferous forest belt. These two regions are found only in the northern hemisphere. South of the chilly pines are temperate forests and grasslands, including the prairies and the steppes. Approaching the tropics, the situation grows more complex. Rainfall and altitude are the dominant influences in areas of savannah, woodland, chapparal (dense, low, shrubby vegetation) and desert. Tropical forests can be roughly divided into two: seasonal or monsoon forests, predominantly deciduous, and tropical evergreen forest, which is generally found close to the equator.

Much the richest of these zones, both in the variety of species and in the total bulk of plant growth, are the tropical evergreen forests. Costa Rica has about 8,000 plant species; Britain, five times larger, has 1,400. Although they cover only about 9 per cent of the land surface, the rain forests contain about 35 per cent of the Earth's plant material. By contrast, deserts and tundra cover more than one quarter of the surface but contain only about 2 per cent of the total plant material. Plant productivity decreases more or less steadily from the equator to the poles, with variations caused by altitude and other factors.

Vegetation at risk
The environmental impact of an expanding human population is perhaps most notable on vegetation. The building of cities, roads and other constructions involves the complete removal of vegetation from sites. Commercial exploitation is rapidly depleting the World's tropical rain forests. Acid rain is a large scale problem in Western Europe and North America, the most heavily industrialized regions on Earth (see ENVIRONMENT*), but locally the same hazards are being experienced in other areas. Desertification is the result of drought and overuse of the land by expanding populations in semi arid regions.*

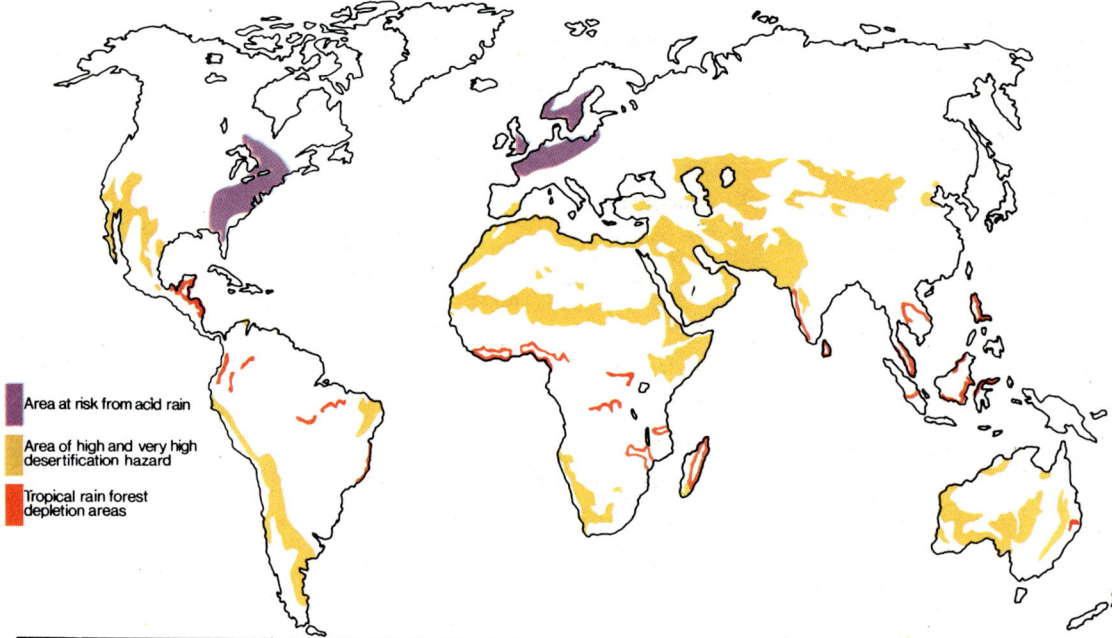

Area at risk from acid rain

Area of high and very high desertification hazard

Tropical rain forest depletion areas

It is worrying that at present tropical forests, by almost any standard the most valuable regions, are dwindling fast, while deserts, the least valuable, are in places increasing.

The dreadful misery suffered by peoples living to the south of the Sahara desert in recent years is the result of drought, over-grazing and over-cultivation. However, the slow but apparently inexorable southward extension of the desert was first detected before a succession of dry years brought on the crisis of the 1970s and 1980s, and it is very difficult to assess the relative importance of low rainfall and poor land management in the deterioration of the area.

In contrast, the decline of the rain forests is due entirely to the activities of people — not those who have lived within them for thousands of years in perfect ecological balance but those who have encroached more recently, bringing their chain-saws and bulldozers. Everyone by now must be aware of the immense damage that will result — and in many places already has resulted — from destroying the rain forests, and all governments make at least token efforts to preserve them, or bits of them. Yet in the current year the Earth's rain forests will shrink by an area about the size of England and Wales. Deserts can be regenerated by irrigation, but once a substantial area of rain forest is destroyed, it can never recover. A forest might grow there again, given the chance, but it would not be the same forest.

This is the latest chapter in a long period of forest decline worldwide. Much of Europe was once forested and it was Europe's need to import wood that initiated the destruction of tropical forests. Today the few remnants of Western Europe's forest are menaced by acid rain, the result of industrial discharge.

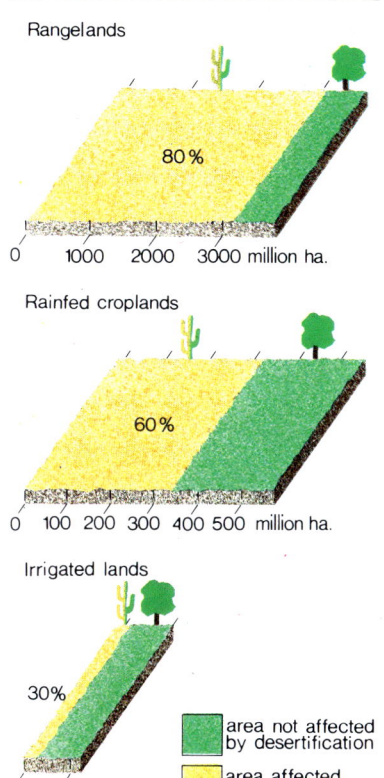

Global extent of desertified land by land-use categories, 1984

According to the United Nations Environment Programme (UNEP) desertification threatens 35 per cent of the Earth's land surface and 19 per cent of its population. The areas shown on the map are those most severely at risk.

Tropical rain forest depletion rates

Country	Area of forest reported to be lost per year (million hectares)
Bangladesh	0.01
Colombia	0.25
Costa Rica	0.06
Ghana	0.05
Ivory Coast	0.40
Laos	0.30
Malaysia	0.15
Papua New Guinea	0.02
Philippines	0.26
Thailand	0.30

WORLD CLIMATE : CLIMATE ZONES

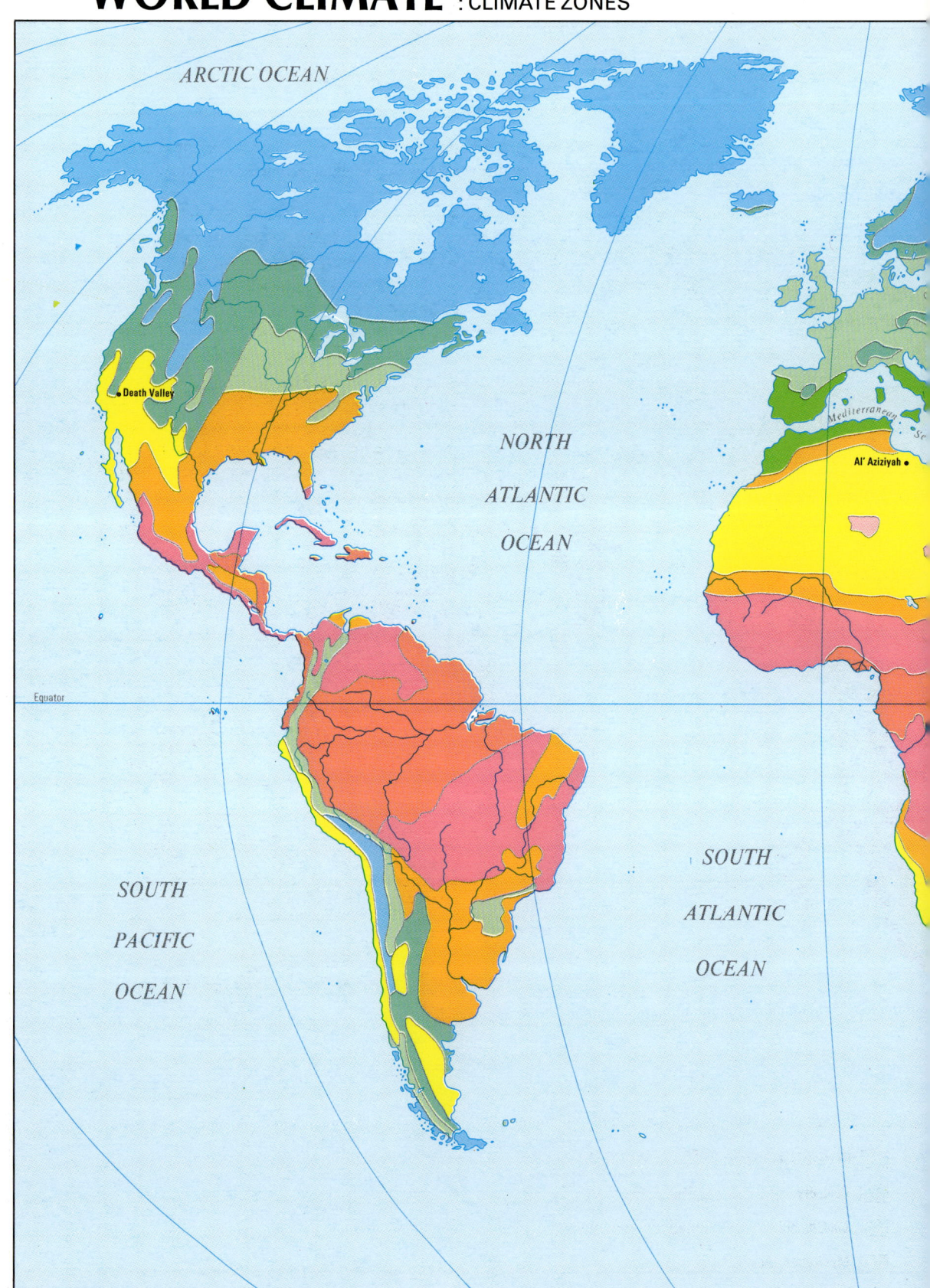

20

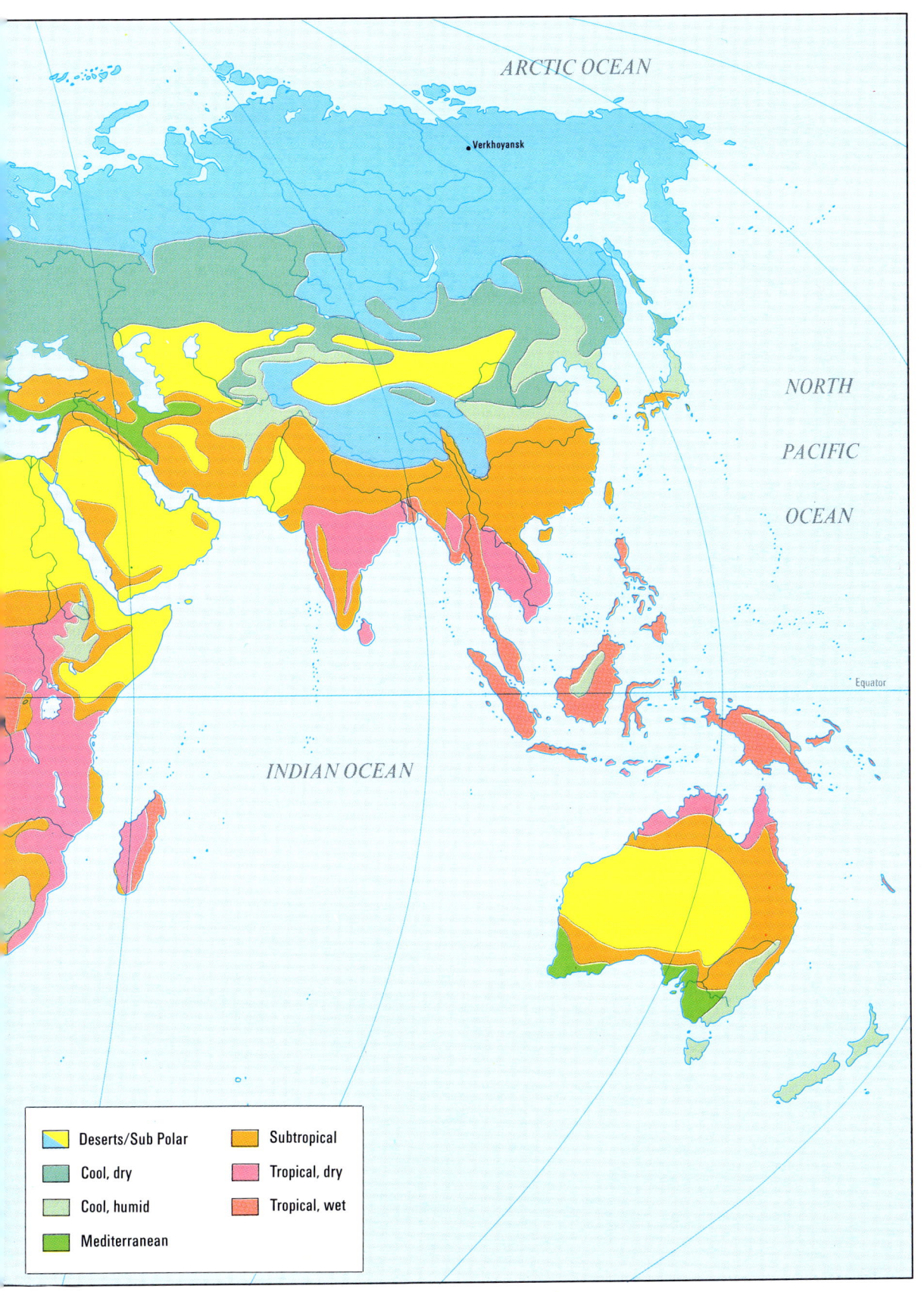

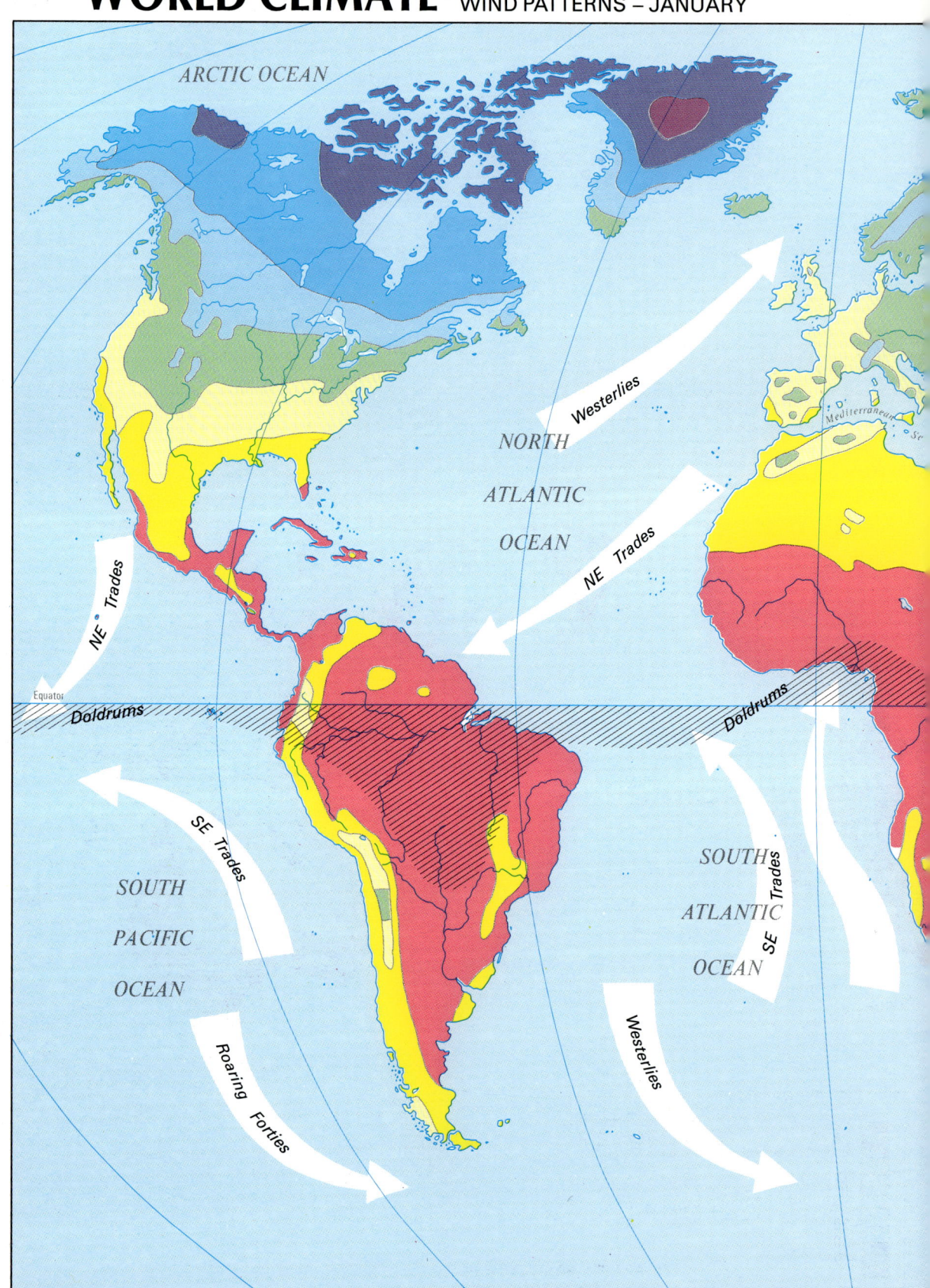

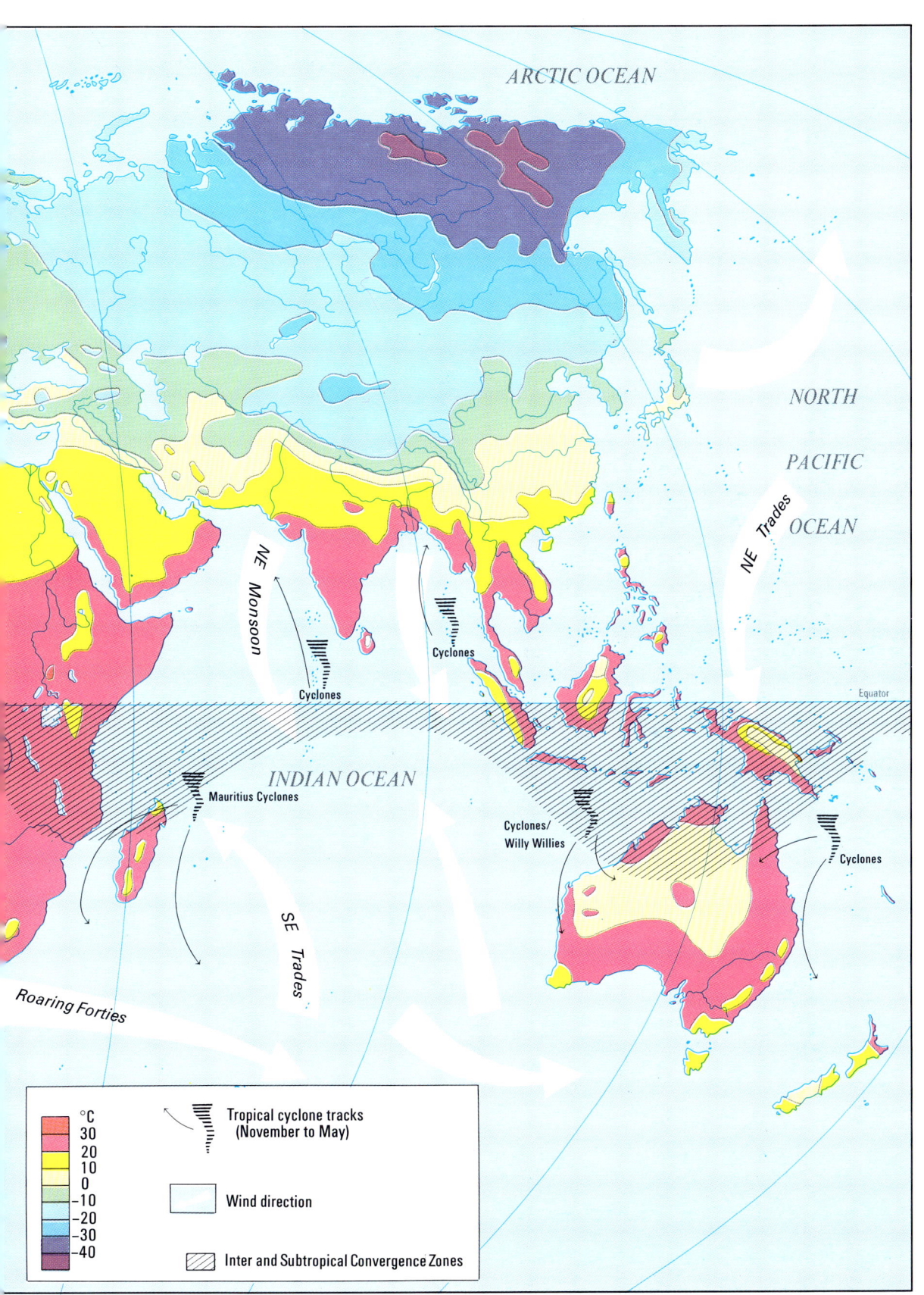

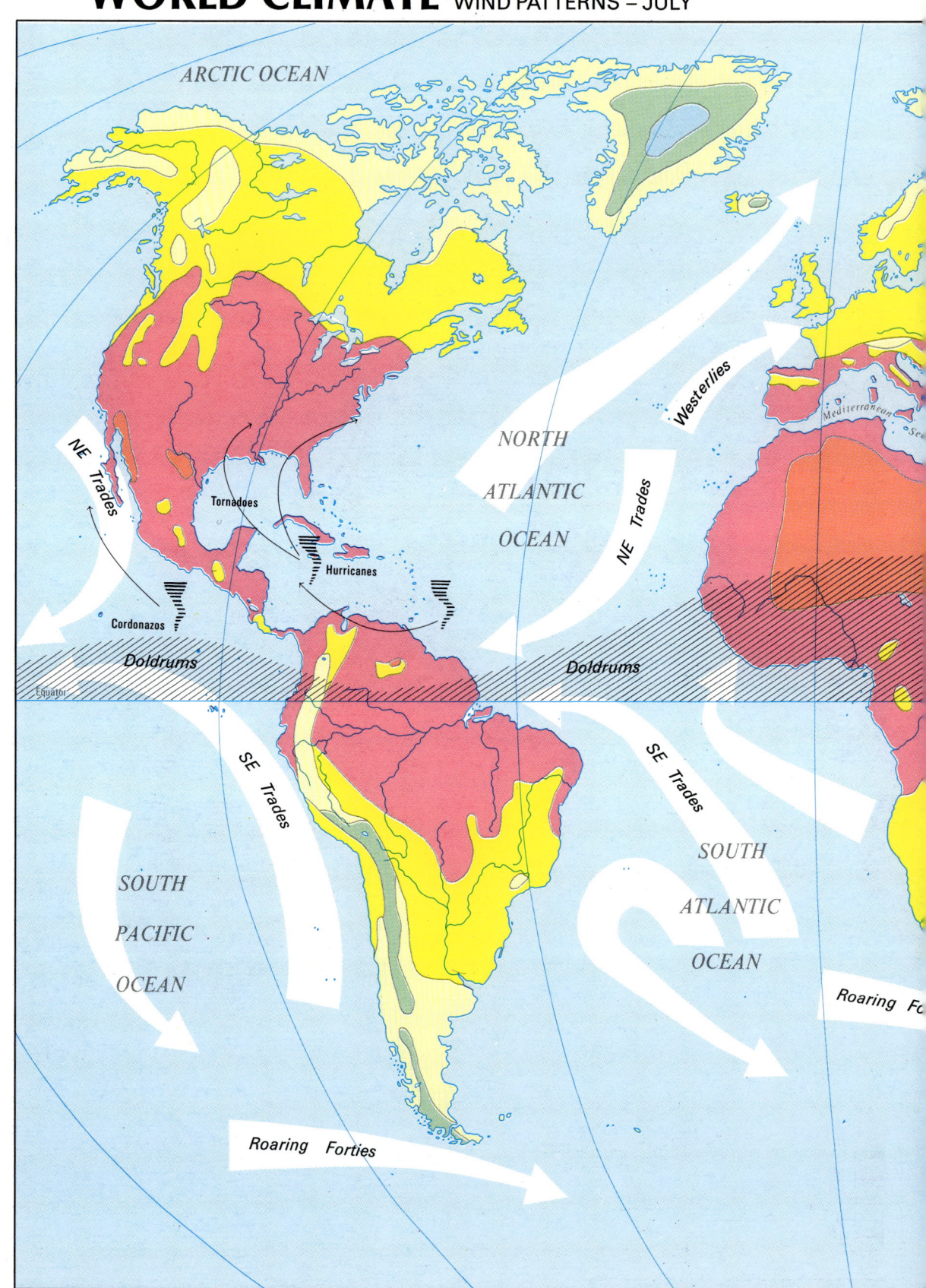

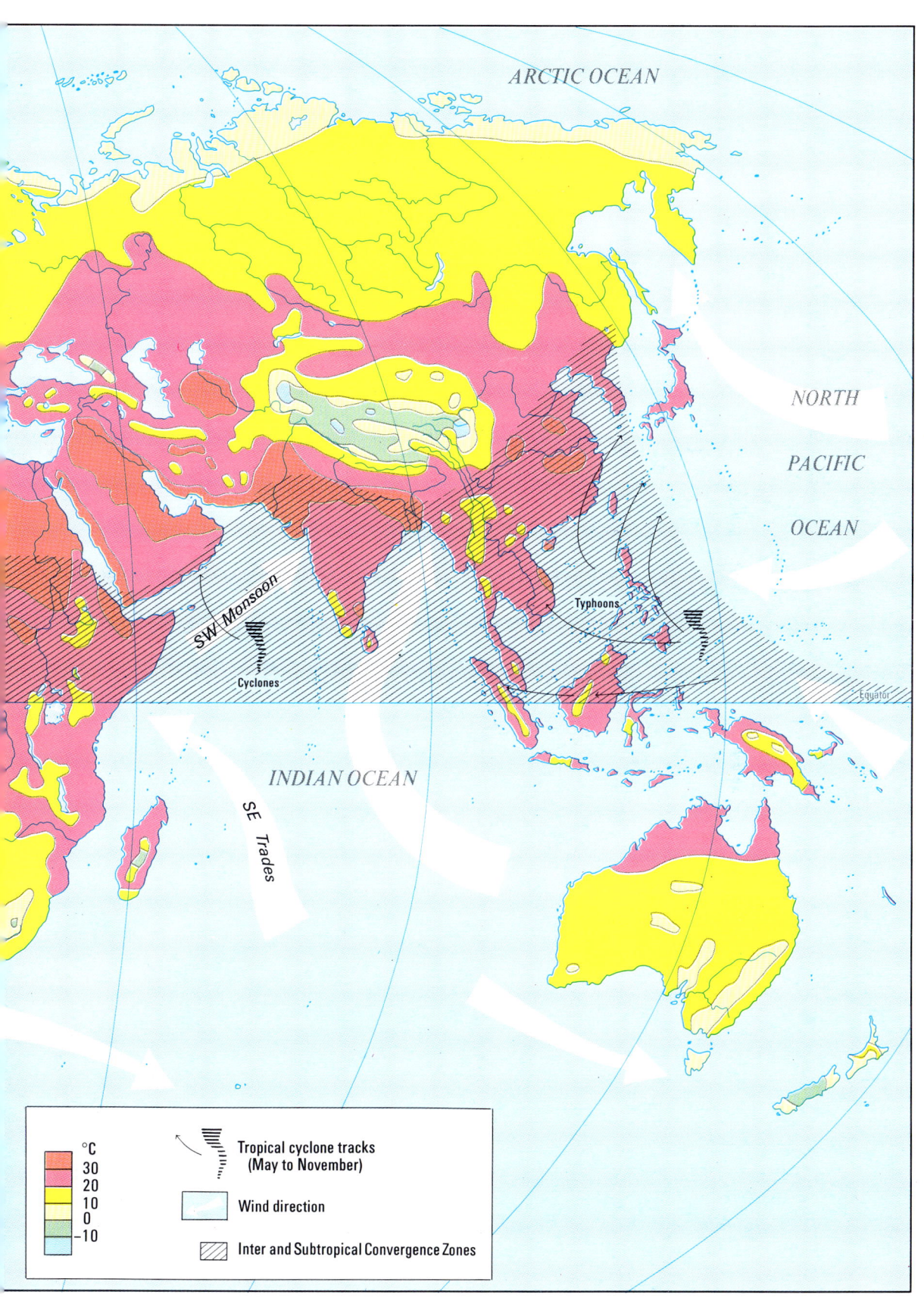

WORLD CLIMATE: RAINFALL

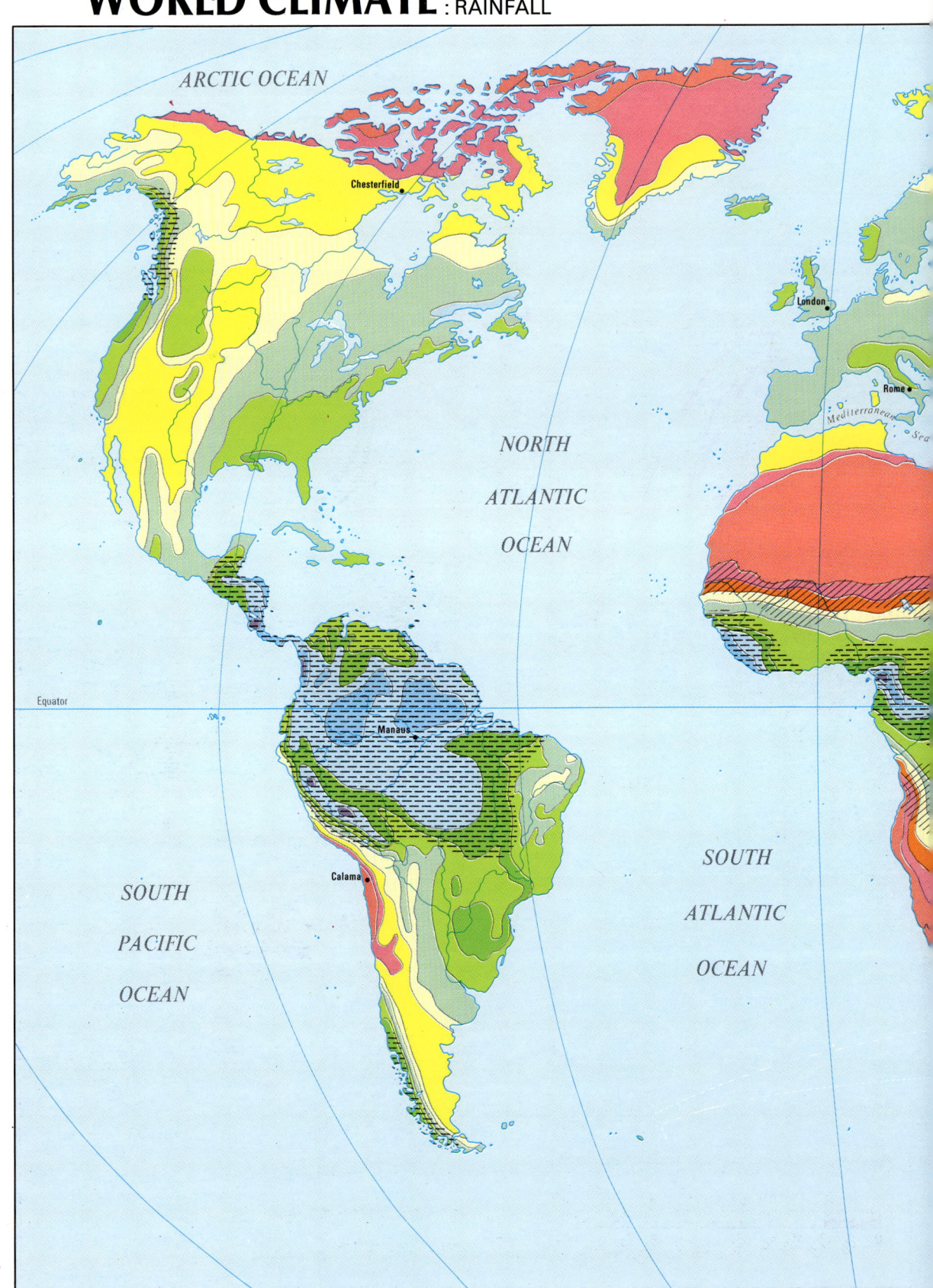

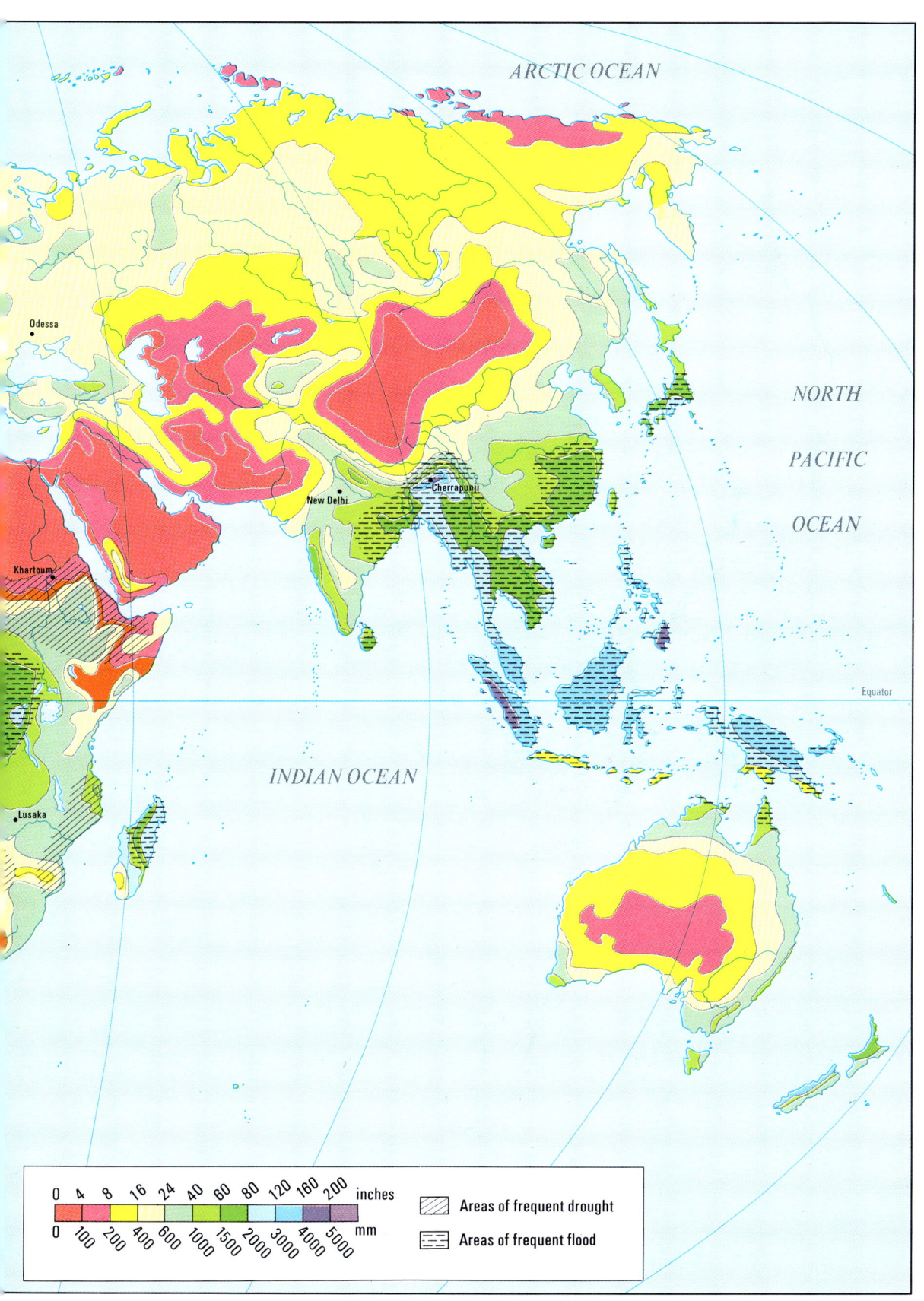

WORLD CLIMATE

Climate is weather averaged out over a long period. If you take your vacation in a place with a hot, dry climate, that will not prevent you having two weeks of wet and chilly weather, if you are unlucky. Weather can change from day to day, but climate is generally constant. Even the smallest variation in climate can have dramatic effects. It would take a worldwide fall in average temperature of less than 5° to plunge us all into a new ice age.

Climate is governed by many factors — latitude, altitude, prevailing winds, distance from the sea — and great variations can occur within a small area. At Quito, high in the mountains of Ecuador, the climate is mild, like a warm English spring, all the year round. Down on the coast a few miles away, it is excessively hot and damp. Local variations cannot be shown on a map of the Earth's major climatic zones, which must deal in general patterns. This map divides the Earth into eight zones, but the zones are far from regular and there are major exceptions, due to altitude and rainfall especially.

The tropical wet zone is entirely confined to the tropics and is characteristic of Central and northern South America, parts of Central and West Africa and most of Southeast Asia and the East Indies. The mean temperature is over 24° and rainfall exceeds 90 inches (about 2,250mm) a year. There is no dry season. It merges into tropical "dry" zone, not in fact particularly dry but having more seasonal rainfall. Typically, summers are hot and wet, winters warm and dry.

A warm and humid or subtropical climate is sometimes called the "China" type. The southeastern United States also lies within this zone. Year-round rainfall and warmth encourage highly productive agriculture where soils permit. The warm, dry climate often described as "Mediterranean" — mild, wet winters, warm but dry

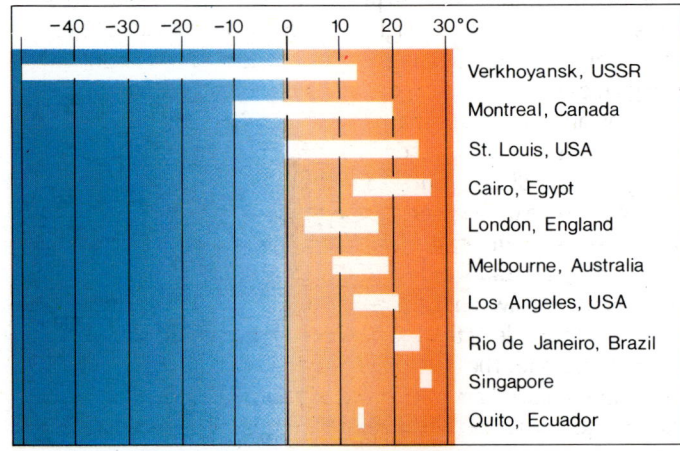

Temperature ranges
Difference between warmest and coldest months at selected locations.

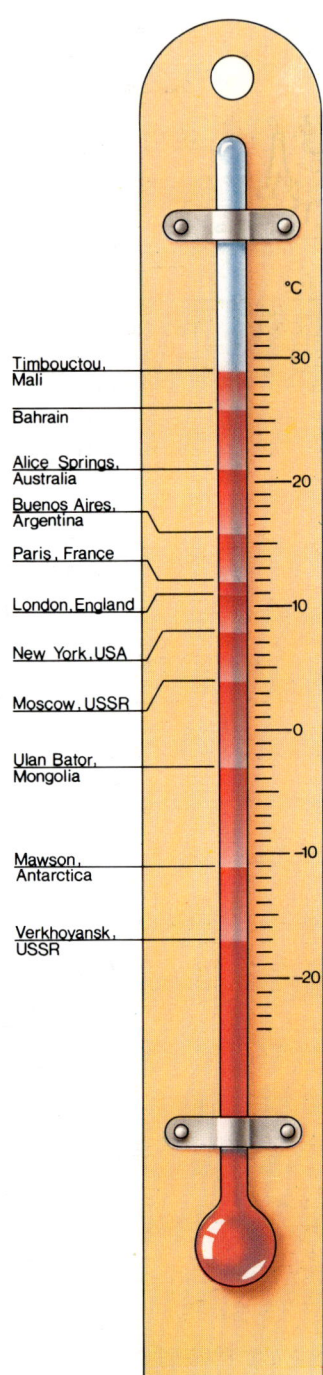

Average annual temperatures
Selected cities worldwide.

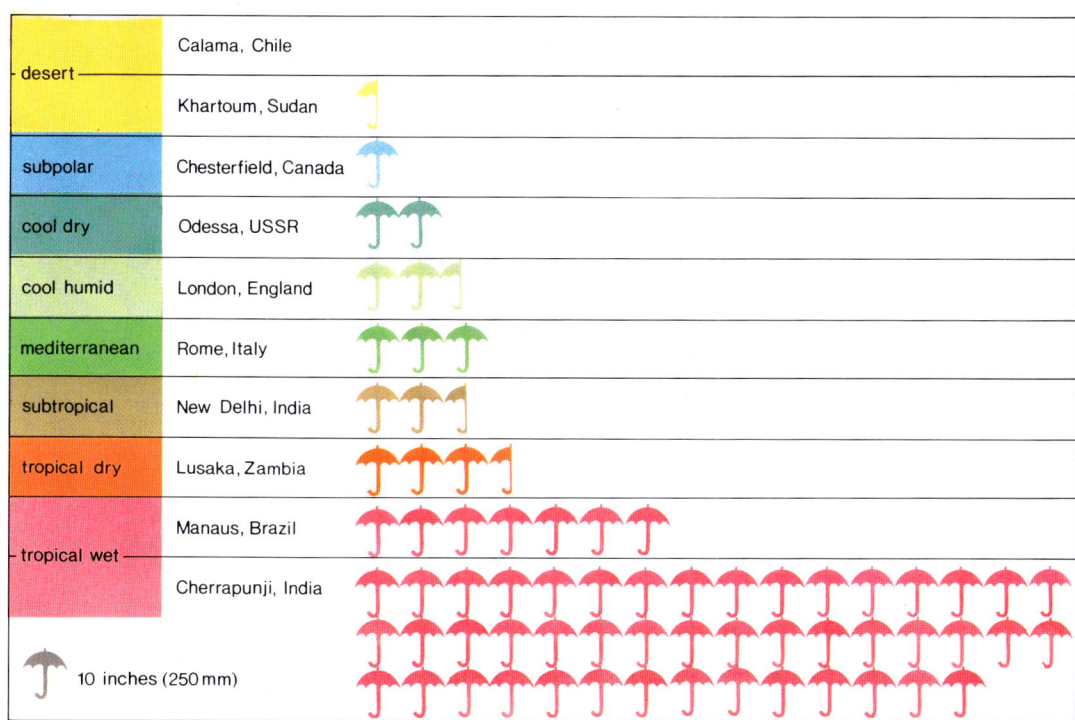

Average annual precipitation
Settlements representative of the eight major climatic zones.

Hottest and coldest places

Highest recorded temperatures

Al Aziziyah, Libya	58.0°C
Death Valley, California, USA	56.7°C

Lowest recorded temperatures

Vostok, Antarctica	−89.2°C
Verkhoyansk, Siberia, USSR	−68.0°C

summers — also occurs in parts of southern Africa and Australia.

The cool humid zone encompasses most of Europe north of the Mediterranean region. In the Southern Hemisphere, New Zealand lies exclusively within this zone. In the great central landmass of Asia, the pattern of regular rainfall gives way to one of dry summers. This cool and dry climate is also characteristic of the Canadian prairies and the South American pampas. The remaining two zones include the land which is too high or too dry or too cold for all but the most selective crop-growing. Deserts are too dry and often too hot; high mountains and sub polar regions are too cold.

Predominant wind patterns are also shown. The most constant are the trade winds (carriers of trade in the days of sailing ships) which, blowing from the direction of the poles, turn west as they approach the Equator, while the Westerlies, blowing from the Equator towards the poles, turn east. Locally and at ground level, wind patterns are complicated by various immediate physical conditions.

The boundary between the trade winds and the tropical air masses on either side of the Equator is called the Intertropical Convergence Zone. The movement of this zone seasonally north-south of the Equator brings the seasonal rainfall to tropical regions. Cyclones and hurricanes originate over oceans in this zone when winds rotate around small but deep troughs of low pressure.

ENVIRONMENT

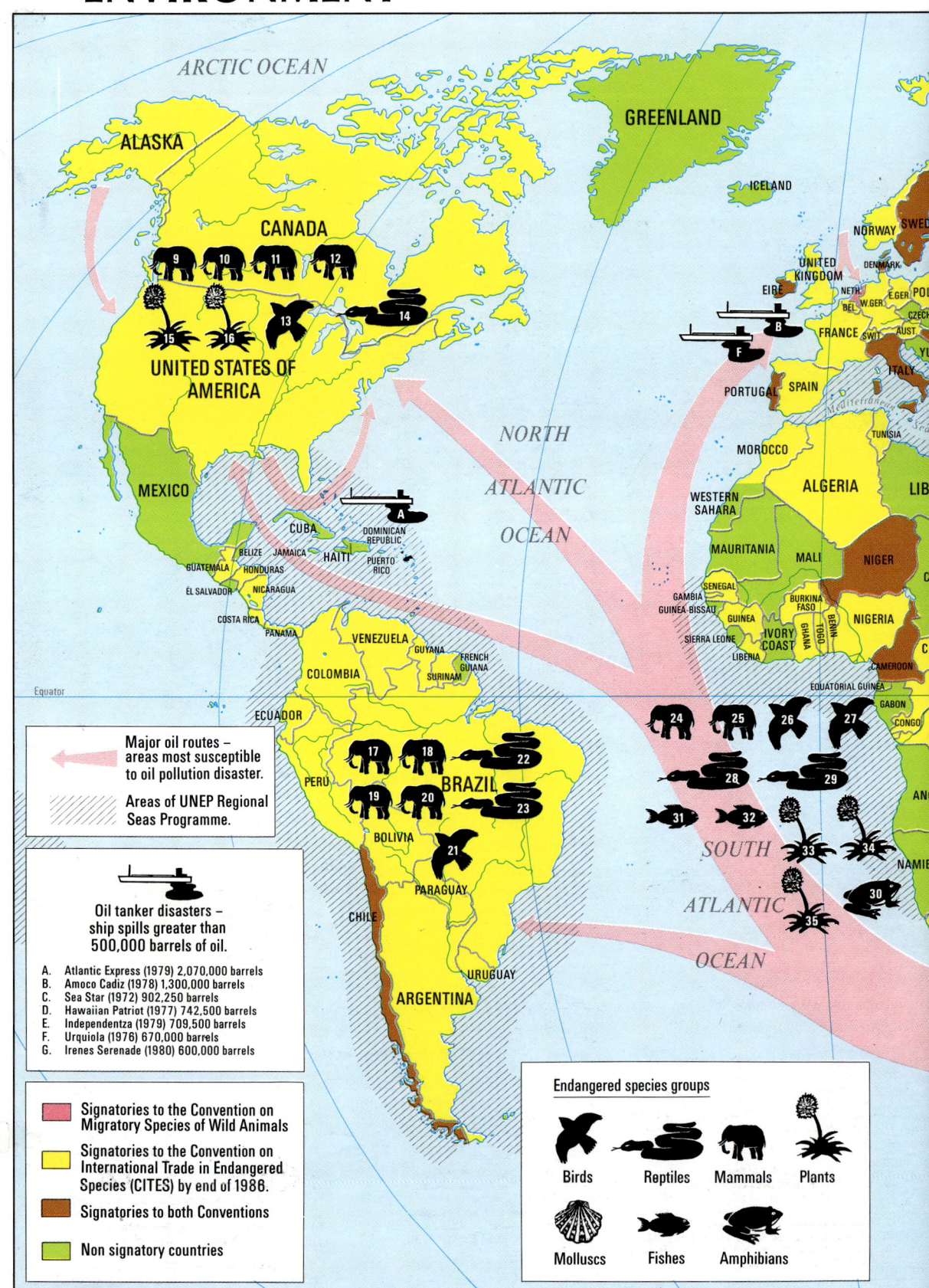

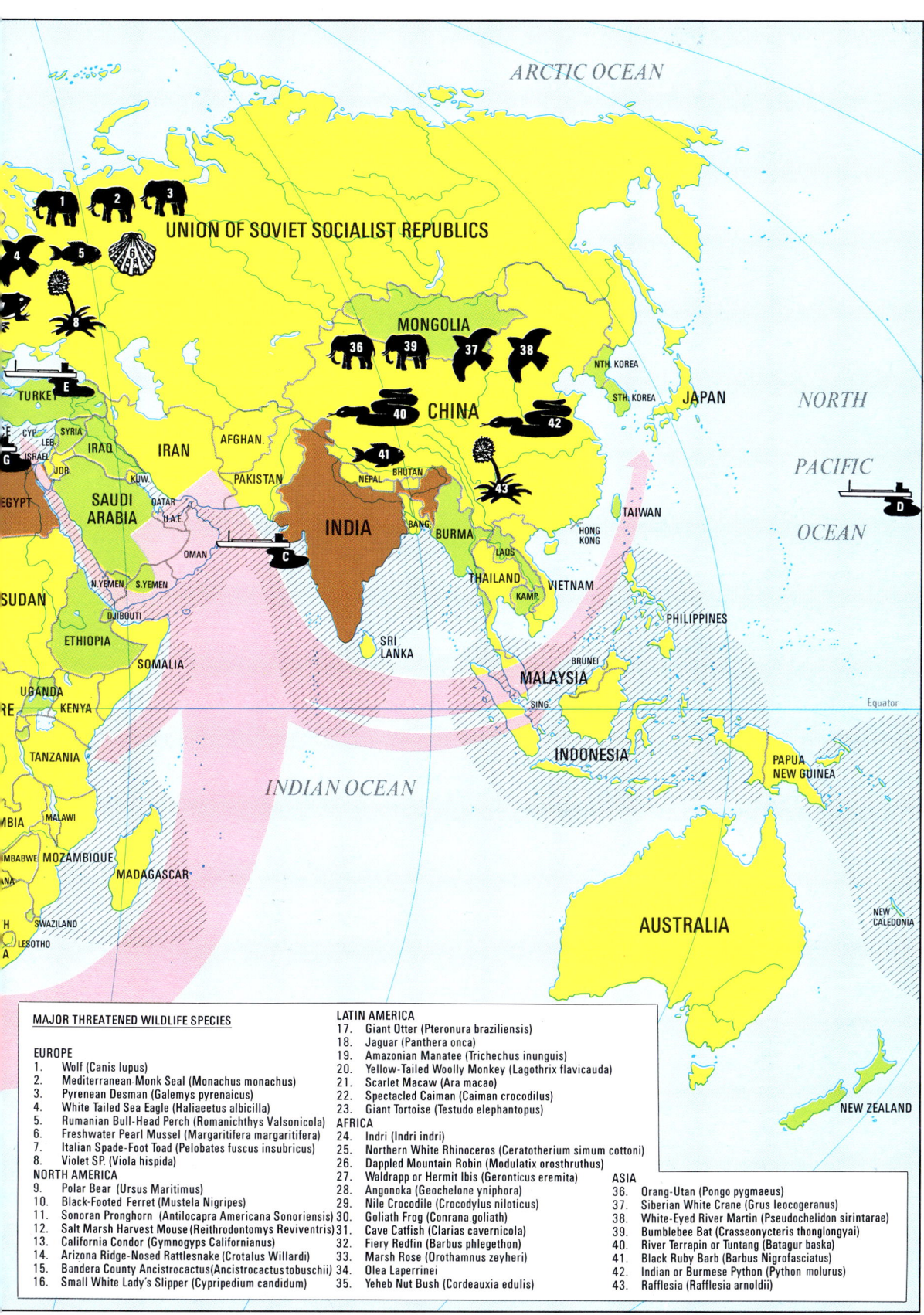

ENVIRONMENT

Of all the cataclysmic threats that hang over us today, perhaps the most dreadful is the continuing destruction of the earth by the ordinary, every-day activities of mankind. We are living on capital, consuming the future.

The single most dangerous aspect of the impending crisis is the irreversible destruction of natural habitats, leading not merely to the extinction of attractive animals like the gorilla or blue whale but, more significantly for the future of humanity, the steady reduction of genetic diversity, which is likely to have incalculable effects on future food production, medicine and science. The rapid depletion of the rain forests, with the rapid and accelerating rate of extinction of uncatalogued plants and animals, is merely the most dramatic example of this trend.

Having become aware of the dangers, we are at last doing something to protect the planet against ourselves. A number of international conventions attempt to retard the process of destruction. Probably the most significant and widest-ranging of these are the Convention on International Trade in Endangered Species (no more leopard-skin coats), and the conventions on migratory animals and on wetlands, the fast-vanishing habitats of waterfowl, which can only be protected by international agreement. Such agreements are at any rate a beginning; unfortunately, it is one thing for a government to ratify a convention, quite another to enforce it.

Pollution in the Mediterranean
Around 100 million people live on the Mediterranean coast and islands, and an estimated 85 per cent of the Mediterranean pollution is carried in rivers from the land to the sea: 430 billion tons of pollution each year. The Mediterranean Action Plan, part of the UNEP Regional Seas Programme, has been instigated to limit land based pollutants at an estimated cost of £6 billion.

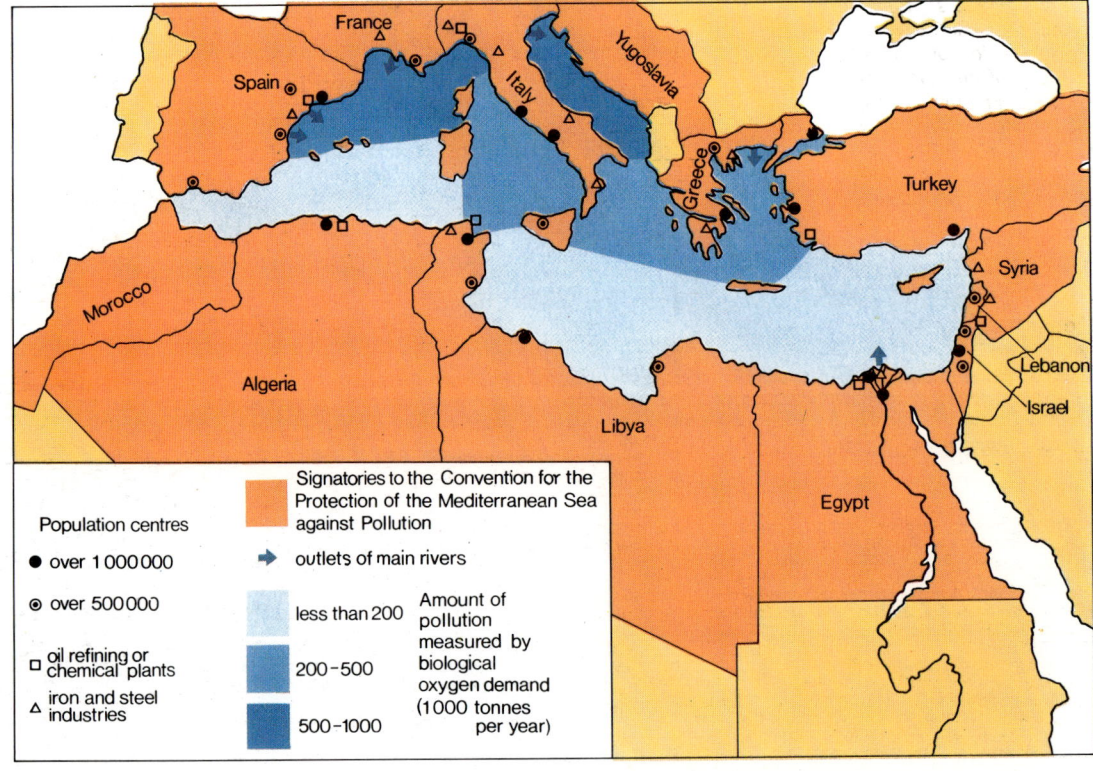

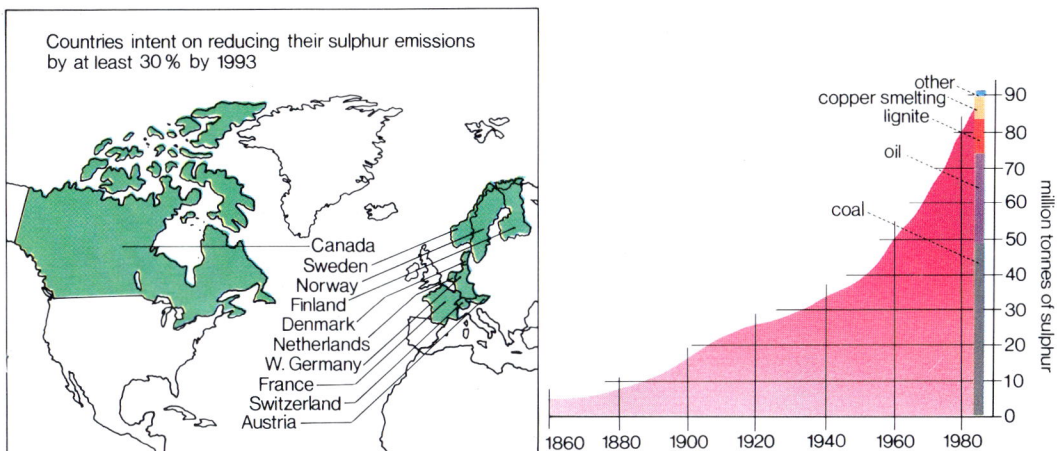

Acid rain

Sulphur dioxide (SO_2) is the gas at the centre of the acid rain debate. It is produced naturally from volcanoes and from rotting vegetable matter, but the increased burning of coal and oil has produced a rapid rise in anthropogenic output this century (see right). Acid rain is now a major political issue, and members of the "30 per cent club" (see above) have agreed to reduce their sulphur emissions by that level by 1993. Our knowledge of the environmental impact of acid rain is currently very basic, however. In some industrial areas SO_2 in the atmosphere actually reduces plant diseases such as black spot which disfigures the leaves of rose bushes.

In spite of growing international awareness of the need to preserve the natural heritage, only a tiny proportion of vulnerable natural habitats are protected as "national parks" and other wildlife reserves.

An estimated 20,000 tons of oil enters the oceans accidentally every year. Most of it comes from the land, and oil tankers (the major routes are shown though there are many others, especially in the Atlantic), providing they obey the rules about washing out tanks at sea, make only a minor contribution except when local disasters occur.

Oil is a major constituent of the disastrous pollution of the Mediterranean, which results from a combination of urban/industrial concentrations around its coasts and the relative lack of tidal movement to spread the muck around. Some success in cleaning up the Mediterranean has been achieved since the Barcelona Convention of 1976, a co-operative clean-up plan (see bottom left). About ten other regional maritime projects of this kind have been started with the encouragement of the UN Environment Programme (see map).

The greenhouse effect

Carbon dioxide (CO_2) is a natural part of the air we breathe, but increasing amounts are being released into the world's atmosphere by burning of fossil fuels and by changing land use, particularly deforestation. The inset shows CO_2 concentrations at Mauna Loa, a remote island in Hawaii far from the immediate effects of industrial pollution. Many experts predict that continued increase of atmospheric CO_2 will lead to global warming, with some possibly disastrous effects for the planet's occupants.

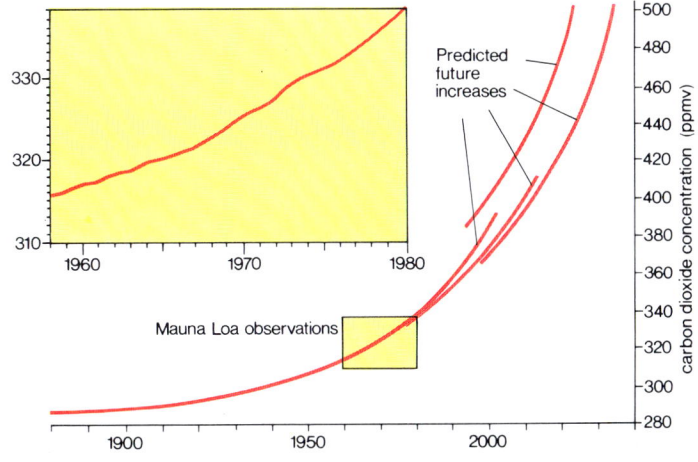

POPULATION DENSITY

POPULATION DENSITY

Population density is given as the number of people per square mile — the total population of the country divided by its area. To a certain extent, population density seems indicative of prosperity. Highly urbanized countries like Britain or the Netherlands are densely populated, and urbanization generally indicates relative prosperity. The most densely populated countries of all are, of course, "city-states" like Singapore, which are too small to feature on the map. However, the most crowded country, excluding city-states, is Bangladesh, where the high fertility of the land supports a dense rural population, albeit in conditions of often extreme poverty. Population density alone is therefore an unreliable guide to living standards.

The countries with the lowest population density are generally those with a large proportion of virtually uninhabitable territory, such as Greenland (mostly ice) or Namibia (largely desert). Although nearly all countries with a very low population density belong to the Third World, that is not necessarily an indication of either under-development or a lack of urbanization. Canada, with about seven people per square mile, is in the lowest bracket of all; Norway and New Zealand each have well under 40 people per square mile.

In a map in which each country was drawn according to the size of its population instead of its area, the world looks very different. The whole of Africa, for example, is smaller than India; China is about three times the size of the Soviet Union. The diagram below left illustrates the striking results of this exercise.

An almost universal feature of world population is the growing proportion of town dwellers (see diagram opposite). The drift from the country to the towns was going on in Europe centuries ago and the industrialization of the 19th century turned a trickle into a torrent. This trend has slowed down markedly in the industrialized countries in recent years, but it nevertheless continues. The slow-down is at least partly the result of the slow-down in population growth overall in many such countries. In many poorer countries the relative rise in urban

Ten largest agglomerations in the World ranked by size, 1970–90

1970	Population (millions)
1 New York/NE New Jersey	16.3
2 Tokyo/Yokohama	14.9
3 Shanghai	11.4
4 London	10.6
5 Rhein-Ruhr	9.3
6 Mexico City	9.2
7 Greater Buenos Aires	8.5
8 Los Angeles/Long Beach	8.4
9 Paris	8.3
10 Beijing	8.3

1980	
1 Tokyo/Yokohama	17.0
2 New York/NE New Jersey	15.6
3 Mexico City	15.0
4 Sao Paulo	12.8
5 Shanghai	11.8
6 Greater Buenos Aires	10.1
7 London	10.0
8 Calcutta	9.5
9 Los Angeles/Long Beach	9.5
10 Rhein-Ruhr	9.3

1990	
1 Mexico City	21.3
2 São Paulo	18.8
3 Tokyo/Yokohama	17.2
4 New York/NE New Jersey	15.3
5 Calcutta	12.6
6 Shanghai	12.0
7 Bombay	11.9
8 Greater Buenos Aires	11.7
9 Seoul	11.5
10 Rio de Janeiro	11.4

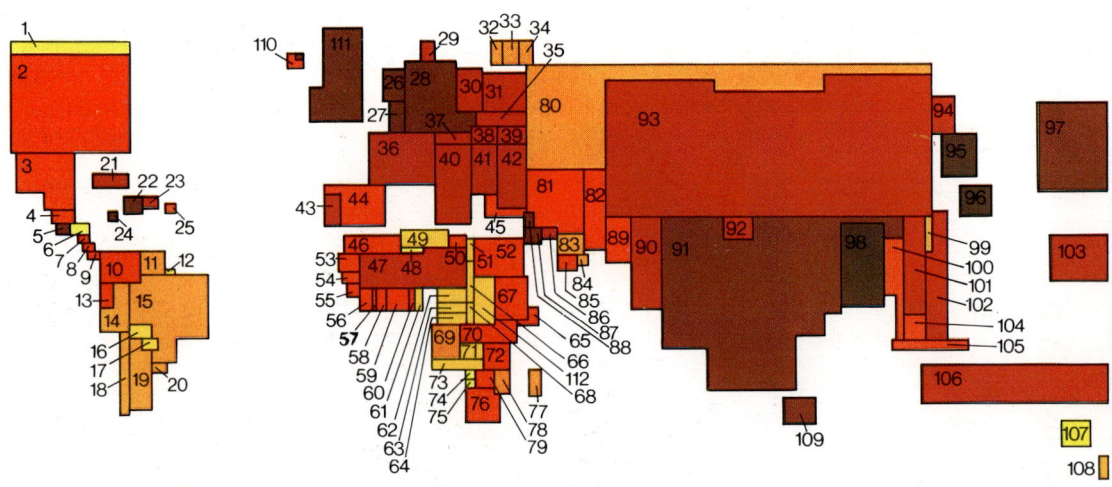

Urban population
Proportion of total population in selected countries that live in urban areas.

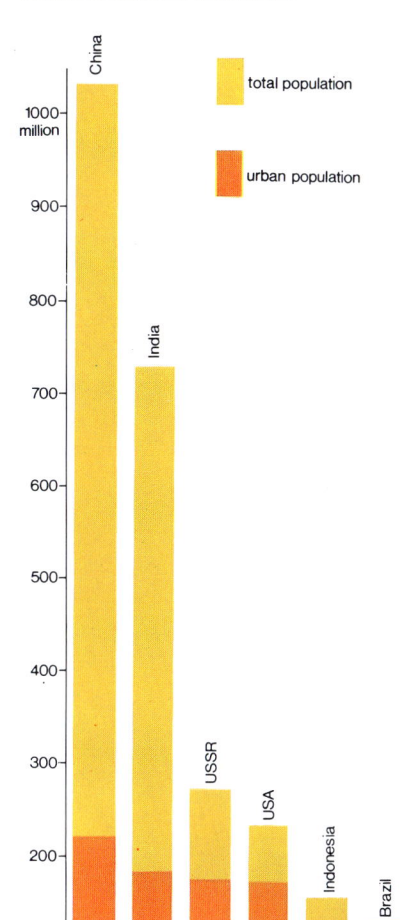

Countries

1 Canada	38 Austria	76 S Africa
2 United States	39 Hungary	77 Madagascar
3 Mexico	40 Italy	78 Mozambique
4 Guatemala	41 Yugoslavia	79 Zimbabwe
5 El Salvador	42 Bulgaria	80 Soviet Union
6 Belize	43 Portugal	81 Turkey
7 Honduras	44 Spain	82 Iran
8 Nicaragua	45 Greece	83 Saudi Arabia
9 Panama	46 Morocco	84 Oman
10 Colombia	47 Nigeria	85 N Yemen
11 Venezuela	48 Mauritania	86 Kuwait
12 Surinam	49 Algeria	87 Israel
13 Ecuador	50 Tunisia	88 Lebanon
14 Peru	51 Libya	89 Afghanistan
15 Brazil	52 Egypt	90 Pakistan
16 Bolivia	53 Senegal	91 India
17 Paraguay	54 Guinea	92 Nepal
18 Chile	55 Sierra Leone	93 China
19 Argentina	56 Burkina	94 N Korea
20 Uruguay	57 Liberia	95 S Korea
21 Cuba	58 Ivory Coast	96 Taiwan
22 Haiti	59 Ghana	97 Japan
23 Dominican Republic	60 Benin	98 Bangladesh
24 Jamaica	61 Mali	99 Laos
25 Puerto Rico	62 Niger	100 Burma
26 Netherlands	63 Congo	101 Thailand
27 Belgium	64 Gabon	102 Vietnam
28 W Germany	65 Somalia	103 Philippines
29 Denmark	66 Chad	104 Malaysia
30 E Germany	67 Ethiopia	105 Kampuchea
31 Poland	68 Central African Republic	106 Indonesia
32 Norway	69 Zaire	107 Australia
33 Sweden	70 Kenya	108 New Zealand
34 Finland	71 Zambia	109 Sri Lanka
35 Czechoslovakia	72 Tanzania	110 Eire
36 France	73 Angola	111 United Kingdom
37 Switzerland	74 Namibia	112 Sudan
	75 Botswana	

Inhabitants per square mile
- less than 10
- 10-25
- 25-50
- 50-200
- 200-500
- 500-1000
- more than 1000

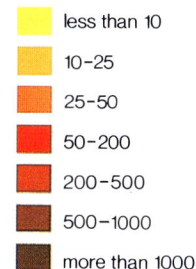

population is a source of grave social concern. It is caused not only by immigrants from the countryside seeking a better living but also by the generally higher standards in cities which result in rising birth rate, higher chances of survival and declining death rate. Sociologists assure us of the truth of this, though the gruesome shanty towns of many large cities in, for example, South America, invite doubts that living standards can really be lower anywhere else.

◀ **Countries according to population size**
For country names, see list above.

WORLD POPULATION GROWTH

RATE OF POPULATION INCREASE (Average 1980-85)

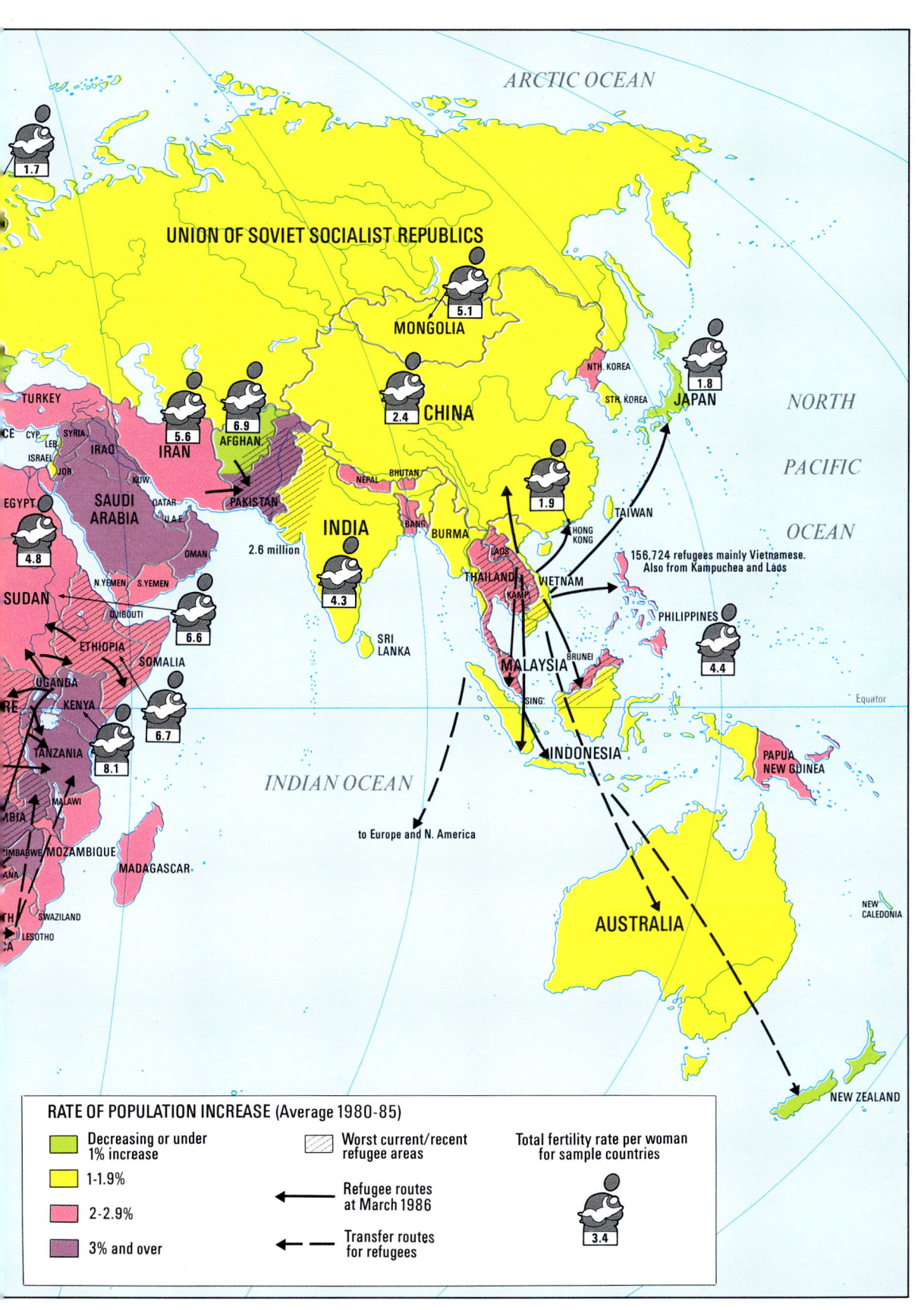

Legend	
Decreasing or under 1% increase	
1-1.9%	
2-2.9%	
3% and over	
Worst current/recent refugee areas	
Refugee routes at March 1986	
Transfer routes for refugees	
Total fertility rate per woman for sample countries	

Countries and fertility rates shown on map:
- USSR: 1.7
- Mongolia: 5.1
- Japan: 1.8
- China: 2.4
- Iran: 5.6
- Afghanistan: 6.9
- Sudan: 4.8
- Ethiopia/Somalia: 6.6
- Kenya/Tanzania: 8.1
- Uganda: 6.7
- India: 4.3
- Thailand area: 1.9
- Philippines: 4.4

India: 2.6 million (refugees)

156,724 refugees mainly Vietnamese. Also from Kampuchea and Laos

to Europe and N. America

39

WORLD POPULATION GROWTH

In 1986 world population was increasing at the rate of over 150 persons a minute, nearly 1,000 an hour.

World population, unlike food production, increases in geometrical proportion: it has doubled in the past 33 years but will need less than 20 years to double again, and projections into the future confront us with figures of awesome size.

Annual growth rate does not have to be very large to maintain this frightening ascent. A country with a growth rate of 3 per cent (Algeria's is for example 3.2 per cent) doubles its population in just 23 years, the total increase being proportionately larger each year. Since many of the countries whose population is increasing at the greatest rate are also among the least well endowed with natural resources, the prospects of winning the world battle against hunger in the foreseeable future are extremely bleak.

Births, deaths and growth rates
A selection of countries showing a large range of annual population growth rates resulting mainly from fluctuations in births and deaths.

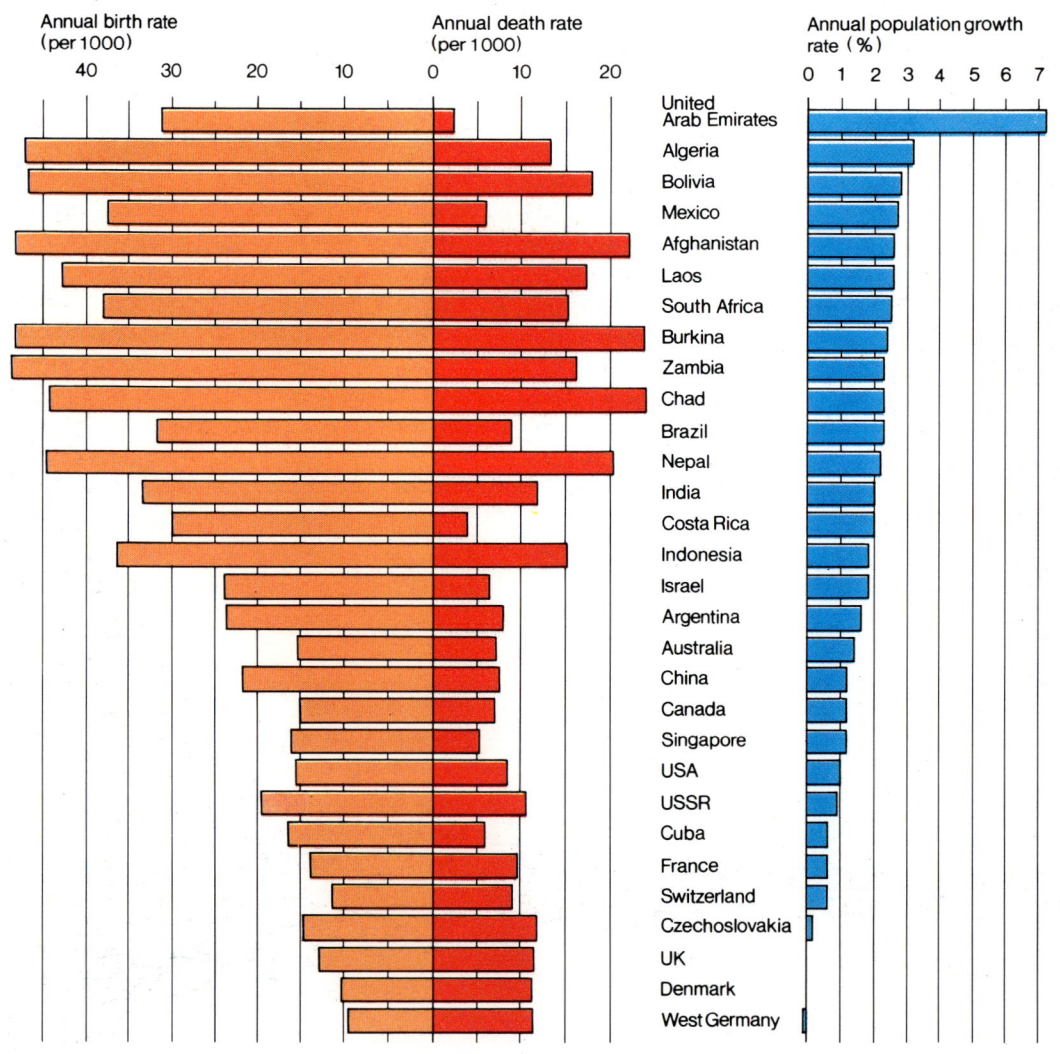

However, world population will not continue indefinitely at the present rate, due, if to nothing more dramatic, to fluctuations of birth and death rates (see diagram left). The rapid increase in poorer countries in recent years is largely due to lower death rates (annual deaths per thousand of the population). In the prosperous, industrialized countries the death rate is often lower still, but there it is combined with low birth rates, and in fact many industrialized countries have now achieved an almost stable population (a balanced birth and death rate).

Since birth rate can, theoretically, be easily controlled, this ought to provide a solution for countries like India where the increasing population constantly threatens to outstrip economic growth. There are many reasons, including religious taboos, why this is not practical, but even when stringent birth control is introduced it does not result immediately in a stable population. Much depends on what demographers call the "age profile": where there is a large proportion of young people, obviously there will be more babies than in a country with a high proportion of elderly people. Thus, China's severe birth-control policy cannot prevent its population rising to probably about one and a half times the present total within the next three generations, and the Chinese population will not stop growing until nearly one hundred years from now. By that time, incidentally, India will probably have overtaken China as the world's most populous nation.

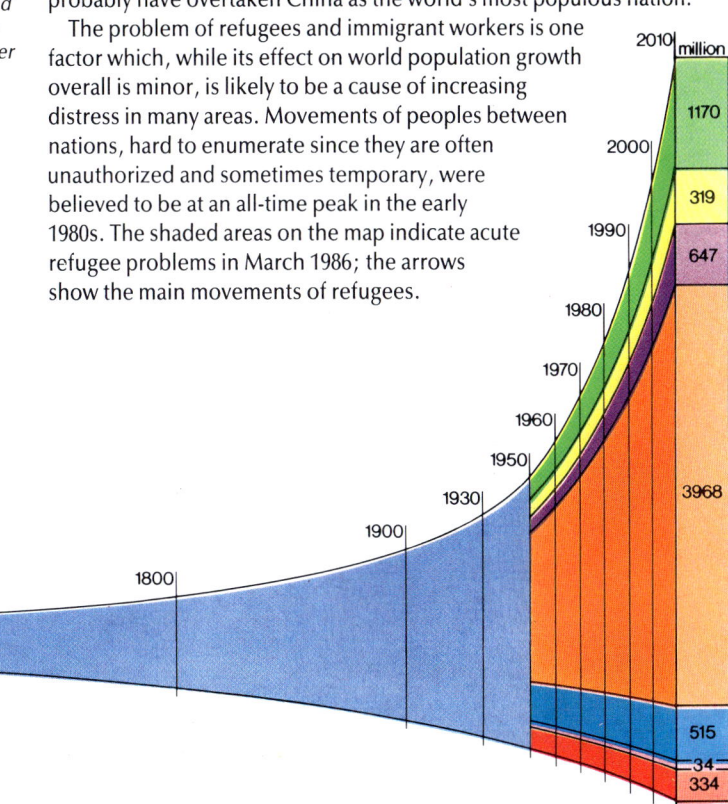

The problem of refugees and immigrant workers is one factor which, while its effect on world population growth overall is minor, is likely to be a cause of increasing distress in many areas. Movements of peoples between nations, hard to enumerate since they are often unauthorized and sometimes temporary, were believed to be at an all-time peak in the early 1980s. The shaded areas on the map indicate acute refugee problems in March 1986; the arrows show the main movements of refugees.

World population by continent
Total world population from 1500 including estimates to the year 2010 as projected by the United Nations. According to United Nations estimates the population of the world will be about 6 billion at the end of this century and will not stabilize until about the end of the following century. At that time it will be over 10 billion. Life expectancy, world-wide, which was about 47 years in 1950, will be almost 65 years by the end of the 20th century.

- World total
- Africa
- North America
- Latin America
- Asia (ex USSR)
- Europe
- Oceania
- USSR

GROSS NATIONAL PRODUCT

GNP PER CAPITA
US dollars (1983)

Color	Range
yellow	less than 200
green	200-500
blue	500-1,000
purple	1,000-2,000
pink	2,000-5,000
orange	5,000-10,000
red	more than 10,000
grey	no data

GROSS NATIONAL PRODUCT

The Gross National Product (GNP) of a country is the total value of the goods and services it produces in one year — more or less the nation's annual wage packet. It is probably the best available indicator of a country's general economic prosperity that we have.

As we can see from the map, North America, Western Europe, Japan, Australasia and some oil states all come within the top two brackets, while most of the Third World is in the lower brackets. The immense disparity between rich and poor countries in terms of GNP is more clearly revealed in the diagram below. If the world total is roughly divided into three, the United States accounts for one third, the European Economic Community plus Japan account for another third, and the whole of the rest of the world — representing about 84 per cent of world population — makes up the remaining third. The United States GNP per capita is not in fact the world's largest, as it is exceeded by several small oil-producing states in the Middle East (see list at right), but these are exceptional, being dependent on virtually a single resource. The diagram below shows graphically just how exceptional, in world terms, is the average income of the United States and other industrialized nations compared with the figure of less than 500 dollars per capita of more than half the world's people.

Although GNP per capita is roughly equivalent to average individual income, it is of course no guide to individual prosperity. An equally

GNP totals
The area for each country is proportional to its total GNP, the colour shows GNP per capita as shown on the map overleaf.

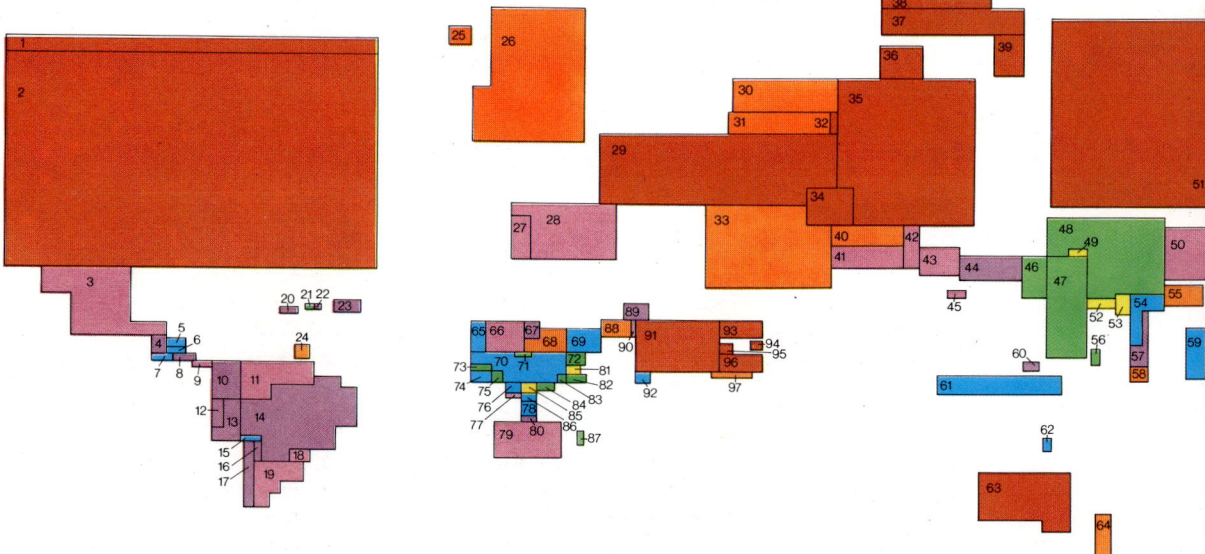

large gap often exists between rich and poor inside each country as between different countries; the wealth may be distributed in unlimited ways, and the proportion taken by the government in taxes differs widely.

There are many objections to GNP as a measure of national prosperity. As it is measured, for the sake of convenience, in US dollars, it is influenced by international exchange rates, so that if a country's

44

Richest and poorest
Richest five countries and poorest five countries as measured by GNP per capita 1983

Richest	GNP per capita (US dollars)
UAE	23,770
Switzerland	16,250
Kuwait	16,200
USA	14,080
Norway	13,990

Poorest	
Zaire	170
Nepal	160
Mali	150
Bangladesh	130
Ethiopia	120

GNP, 1983
List of countries, right, refer to map at left.

currency happens to fall against the dollar, perhaps due to higher interest rates in the United States, its GNP falls proportionately, though clearly the actual value of its product does not fall in that way. Many countries have a flourishing "black market economy", which naturally does not feature in official figures. Services and labour which are unpaid — for example, the subsistence farming common in many Third World countries — tend to be underestimated or ignored altogether. Finally, different governments set about compiling their figures in different ways, which are often not strictly comparable. Communist countries do not publish a figure for GNP as it is interpreted elsewhere, since services are not included. Others supply no figures, due to civil disturbance or other cause, and some publish figures which are regarded as unreliable.

However, with all its imperfections, GNP comparisons reveal incontrovertibly the vast gap in per capita income between the world's rich and the world's poor.

1 Canada	33 Italy	65 Morocco
2 USA	34 Switzerland	66 Algeria
3 Mexico	35 W Germany	67 Tunisia
4 Guatemala	36 Denmark	68 Libya
5 Honduras	37 Sweden	69 Egypt
6 Nicaragua	38 Norway	70 Nigeria
7 El Salvador	39 Finland	71 Niger
8 Costa Rica	40 Austria	72 Sudan
9 Panama	41 Yugoslavia	73 Senegal
10 Colombia	42 Hungary	74 Ivory Coast
11 Venezuela	43 Greece	75 Ghana
12 Ecuador	44 Turkey	76 Cameroon
13 Peru	45 Cyprus	77 Gabon
14 Brazil	46 Pakistan	78 Zimbabwe
15 Bolivia	47 India	79 South Africa
16 Paraguay	48 China	80 Namibia
17 Chile	49 Nepal	81 Ethiopia
18 Uruguay	50 S Korea	82 Kenya
19 Argentina	51 Japan	83 Uganda
20 Jamaica	52 Bangladesh	84 Tanzania
21 Haiti	53 Burma	85 Zaire
22 Dominican Republic	54 Thailand	86 Zambia
23 Puerto Rico	55 Hong Kong	87 Madagascar
24 Trinidad & Tobago	56 Sri Lanka	88 Israel
25 Ireland	57 Malaysia	89 Syria
26 Great Britain	58 Singapore	90 Jordan
27 Portugal	59 Philippines	91 Saudi Arabia
28 Spain	60 Brunei	92 S Yemen
29 France	61 Indonesia	93 Kuwait
30 Netherlands	62 Papua New Guinea	94 Bahrain
31 Belgium	63 Australia	95 Qatar
32 Luxembourg	64 New Zealand	96 UAE
		97 Oman

GNP GROWTH RATE

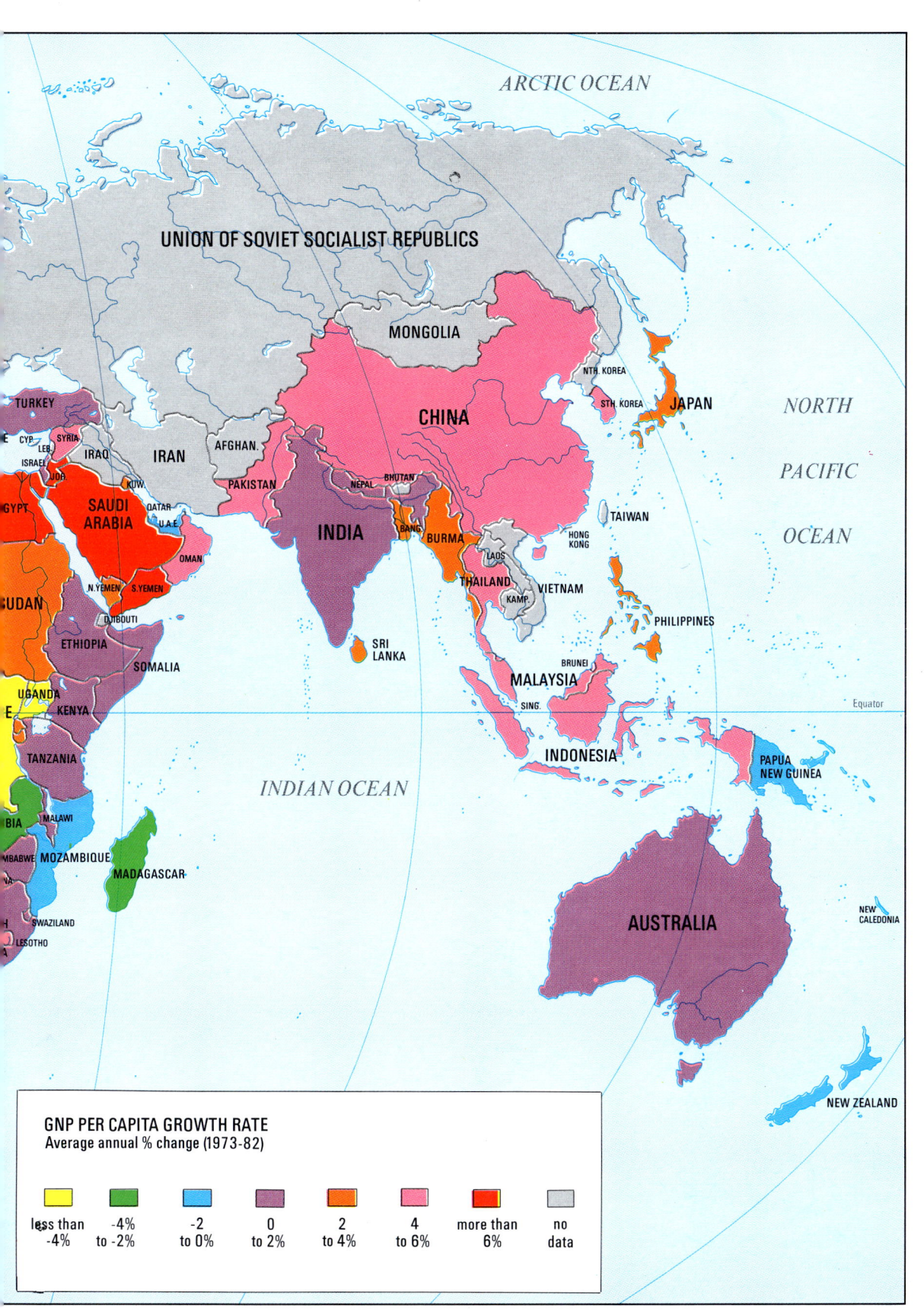

GNP PER CAPITA GROWTH RATE
Average annual % change (1973-82)

Color	Range
yellow	less than -4%
green	-4% to -2%
blue	-2 to 0%
purple	0 to 2%
orange	2 to 4%
pink	4 to 6%
red	more than 6%
grey	no data

GNP GROWTH RATE

The gap in GNP between rich and poor countries is not only enormous, it is in many cases increasing. Obviously, the difference between countries that average 10,000 dollars and 500 dollars becomes steadily larger if both figures increase by 2 per cent a year but, as the map shows, this is not just a matter of percentages. During the decade ending in 1982 practically all the rich nations registered a modest increase in average annual GNP per capita, while many of the world's poorer nations registered a decrease. This is particularly noticeable in Africa south of the Sahara.

Fluctuations in GNP per capita are caused not only by changing rates of production but also by changing population. If GNP is unchanged while population increases, then GNP per capita falls: the cake is the

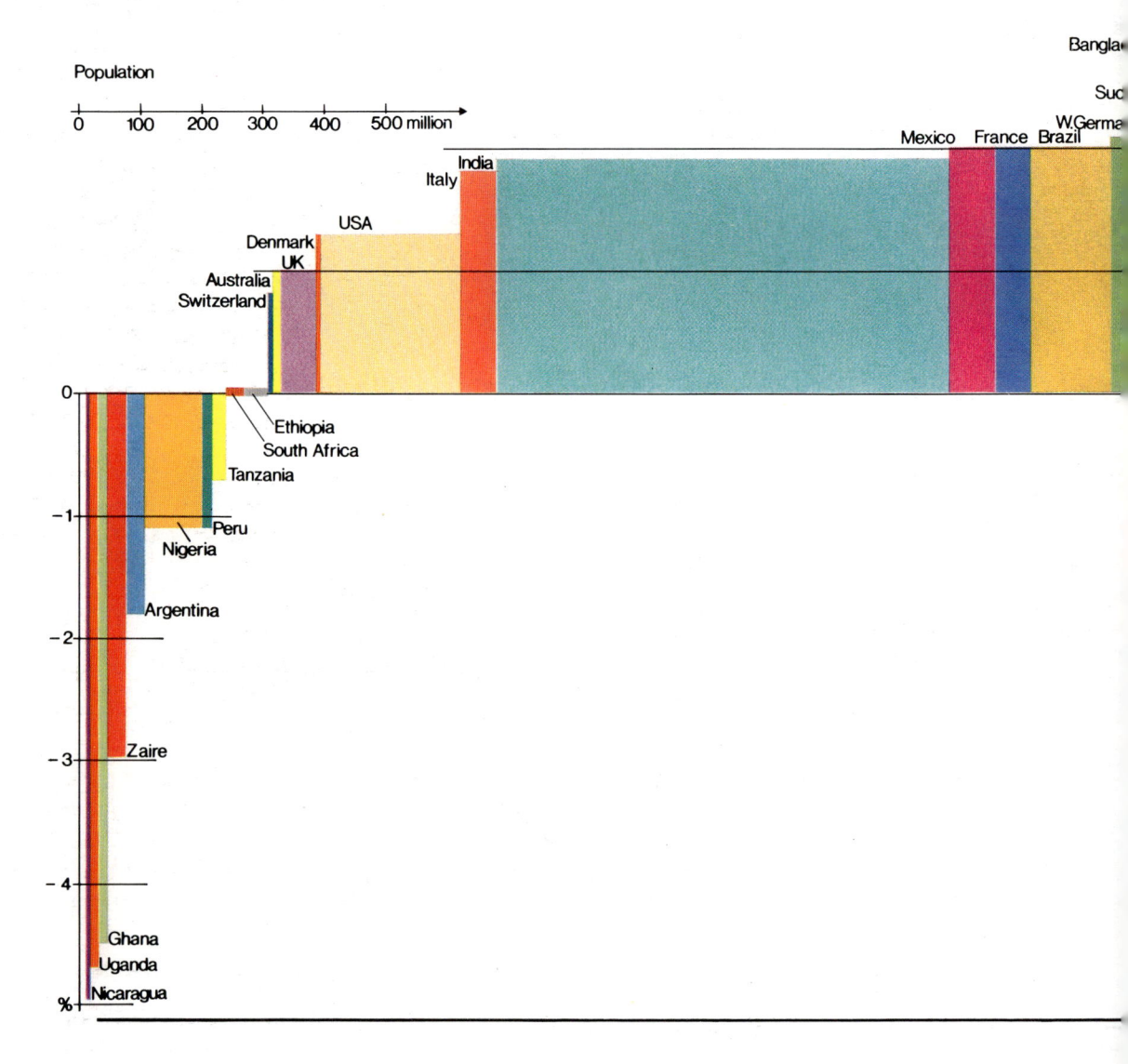

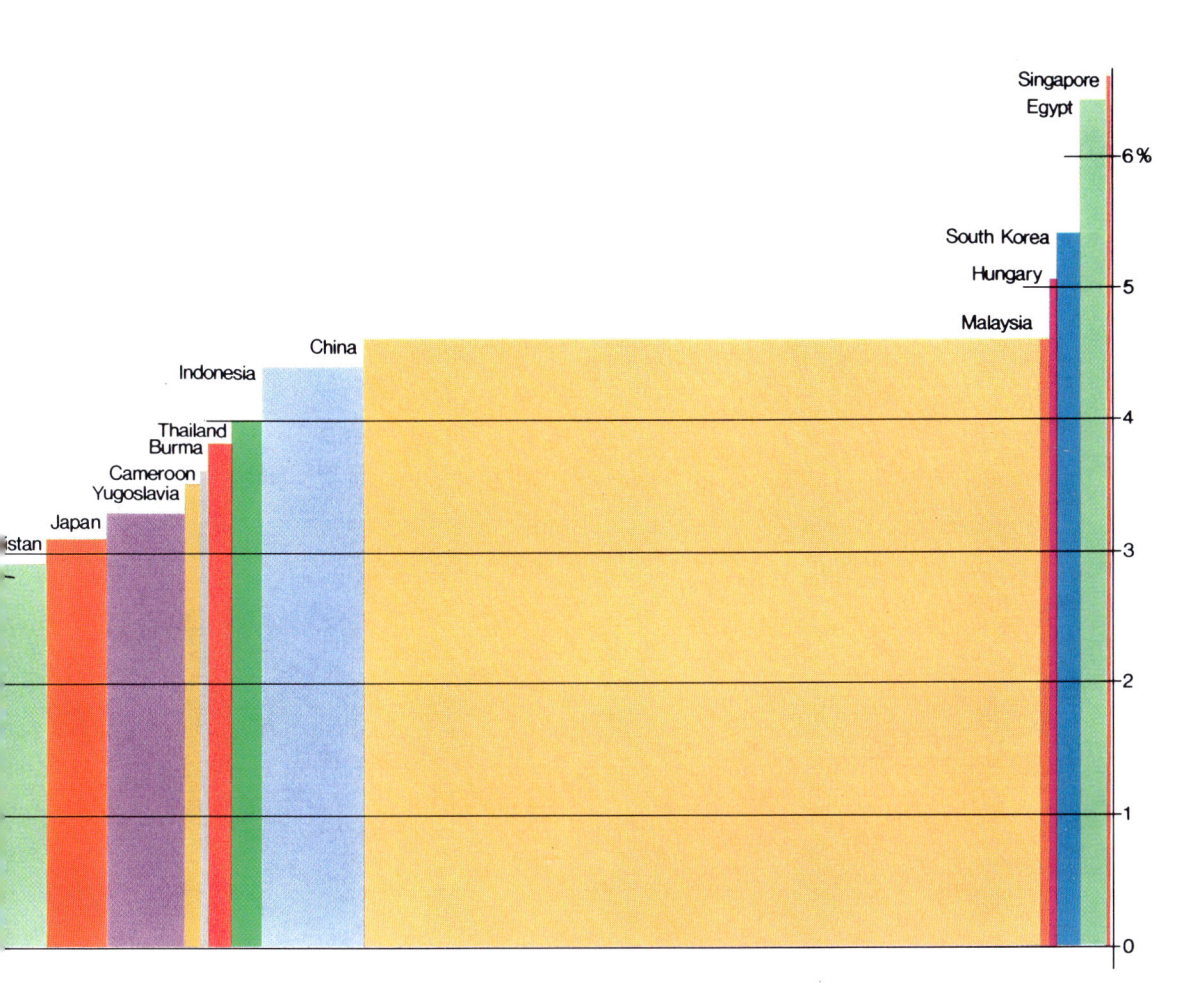

GNP per capita growth rates

A selection of countries showing growth rate 1973–83 (per year) and population in 1983. Some of the fastest growing economies are in Eastern Asia built on low labour costs and growing "high-tech" industries. The countries showing a decline in GNP over this decade have all experienced internal political unrest.

same size but must be cut in smaller slices. In some countries, the decline is due to special circumstances. Years of unrest have obviously had a disastrous effect on the economy generally in countries like Uganda or Vietnam. But in a number of Third World countries relatively little affected by war or civil strife, population growth is outstripping the rise — if any — in production.

But there are exceptions. The world pattern of rich and poor, developed and developing countries, as suggested by GNP or by other measures of prosperity, does not appear in this comparison of GNP growth rates as these depend on factors not directly related to national income. Thus Egypt, a comparatively poor country with severe economic difficulties such as international debt and unemployment, recorded one of the highest average annual growth rates of any country. It should also be remembered that this decade, the latest for which figures are widely available, included several years of unusually severe economic recession — but then, no decade is typical.

RELIGIONS OF THE WORLD

Religions of Asia

■ Atheism (and Communism)	■ Christian, Orthodox	■ Traditional/Tribal
■ Buddhism	■ Christian, Protestant	■ Others
■ Christian, no major sect	■ Hindu	Religious Capitals and centres
■ Christian, Roman Catholic	■ Muslim	

51

RELIGIONS OF THE WORLD

Religion is obviously a difficult subject to reduce to statistics or to represent on a map. For a start it is not simple to define what "religion" means. It is often said, for example, that Confucianism and even Buddhism in some aspects are better described as social systems than as religions, and most great religions contain within them sects so various that they are sometimes more easily defined by their differences than their agreements. In the United States alone there are about 35 substantial (over 50,000 members) Christian Churches, as well as many smaller ones.

Equally, it is difficult to convey the weight of religious belief in governing the way people think or act. Many of the conflicts that plague the modern world have a religious content, but religion is seldom the only or even the chief ingredient. To what extent are religious differences responsible for the troubles in the Middle East or Northern Ireland? Some people would say very little, yet when the chief opponents in any conflict belong exclusively to different religions, that fact can hardly be regarded as unimportant.

A map of world religions can only show the dominant faith(s) in each region. In most large cosmopolitan cities it would be possible to find substantial minorities belonging to every religion ever recorded, and no doubt others scarcely known outside a small circle of devotees. Small minorities cannot be shown here, nor can the strength of the faith of the adherents of a given religion. Many people adhere to a religion in much the same way as they adhere to the law, without giving the matter much thought, while others profess a religion for the sake of social convenience without themselves possessing a vestige of faith. In the

Division of world population by religions

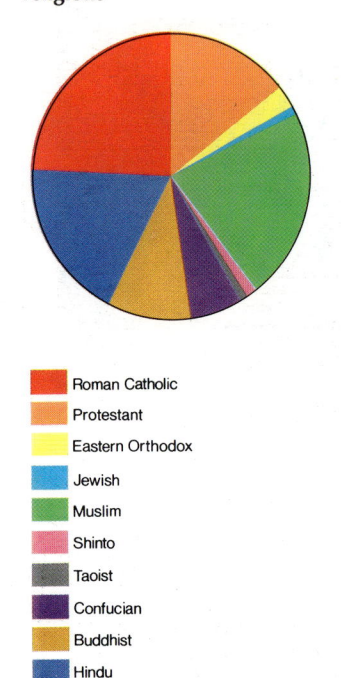

- Roman Catholic
- Protestant
- Eastern Orthodox
- Jewish
- Muslim
- Shinto
- Taoist
- Confucian
- Buddhist
- Hindu

Estimated membership of principal world religions by continent

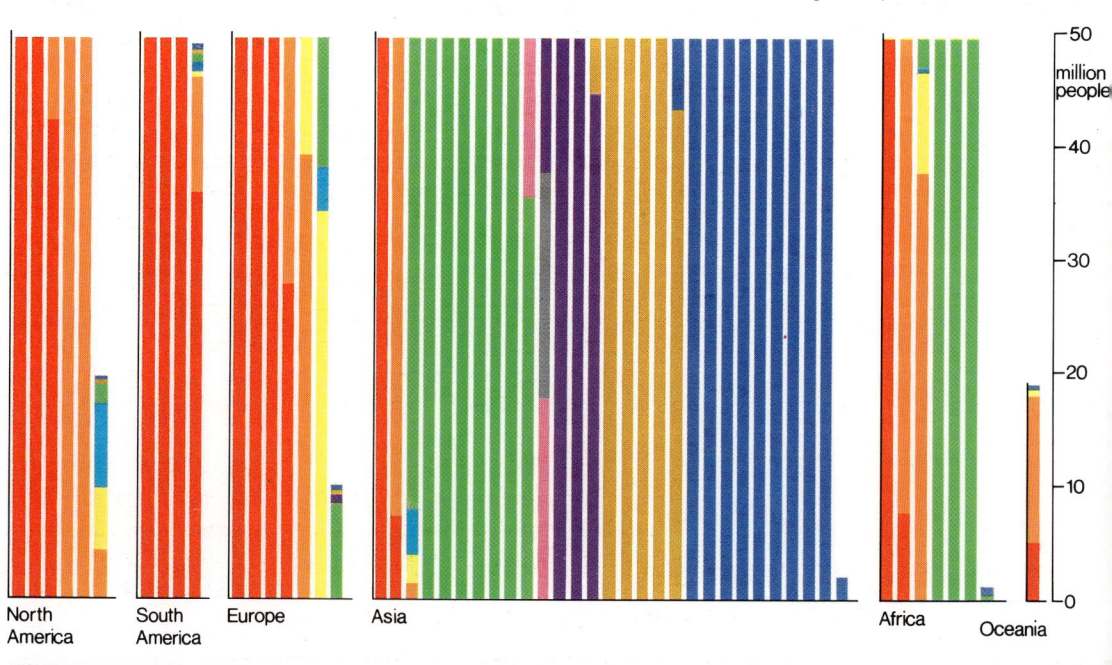

North America | South America | Europe | Asia | Africa | Oceania

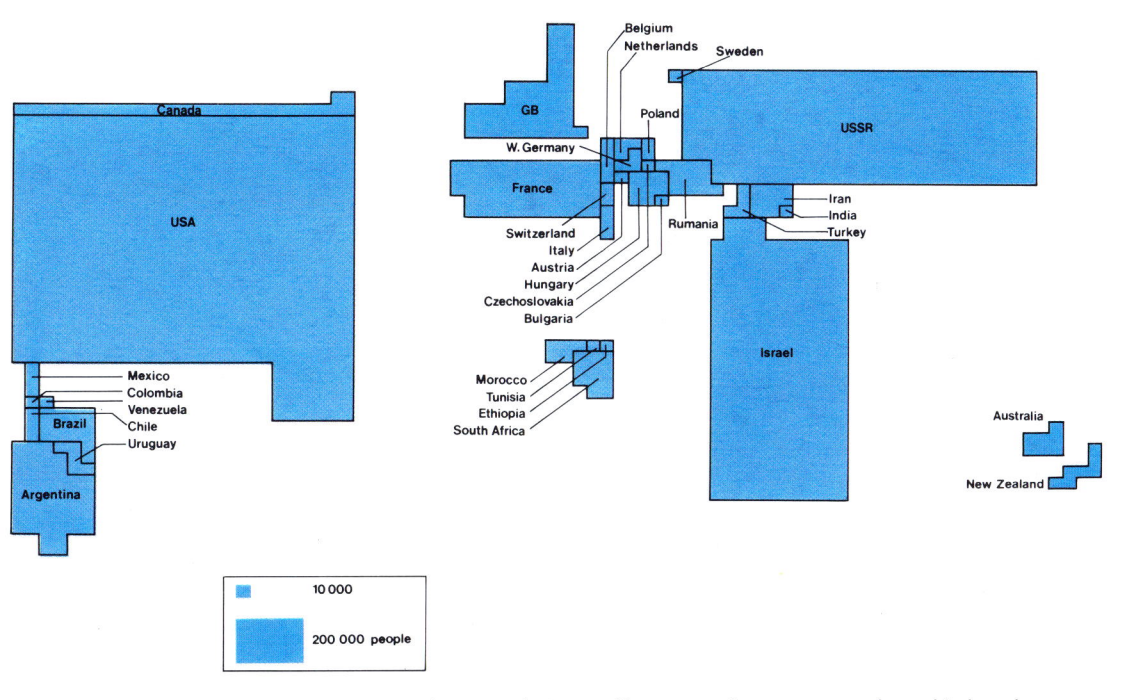

Distribution of Jews around the world
Since the formation of a Jewish state in 1948, Israel has absorbed Jews from all parts of the globe. Nevertheless, there are still more Jews resident in the United States than in Israel, and more Jews live in New York than in Jerusalem.

Christian religion, unlike some others, communal worship has always played a vital part, yet many professing Christians attend a church seldom or never.

A further difficulty arises in the case of a government which professes a different religion from that traditionally followed by the majority of the people it governs. Marxist governments officially exclude all religions, yet clearly the Eastern Orthodox Church retains some hold in Russia much as Islam does in other parts of the Soviet Union or Roman Catholicism does in Poland. Many people would argue that Marxism is itself a religion, and its rejection of more traditional faiths could be seen as evidence for that argument (all religions being mutually exclusive). Certainly the workers' paradise seems no nearer than the Christian one.

In Islam, some at least of the internal tensions and conflicts stem from the two main divisions, Sunni and Shi'a. Very broadly, the ruling class has tended, traditionally, to belong to the former and the popular masses to the latter. The recent political success of Shi'ism in Iran in an extreme and zealous form has been an element in provoking hostility both within Islam and with the rest of the world. Its encouragement of Muslim fundamentalism throughout Islam is likely to remain a considerable influence for revolutionary change.

Religion is, to some extent, a matter of geographical distribution. If you are a Hindu you may very likely be an Indian; it would be surprising if you were a Japanese. Some religions, however, are more widely spread, such as Roman Catholicism, and despite the existence of a Jewish state in Israel, Judaism claims substantial numbers of adherents worldwide.

LANGUAGES OF THE WORLD

1 Quechua	25 Kinyarwanda
2 Dutch	26 Kirundi
3 Danish	27 Chichewa
4 Icelandic	28 Malagasy
5 Norwegian	29 Afrikaans
6 Swedish	30 Pushtu Dari
7 Finnish	31 Urdu
8 German	32 Hindi
9 Polish	33 Nepali
10 Czech/Slovak	34 Dzongkha
11 Magyar	35 Bengali
12 Rumanian	36 Burmese
13 Bulgarian	37 Thai
14 Serbo-Croatian	38 Lao
15 Italian	39 Khmer
16 Albanian	40 Bahasa Malay
17 Greek	41 Bahasa Indonesia
18 Turkish	42 Vietnamese
19 Hebrew	43 Philippino
20 Farsi	44 Sinhala
21 Somali	45 Korean
22 Amharic	46 Japanese
23 Sango	47 Mongolian
24 Swahili	

Asia and Oceania — Languages Map

ARCTIC OCEAN

UNION OF SOVIET SOCIALIST REPUBLICS

MONGOLIA 47
NTH. KOREA 45
STH. KOREA 46
JAPAN
CHINA
TAIWAN
HONG KONG
TURKEY 18
CYP
LEB
SYRIA
ISRAEL 19
JOR
IRAQ
IRAN 20
AFGHAN 30
PAKISTAN 31
NEPAL 33
BHUTAN 34
INDIA 32
BANG 35
BURMA 36
LAOS 38
THAILAND 37
KAMP 39
VIETNAM 42
PHILIPPINES 43
SAUDI ARABIA
KUW
QATAR
U.A.E.
OMAN
N. YEMEN
S. YEMEN
DJIBOUTI
EGYPT
SUDAN
ETHIOPIA 22
SOMALIA 21
UGANDA 24
KENYA 24
25 26
TANZANIA 24
SRI LANKA 44
MALAYSIA 40
BRUNEI
SING 41
INDONESIA
PAPUA NEW GUINEA
MALAWI 27
MOZAMBIQUE 28
ZIMBABWE
MADAGASCAR
SWAZILAND
LESOTHO

NORTH PACIFIC OCEAN

INDIAN OCEAN

Equator

AUSTRALIA

NEW CALEDONIA

NEW ZEALAND

Legend

- 🟦 English
- 🟪 French
- 🟧 Spanish
- 🟨 Portuguese
- 🟩 Chinese
- 🟩 Russian
- 🟫 Arabic
- 🟥 Others (see list)

Not the language of majority or of a significant proportion of the population ★

55

LANGUAGES OF THE WORLD

Estimates of the number of languages spoken in the world today vary enormously mainly as a result of the difficulty of defining a language as distinct from a dialect. Conservative estimates put the total at about 2,800, but a figure as high as 5,000 is often quoted.

The region of greatest linguistic diversity is the Americas, whose aboriginal inhabitants speak at least 1200 languages. The variety and richness of American languages (Chippewa is said to have up to 6,000 verb forms) is something of a mystery.

The number of American languages, however, is decreasing, and the majority are spoken by a small and diminishing number of people. In fact, the great majority of languages are spoken by relatively few. Only about 100 languages are spoken by more than 1 million people, and only 20 by 50 million or more (see below).

Although more people speak Chinese than any other language, it is spoken by very few non-Chinese, and the languages most widely spoken across the world either as the native tongue or as a second language are English, French and Spanish. This is a result of European imperialism, just as the prevalence of Latin in medieval Europe was a legacy of the Roman Empire. The persistence of these "colonial" languages, even in countries of Asia and Africa where they have never been a native language and where cultural nationalism is often eager to discard the symptoms of a colonial past, is helped by the frequent absence of any other single language in common. There are, for instance, about 500 languages in Africa south of the Sahara and probably a larger number in India. The reason why the Indian cricket team speak to each other in English is that they have no other mutually intelligible tongue.

World's principal languages
One per cent of the world population is roughly equal to 50 million people. The geographical location of speakers of different languages is aptly contrasted between the two most widely spoken. The very large majority of Guoyo speakers live in mainland China. English, on the other hand, is widely spoken in Australia, Bahamas, Canada, Sri Lanka, Cyprus, Gambia, Ghana, Guyana, India, Eire, Jamaica, Kenya, Malaysia, Malta, New Zealand, Nigeria, Pakistan, Sierra Leone, Singapore, South Africa, Tanzania, Trinadad and Tobago, Uganda, UK, USA and Zimbabwe. It is also used widely as the second language of educated Europeans and of citizens of the USSR.

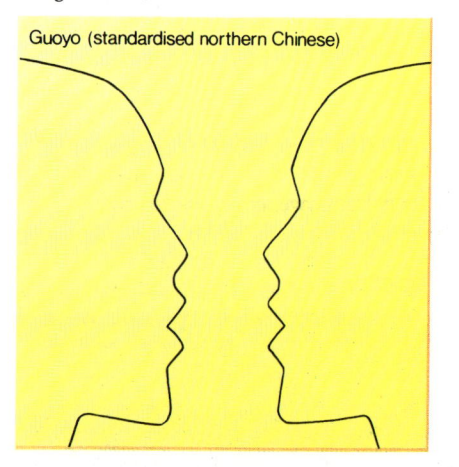

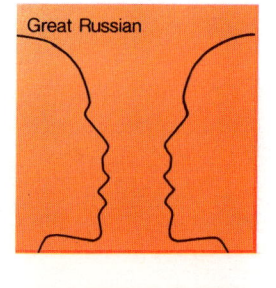

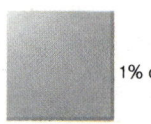

Guoyo (standardised northern Chinese)

English

Great Russian

Spanish

1% of world population

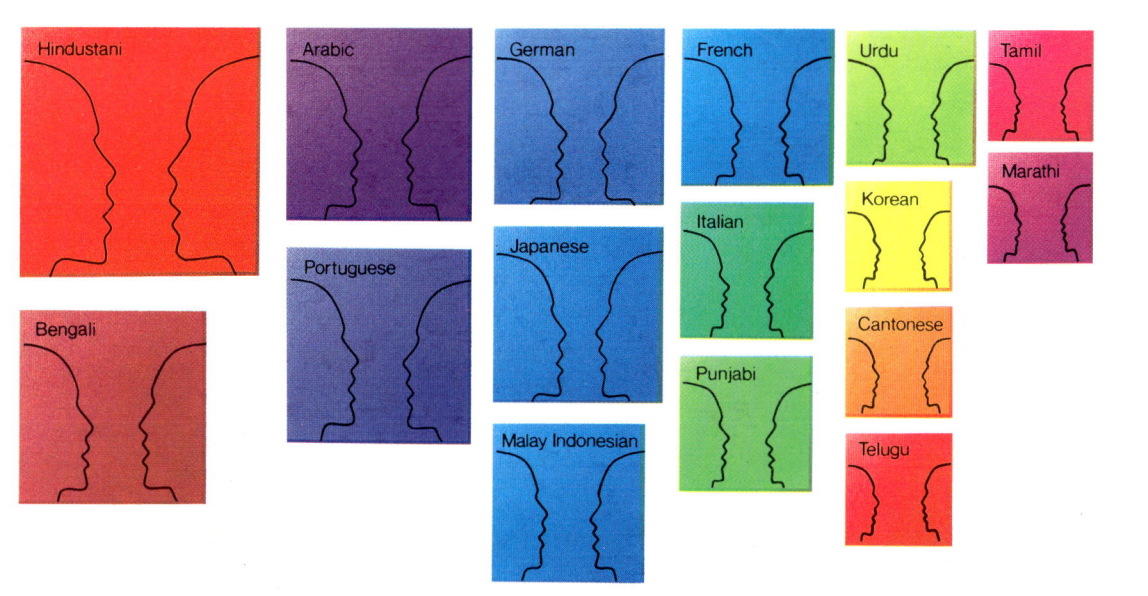

World's principal languages
The twenty most widely spoken languages are illustrated here. In total, these twenty languages are spoken by over three billion people across the globe, or 66 per cent of the world's population. There are estimated to be 5,000 languages which are spoken by the people of the world.

One effect of the prevalence of "colonial" languages is the perpetuation of social and economic divisions. In many African and Asian countries, a European language such as English or French is spoken by the political, social and/or economic elite — by generals and businessmen — but not by the mass of the people. Those who speak only the local language are at an obvious disadvantage, as they discover at an early age when, going to school, they often find appropriate teaching materials in their language are inferior or unobtainable.

Once a language gains a degree of international currency such as English has attained, for instance as the language of scholarship in which scientists and others communicate internationally, that status tends to reinforce its dominant position. However, such a situation may be reversed, as is evident from the example of Latin. Attempts have often been made to devise an international language, easily learned and spoken, but they have not been successful.

A language represents a culture, and the loss of a language is therefore a cultural impoverishment. It is perhaps ironic that attempts to sustain minor languages are no less vigorous, or necessary, in countries like Britain and France than they are in countries trying to adjust to a post-colonial status.

The map shows the main languages spoken in most countries, and indicates the many areas of the world where the "official" language, or the language of the political/commercial elite, is not that of a large proportion of the people. The diagram shows the major languages of the world and the proportion of the world's population that speak them.

WORLD FOOD PRODUCTION

Countries where agricultural exports account for more than 50% of all exports by value (1983) are indicated by their major cash crop.

Major cash crops

- Coffee
- Groundnuts
- Oil palms
- Cotton
- Pepper
- Cloves
- Cereals
- Bananas
- Sugar
- Rice
- Tea
- Dairy products

Predominant agricultural regions

- Little or no agricultural activity
- Nomadic herding
- Hunting, gathering, fishing and primitive cultivation
- Shifting and marginal cultivation
- Commerical forestry
- Extensive grazing or stock raising
- Subsistence agriculture: mainly rice
- Subsistence agriculture: other crops
- Subsistence agriculture: mixed crop and livestock
- Mediterranean agriculture: citrus, vines and olives
- Plantation crops
- Specialized horticulture
- Other commercial crops: grain dominant
- Commercial agriculture: mixed crop and livestock
- Dairy farming
- Manufacturing and service industries
- Principal fishing grounds

59

WORLD FOOD PRODUCTION

Only a small proportion of the total land surface of the Earth can be classed as of high natural fertility, though a considerably larger proportion (still, however, less than 25 per cent of the total) is capable of productive agriculture. This is more than double the area being cultivated at present. The fact that nearly two-thirds of the world's population do not get enough to eat is therefore not due to a shortage of cultivatable land.

The most striking aspect of world food production is the disparity in methods. In many parts of the world subsistence farming is carried on in a manner which has changed very little since man or, very likely, woman, first took up a hoe. In other parts, agriculture has become a highly technical industry exploiting all the resources of the technological revolution. The vast surplus yields of the North American prairies compared with, for example, the bare subsistence of much of Africa, are due not so much to Nature's generosity with soil and rainfall as to a rich nation's aptitude with fertilizers and irrigation.

There are many worrying aspects of modern high-yield agriculture, not least its dependence on fertilizers derived from nonrenewable resources; increase in world food production since 1960 is

World cereal stocks, 1971–83
Note the depletion in stocks in the early 1970s, a result of the African food crisis (see WORLD FOOD CONSUMPTION).

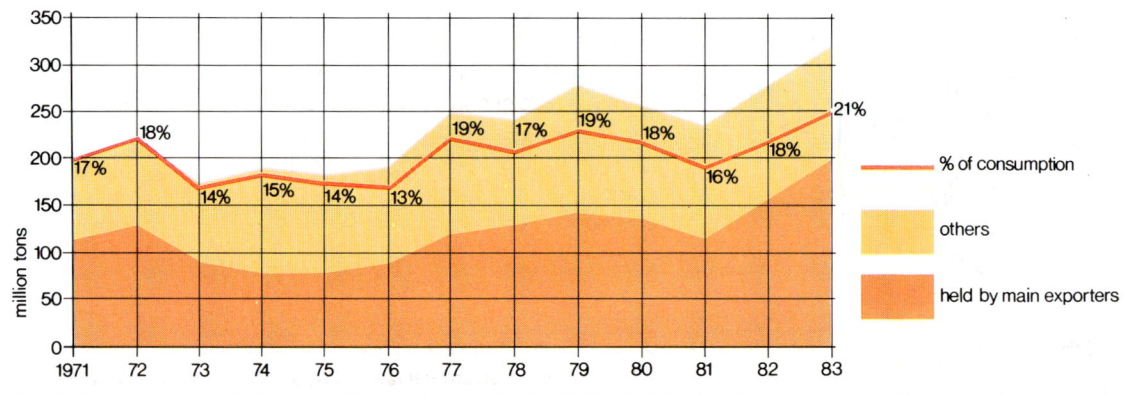

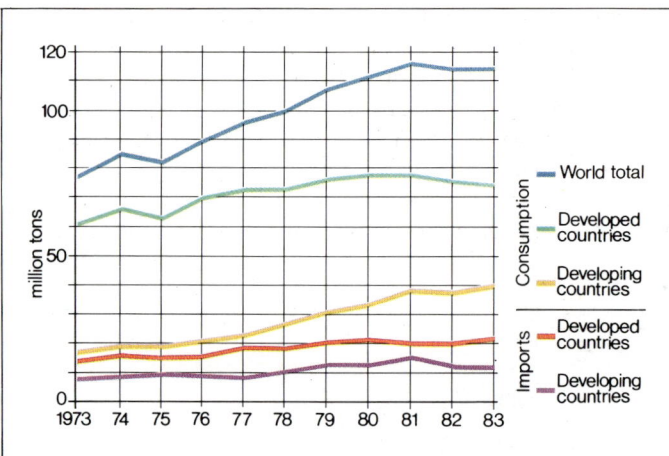

Consumption and imports of fertilizers, 1973–83

In the early 1970s fertilizer consumption levelled off in developing countries and declined in developed ones for the first time since World War II, due to fertilizer shortages and high world prices. These high prices generated new investment in fertilizer capacity. However, prices fell and consumption expanded during the rest of the 1970s. Since 1980 consumption has again levelled off as world prices again soared after the second oil shock of 1979, the effects of recession on agriculture and the international debt burdens of many developing countries that cut back imports.

Fishery production indices, 1971–83

The years 1969–71 are taken as the base of 100 per cent and all subsequent figures relate to those base years.

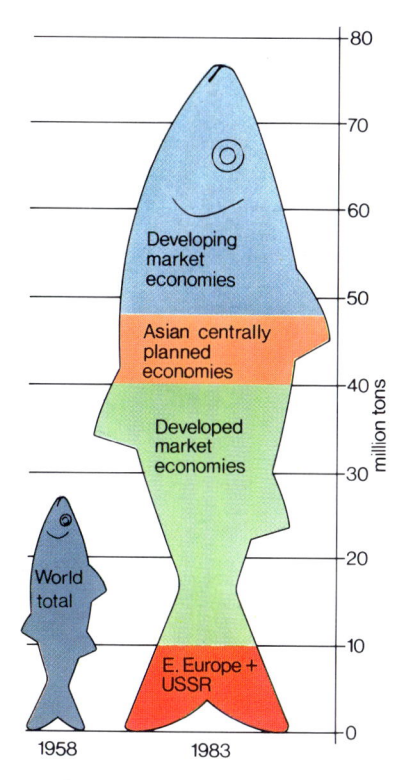

Prices
— weighted
— unweighted

World catch of fish

The total world fish catch in 1983 was almost exactly divided half and half between developing and developed countries. A further subdivision is made above between countries with free market economies and those with socialist centrally planned economies. The catch of the Asian centrally planned economies is largely attributable to China and North Korea.

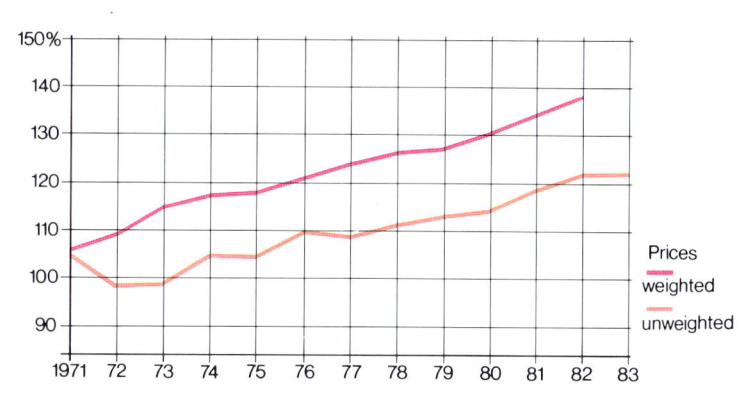

proportionately very close to the increase in the use of fertilizers. But of more immediate concern is the failure of so much of the rest of the world to produce enough food for its inhabitants. In spite of many heartening improvements, notably in China and India, the world situation overall cannot be said to have improved greatly since the Food and Agriculture Organization was founded in 1945.

A map of world food production is not, however, a reliable guide to what people eat — or, do *not* eat (see WORLD FOOD CONSUMPTION). One unfortunate tendency in many Third World countries has been for the growth of large-scale agricultural enterprises producing export cash crops at the expense of traditional, small-scale largely subsistence farming. The result may be an increase in national food production, and profits for the rich farmer or the big corporation, while local peasant farmers are further impoverished.

The oceans offer vast food resources, particularly of protein, the lack of which is the most serious deficiency in most of the world's undernourished populations. Japan, with very little farmland, is the country most dependent on fish; others with high consumption include Iceland, Norway and Denmark. Between 1950 and 1970 the world total fish catch increased at an annual rate of about 7 per cent, due to larger and more numerous fishing fleets plus more efficient methods.

However, since the 1970s the rate of increase has been sharply reduced, and a number of fisheries, including Californian sardines, North Sea herrings, South African pilchards and Peruvian anchovies, have been practically extinguished, at least temporarily. Over-fishing is the chief cause and, if the productivity of the oceans is to be maintained, much tighter regulation of fisheries is clearly needed than is provided by the numerous organizations currently struggling with these problems.

WORLD GRAIN TRADE

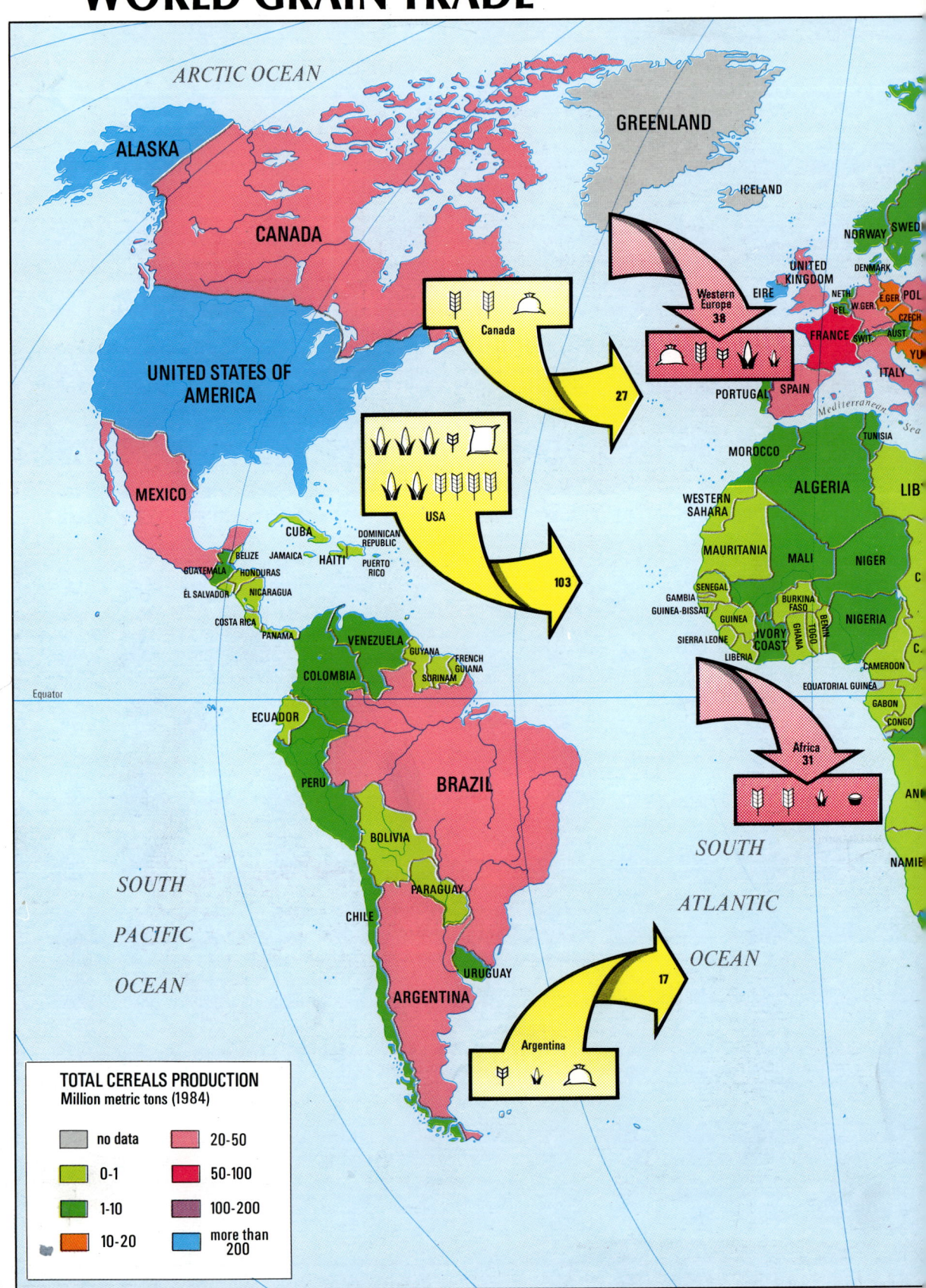

TOTAL CEREALS PRODUCTION
Million metric tons (1984)

- no data
- 0-1
- 1-10
- 10-20
- 20-50
- 50-100
- 100-200
- more than 200

Canada 27
USA 103
Argentina 17
Western Europe 38
Africa 31

63

WORLD GRAIN TRADE

Cereals are the largest single source of food for practically everybody and for a large proportion they constitute the chief item of diet. The trade in cereals thus provides a fair index of available food resources.

The overpowering predominance of North America in the world grain trade is immediately obvious. The United States accounts for about 16 per cent of the world total production of wheat, about 21 per cent of oats, and about 47 per cent of maize (corn), and it is far the largest exporter of cereals. Other major net exporters of grain are Canada, France, Australia, Argentina and Thailand, but the total from those countries is little more than half the United States total alone (see top right). Figures are obviously subject to considerable fluctuations from year to year, due to varying harvests, particularly in the Soviet Union which is the largest net importer of grain.

A major feature of the world grain trade during the past decade has been the continuing success of the United States and the comparative failure of the Soviet Union. The main grain producers between 1971 and 1981 recorded considerable increases in production — as much as 90 per cent up in Australia, about 70 per cent in Canada and the United States (in spite of the federal governments' efforts to restrict production) — while the Soviet Union, though still the largest grain producer after the United States, recorded a decrease in the same period. Soviet efforts to end their dependence on the United States farmers have so far met with no success.

The map also shows the inevitably small part played by the poorest countries in the world grain trade. Nearly every African country is a net importer of grain, but few can afford to import as much as they need. In spite of booming production worldwide, which just about kept pace with population growth up to the early 1980s, in some African countries, which were already suffering from food shortages, production fell. Egypt was self-sufficient in grain in the 1950s, but today it imports more than it grows in order to meet domestic requirements. Total grain imports in the whole of Africa are less than the total for Japan, but this is explained less by Japan's low cereal production than by its greater ability

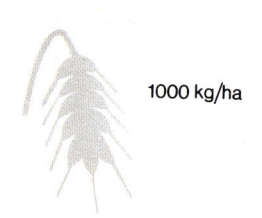

West Europe
USA
China
South America
USSR
Africa

1000 kg/ha

Cereal yields, 1984

Yields per hectare in Western Europe and in the United States are nearly twice the World average of about 2,500 kilograms. These high yields are achieved by an increasing level of mechanization, the intense use of fertilizers and the development of high-yield cereal strains. The Soviet Union by contrast is plagued by a general lack of investment in agriculture and inefficient transport and grain storage facilities. In Africa, where yields are less than half the World average, production is generally on a small scale with a much lower degree of mechanization and fertilizer use.

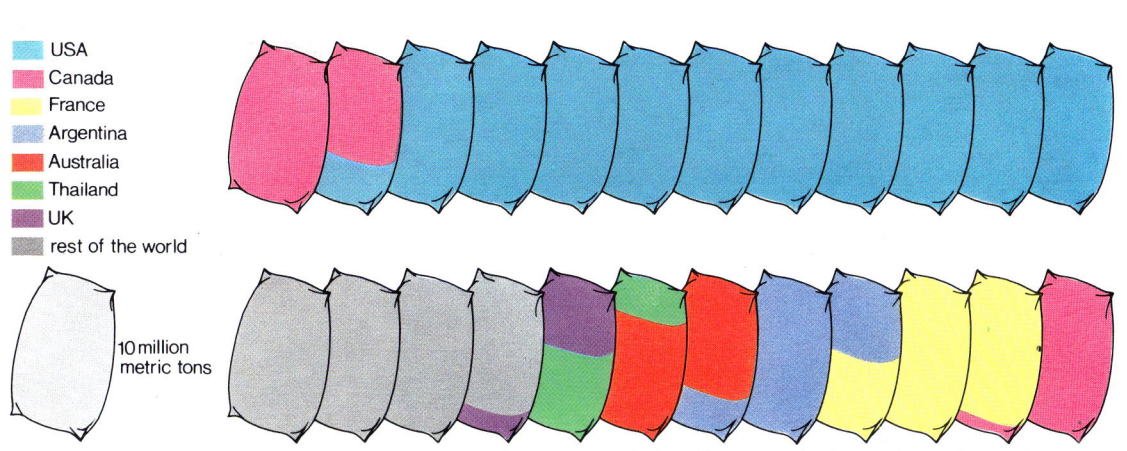

- USA
- Canada
- France
- Argentina
- Australia
- Thailand
- UK
- rest of the world

10 million metric tons

Principal grain exporters, 1984
The dominance of the United States is clear, contributing 44 per cent of the total World grain exports in 1984.

to pay. The map nonetheless illustrates the heavy dependence of African nations generally on imported grain, though it should be noted that in many tropical Third World countries other staple crops, such as cassava, are grown which reduce reliance on cereals.

In the early 1980s world grain production per capita fell sharply, though the reasons for this appear to have been temporary — largely the drought which brought such disaster to northeast Africa in particular. The main problem of world cereal resources remains one of distribution and use. For example, approximately one-third of the world total grain production is at present used as animal feed.

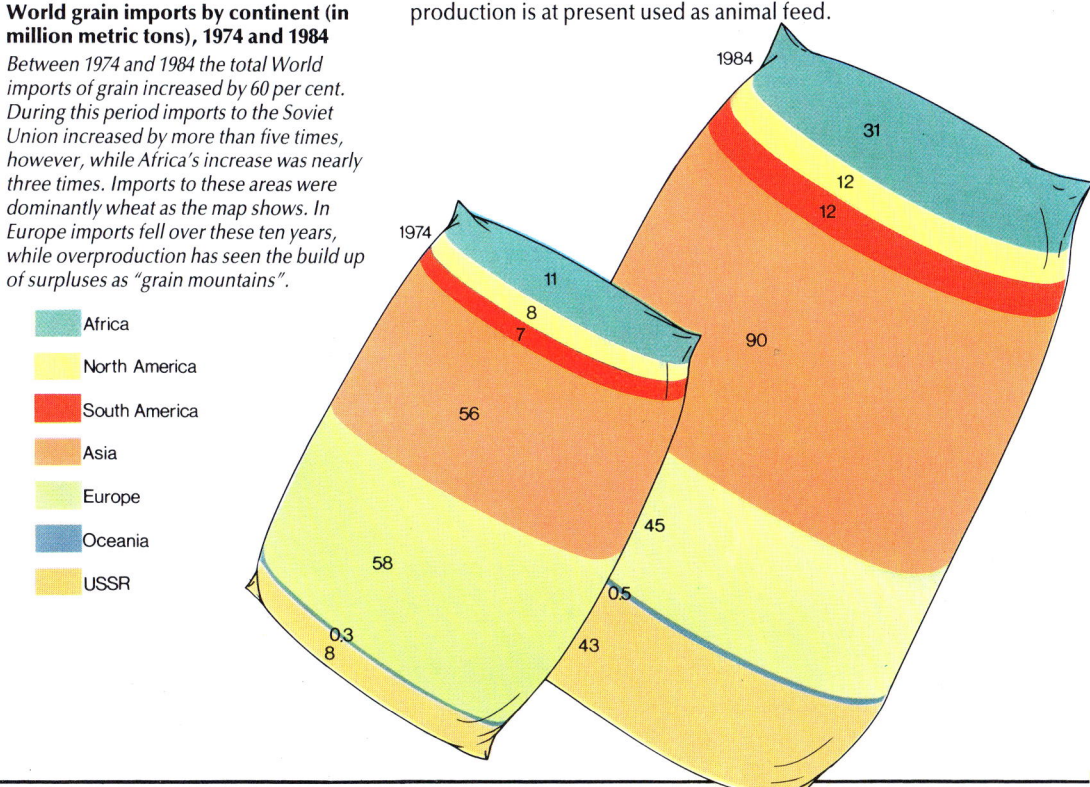

World grain imports by continent (in million metric tons), 1974 and 1984
Between 1974 and 1984 the total World imports of grain increased by 60 per cent. During this period imports to the Soviet Union increased by more than five times, however, while Africa's increase was nearly three times. Imports to these areas were dominantly wheat as the map shows. In Europe imports fell over these ten years, while overproduction has seen the build up of surpluses as "grain mountains".

- Africa
- North America
- South America
- Asia
- Europe
- Oceania
- USSR

1974: 11, 8, 7, 56, 58, 0.3, 8

1984: 31, 12, 12, 90, 45, 0.5, 43

WORLD FOOD CONSUMPTION

DIETARY ENERGY SUPPLIES PER CAPITA
Percentage above or below requirements (1981–83)

- worse than 15% below
- 15-10% below
- 10-5% below
- 0-5% below
- 0-5% over
- 5-15% over
- 15-30% over
- more than 30% over

PROTEINS PER CAPITA
Grams per day (1981–83)

- 50
- 0
- Vegetable
- Animal
- no data

67

WORLD FOOD CONSUMPTION

The crux of the world's food problem is dramatically illustrated by the colours on the map, which demonstrate that the problem is not simply one of surfeit or scarcity but one of distribution. While many countries, including all of Europe and North America, have food supplies greater than they need, in many others, particularly in Africa but also in other regions of the Third World, the average diet is insufficient to preserve ordinary standards of life and health. In the Sahel, thousands die annually of starvation; in the EEC and the United States, embarrassingly large agricultural surpluses are stockpiled, and a substantial number of deaths result from eating too much — or too rich — food.

Dietary requirements, as shown on the map, are the minimum amounts of animal and vegetable foods regarded by the World Health Organization as necessary to preserve health. This amount varies according to age, weight, climate — people need to eat more in cold climates than in hot ones — and other factors, while the national totals given here cannot indicate local variations, as between a middle-class town dweller and a nomadic pastoralist. In many countries, such as Argentina or Mexico, where the food supply is more than adequate on a national level, many people do not get enough to eat. There are also

Areas of food avoidance
Avoidance of these foods are mainly for religious reasons.

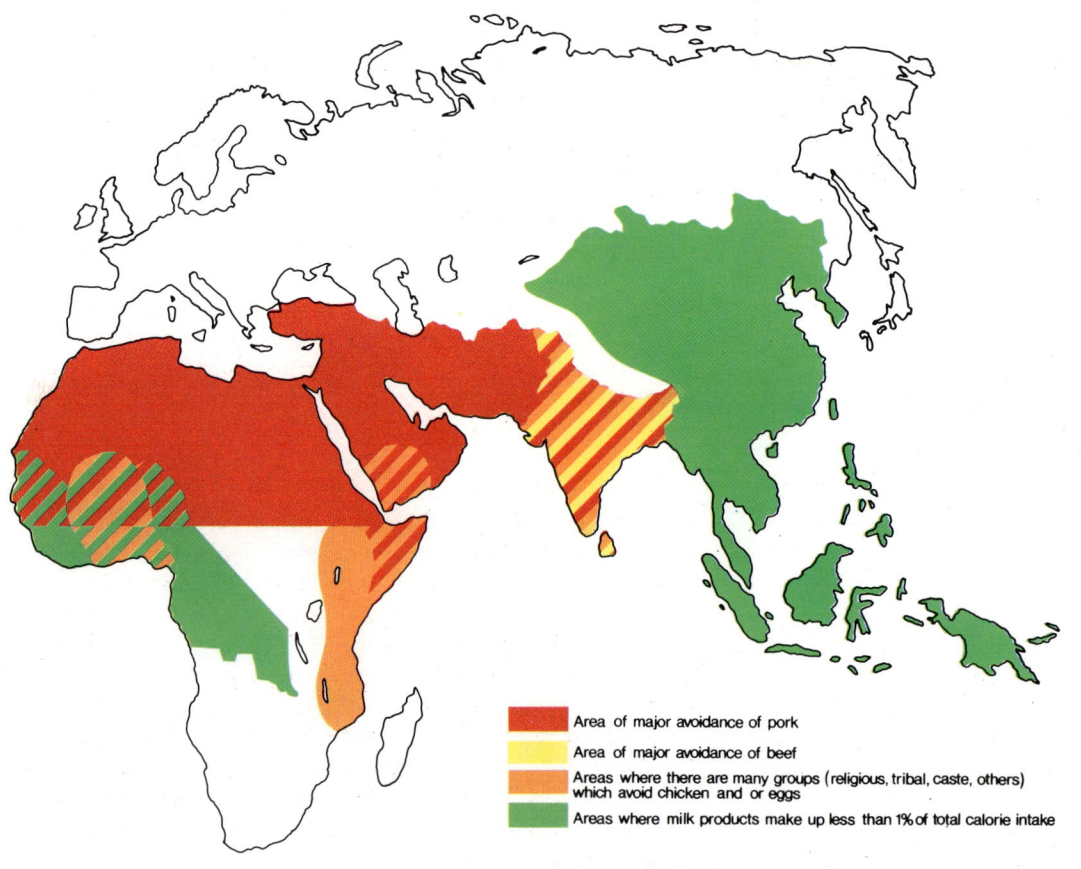

- Area of major avoidance of pork
- Area of major avoidance of beef
- Areas where there are many groups (religious, tribal, caste, others) which avoid chicken and or eggs
- Areas where milk products make up less than 1% of total calorie intake

African food aid in cereals, 1984
The shipment of food aid is not a straightforward operation. The passage of large quantities of cereals, the most critical commodity, faces several potential problems. Ports are frequently congested, unloading is delayed and storage facilities too often inadequate. Transport networks are often unable to manage the rapid movement of large volumes and land-locked countries particularly suffer as a consequence. Bureaucracy and corruption amongst officals also hamper relief operations.

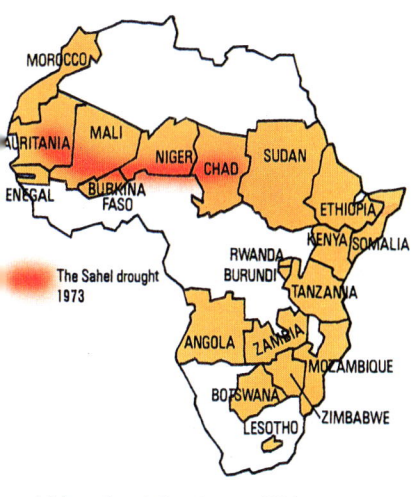

USA
EEC
Canada
Japan
Australia
Sweden
others

500 tons

African food shortages, 1984
Many African countries faced abnormal food shortages in the early 1980s. These were years of drought in nearly half the countries of Africa. The result of poor crops, cereal production in 1983/84 in 24 African countries was 15% less than the previous normal crop of 1981, and has been worsened in some areas by political unrest. The African food emergency has continued into 1985 and 1986.

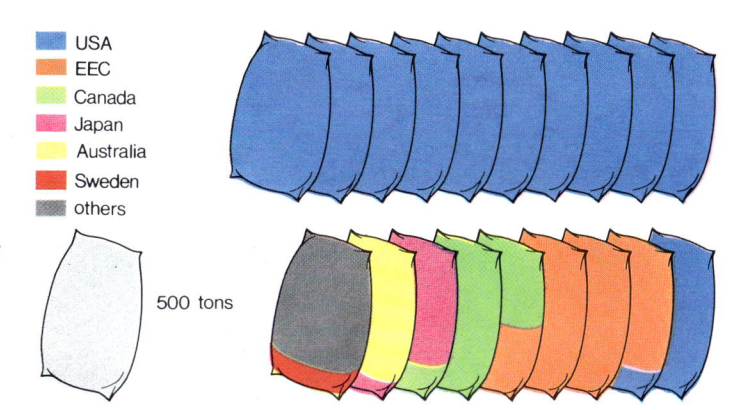

greater national extremes than are revealed within the range from over 30 per cent above to over 15 per cent below normal requirements. The figure of Eire is over 50 per cent above, for Ethiopia nearly 30 per cent below.

In many Third World countries suffering from deficiencies, the major problem is lack of protein, necessary for physical growth and regeneration. The map also shows annual average consumption of protein per capita, divided into animal and vegetable protein. A high proportion of animal protein is characteristic of rich countries. It is a wasteful method of fulfilling dietary requirements since, for example, the quantity of cereals necessary to produce one pound of beefsteak could have fed hundreds of people.

The picture of world food consumption in the past thirty years presents several cruel ironies. For example, while food production in developed countries has generally increased, often at remarkable and still-continuing rates, in many African countries it has actually decreased markedly in that period. Social and economic policies are partly to blame; so are climatic conditions. In the Sahel, drought is always a danger, but that which has continued more-or-less unabated from the late 1960s into the mid-1980s is the longest this century, causing the extension of the desert into former grasslands. Only time will tell how permanent these changes are.

Before the Industrial Revolution famine occurred even in Western Europe, whereas today it is confined almost without exception to countries south of a line drawn through the Mediterranean. Famine is hard to categorize: contemporary statistics probably do not tell the whole story and until about thirty years ago it was impossible to compile an accurate survey. Nevertheless, the evidence suggests that famine is increasing. The map at left shows 20 countries where serious food shortages, many amounting to famine, were recorded during 1984.

Food shortages cannot be dealt with in isolation, and emergency aid programmes supply, at best, temporary solutions. However, in view of the world surplus of food production, no explanation of current world politics and economics is likely to erase the resentment of ordinary — hungry — people.

WORLD HEALTH

70

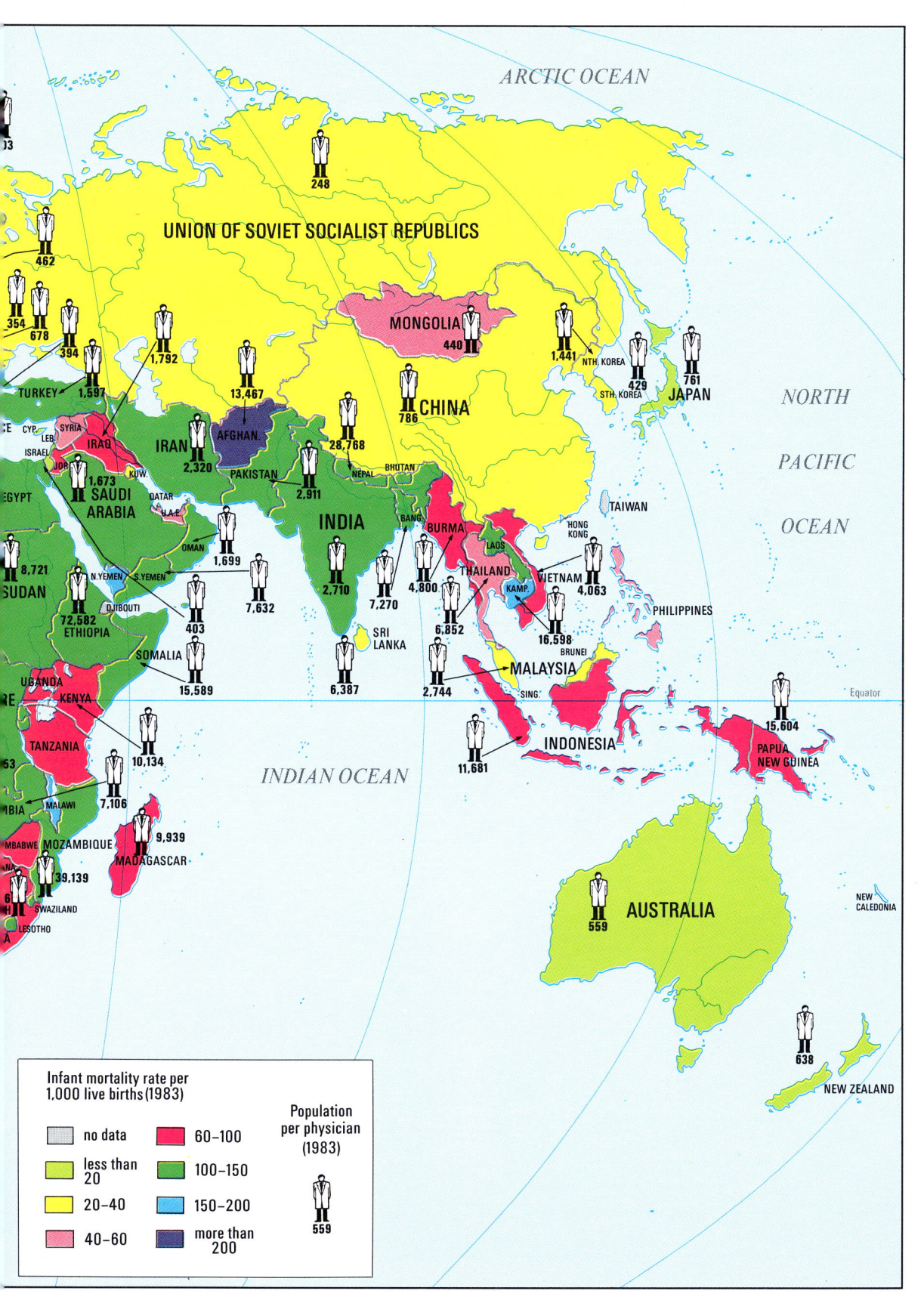

Asia and Oceania: Infant Mortality and Population per Physician (1983)

Map Labels

Oceans and Regions:
- ARCTIC OCEAN
- NORTH PACIFIC OCEAN
- INDIAN OCEAN
- Equator

Countries and Population per Physician:

- UNION OF SOVIET SOCIALIST REPUBLICS — 248
- MONGOLIA — 440
- CHINA — 786
- NTH. KOREA — 1,441
- STH. KOREA — 429
- JAPAN — 761
- TURKEY — 1,597
- (unlabeled) — 462
- (unlabeled) — 354
- (unlabeled) — 678
- (unlabeled) — 394
- (unlabeled) — 1,792
- SYRIA / IRAQ — 1,673
- CYP, LEB, ISRAEL, JOR, KUW
- SAUDI ARABIA
- QATAR, U.A.E.
- IRAN — 2,320
- AFGHAN. — 13,467
- PAKISTAN — 2,911
- NEPAL, BHUTAN
- INDIA — 2,710
- BANG. — 7,270
- BURMA — 4,800
- LAOS
- THAILAND — 6,852
- KAMP. — 16,598
- VIETNAM — 4,063
- HONG KONG
- TAIWAN
- PHILIPPINES
- MALAYSIA — 2,744
- BRUNEI, SING.
- INDONESIA — 11,681
- PAPUA NEW GUINEA — 15,604
- SRI LANKA — 6,387
- OMAN — 1,699
- N.YEMEN, S.YEMEN — 7,632
- EGYPT
- SUDAN — 8,721
- DJIBOUTI
- ETHIOPIA — 72,582
- SOMALIA — 15,589
- UGANDA
- KENYA — 10,134
- TANZANIA — 7,106
- MALAWI
- MOZAMBIQUE
- MADAGASCAR — 9,939
- ZIMBABWE — 39,139
- SWAZILAND, LESOTHO
- AUSTRALIA — 559
- NEW CALEDONIA
- NEW ZEALAND — 638
- (unlabeled) — 403

Legend

Infant mortality rate per 1,000 live births (1983)
- no data
- less than 20
- 20–40
- 40–60
- 60–100
- 100–150
- 150–200
- more than 200

Population per physician (1983) — 559

WORLD HEALTH

A major influence in life expectancy is the infant mortality rate, which is the number of babies per 1,000 born alive who die before their first birthday. No one will be surprised to note the close relationship between health and wealth indicated on the map. In most Western industrialized countries this figure is less than 12. In Japan it is 7, which is the lowest. In most of the poorest countries of the Third World it is over 100, and in many, over 150. The estimate for Ethiopia, before the drought, was approaching 200. Of all the dire comparisons between the rich and the poor of the world, no figures are more shocking than these.

Although many poor tropical countries suffer from endemic diseases hard to eradicate, a total revolution in figures for infant mortality and life expectancy could be achieved by what are, in theory, very simple measures. For example, if the current campaign of the World Health Organization for clean water and sanitation were to be fully successful by its projected finishing date in 1990, the effect on world health would be much greater than any conceivable breakthrough in the medical laboratories of the West.

The ratio between the number of physicians and the total population is a rather rough-and-ready guide to health care. Obviously, where doctors are scarce, mortality is likely to be high, and doctors are notably scarce in countries where infant mortality is high. The Soviet Union, nevertheless, has a very large number of doctors, more than double the proportion in the United States, but infant mortality rate is lower in the United States and life expectancy four years longer. Soviet doctors tend to have a lower social status than they do in Western countries, but it would be unwise to draw any dogmatic inferences from that. The number of physicians includes all medical graduates engaged in research, administration and teaching, and if it were possible to obtain figures for physicians involved directly in medical practice, the results might look different, as they would if "paramedics" and workers outside conventional Western ideas of medicine were included.

Population per hospital bed
Selected countries

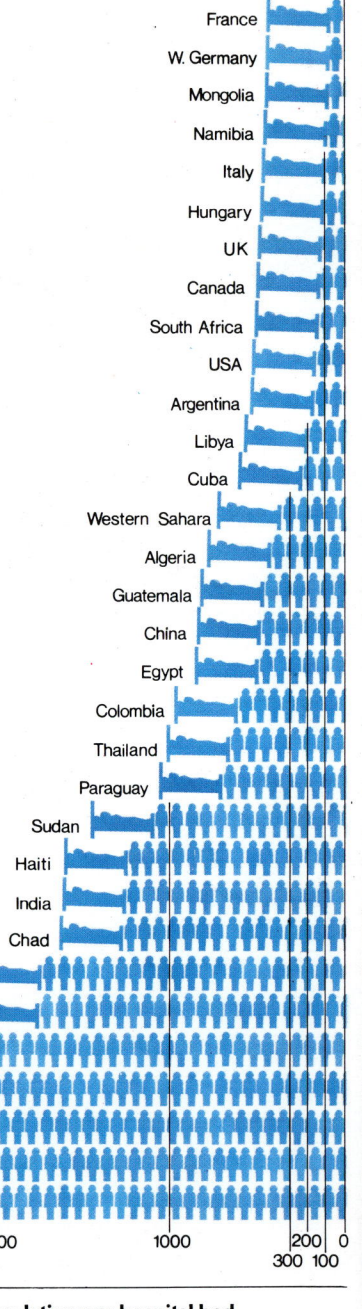

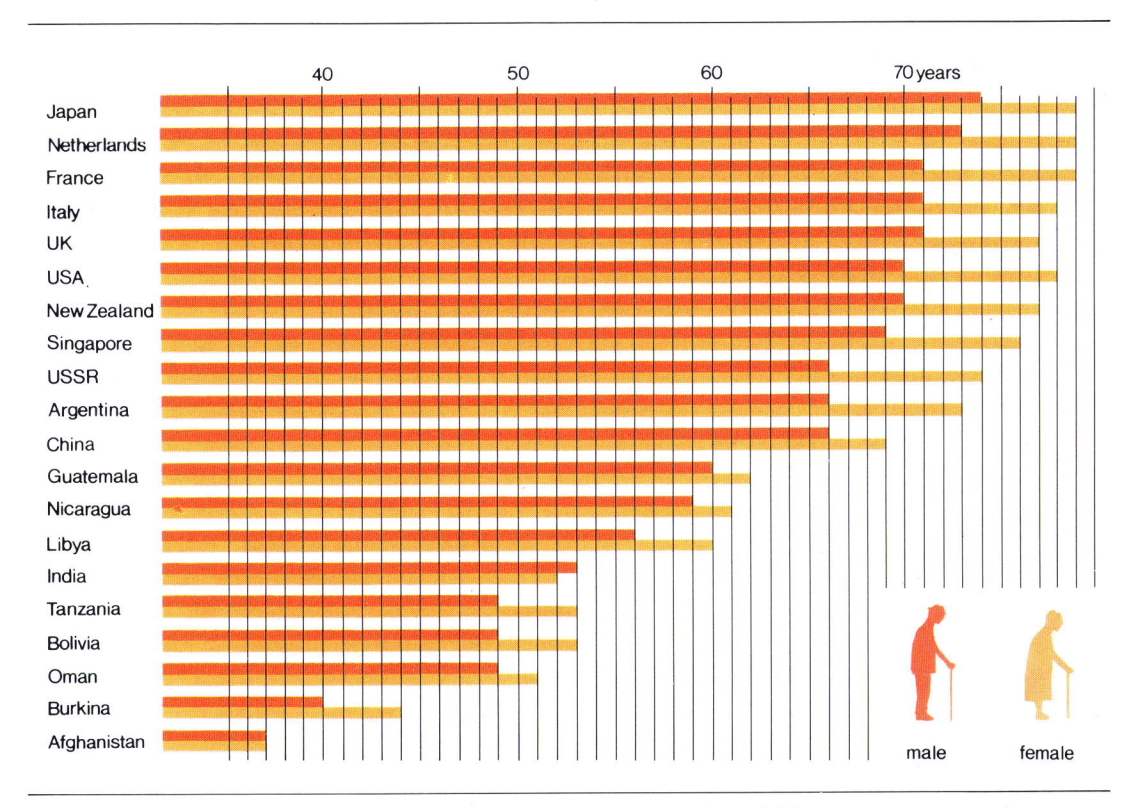

Life expectancy at birth
Only in India do men live on average longer than women. Otherwise female life expectancy is greater and the difference between male and female longevity appears to increase with increasing overall life expectancy.

The number of hospital beds available in proportion to total population (see left) also shows wide discrepancies between rich and poor. In Bangladesh, where life expectancy is about 47 years, there is only 1 hospital bed for every 4,500 people; in Nepal, where life expectancy is about 44, only 1 bed for 5,000. However, North Korea, where life expectancy is three years shorter than in South Korea, has more than six times as many hospital beds proportionately, or so it says. In such cases the suspicion arises that the figures are based on different criteria and that wishful thinking may play a part. Medical qualifications and medical practice also vary. The "traditional" medicine of China and some other countries is not included.

The average life expectancy in a country is another indication of the general state of health care. In the poorest countries of Africa average life expectancy at birth is less than 50 and in Ethiopia it is less than 40, while in the rich, industrialized countries it is over 70. It is almost invariably the case that women live on average longer than men, and in a few countries the life expectancy of women is now not far short of 80, for example 79 in Norway, Japan, Switzerland and France, 78 in the United States. However, it is thought that current life expectancy in these countries is near the realistic limit: the Bible's estimate of "three-score years and ten" has been exceeded, but is not likely to be exceeded by much more.

WORLD DISEASE

HEART DISEASE
Coronary Heart Disease: Mortality rate per 100,000 (males 35-64 years)

- 292 and over
- 211-291
- 122-211
- 54-121
- 1-53
- no data

CEREBROVASCULAR DISEASE
Cerebrovascular Disease: Mortality rate per 100,000 (males 35-64 years)

- 105 and over
- 64-104
- 18-63
- no data

TYPHOID, CHOLERA AND SCHISTOSOMIASIS

- Countries where vaccination against Typhoid recommended
- Countries where vaccination against Typhoid and Cholera recommended
- Areas where Schistosomiasis prevalent
- C Vaccination against Cholera essential and certificate required

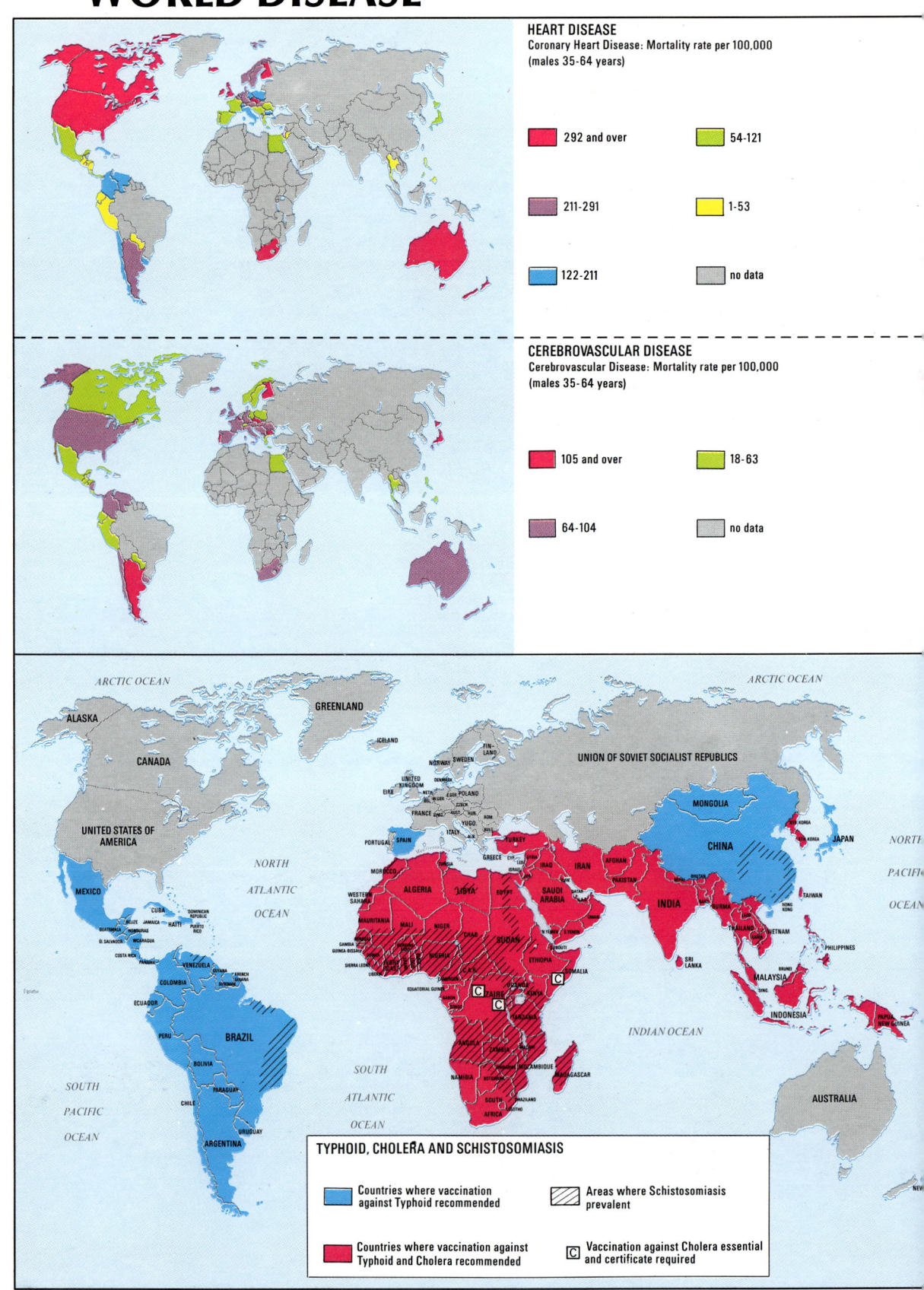

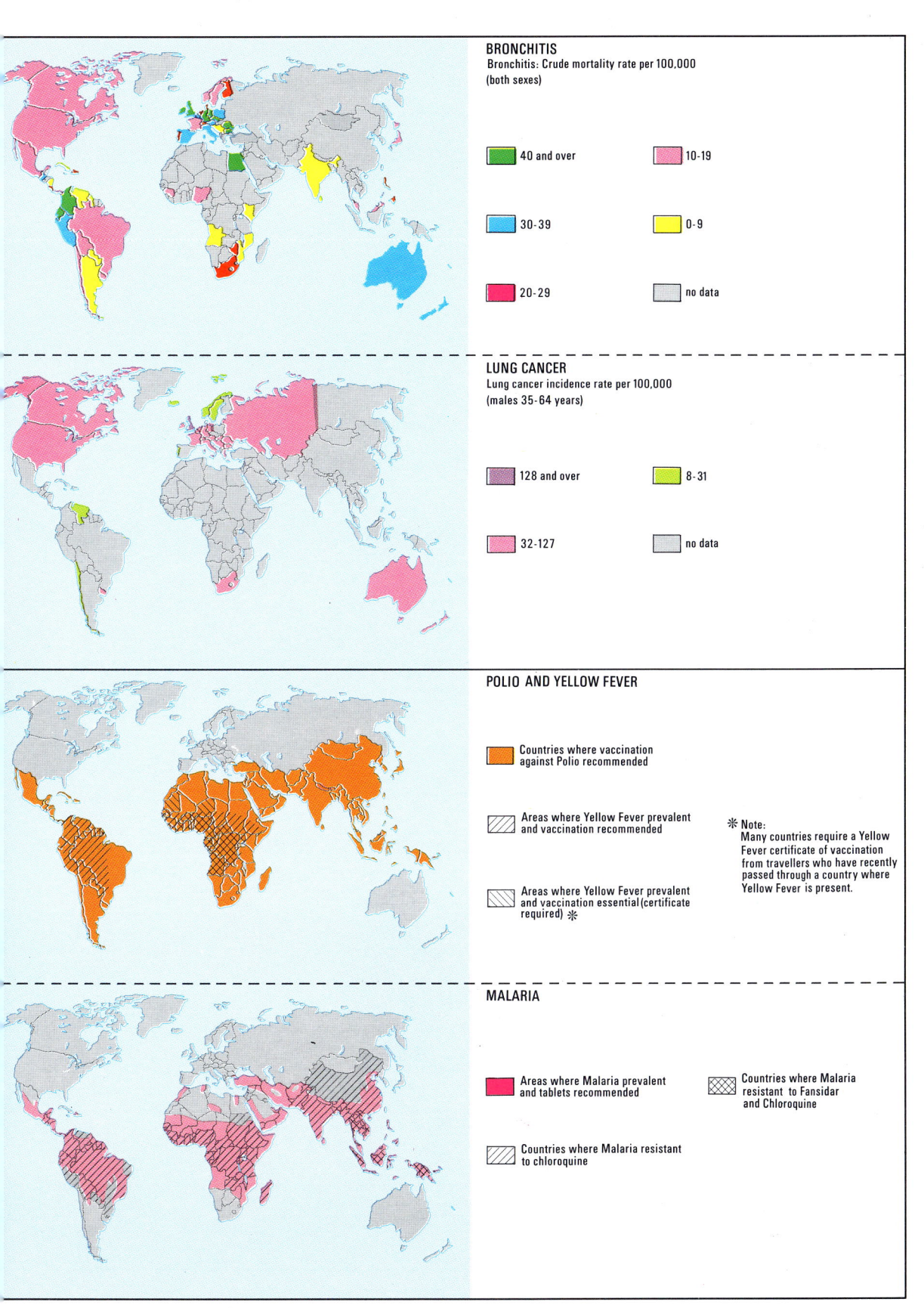

BRONCHITIS

Bronchitis: Crude mortality rate per 100,000 (both sexes)

- 🟩 40 and over
- 🟦 30-39
- 🟥 20-29
- 🟪 10-19
- 🟨 0-9
- ⬜ no data

LUNG CANCER

Lung cancer incidence rate per 100,000 (males 35-64 years)

- 128 and over
- 32-127
- 8-31
- no data

POLIO AND YELLOW FEVER

- Countries where vaccination against Polio recommended
- Areas where Yellow Fever prevalent and vaccination recommended
- Areas where Yellow Fever prevalent and vaccination essential (certificate required) ✴

✴ Note:
Many countries require a Yellow Fever certificate of vaccination from travellers who have recently passed through a country where Yellow Fever is present.

MALARIA

- Areas where Malaria prevalent and tablets recommended
- Countries where Malaria resistant to chloroquine
- Countries where Malaria resistant to Fansidar and Chloroquine

WORLD DISEASE

Much more money is spent on curing disease than on preventing it although, as everybody knows, prevention is better than cure. Most of the world's premature deaths from disease are fundamentally due to poverty — malnutrition, contaminated water, inadequate sanitation, lack of medical care and ignorance. However, these problems have largely been eradicated from industrialized Europe and North America, as a result of ample food, and past investment in and current expenditure on safe water supplies, sewage disposal and inoculation programmes. Even so, roughly 90 per cent of the world's current health expenditure is still spent in these areas on additional medical services.

It is said that in the North (Europe, North America) people die of the diseases of abundance and old age, while in the South (Africa, Asia, South America) they die of the diseases of deprivation. Thus, in the North about one half of the deaths are caused by coronary heart and cerebrovascular diseases, associated with a rich diet high in animal fats, lack of exercise and tobacco. Nearly a quarter are due to cancer, smoking being involved especially with lung cancer as well as bronchitis. Other degenerative diseases such as arthritis accompany a longer life expectancy.

Another contributory factor, hard to measure, is mental stress: expenditure on tranquillizers in Europe and North America exceeds the entire health budget of the world's sixty poorest countries. Suicide rates and occupants of mental hospitals are also higher. Alcoholism and now drugs of addiction play a part.

A growing number of minor illnesses and more serious infectious diseases such as lassa fever and "legionnaires' disease" have appeared comparatively recently. Though worrying, they are statistically insignificant in a world picture. AIDS (see top right) may prove to be an exception unless the vast resources currently devoted to the search for a vaccine prove successful.

Infectious and parasitic diseases
Chance per 1,000 of 45-year-old males dying in selected countries.

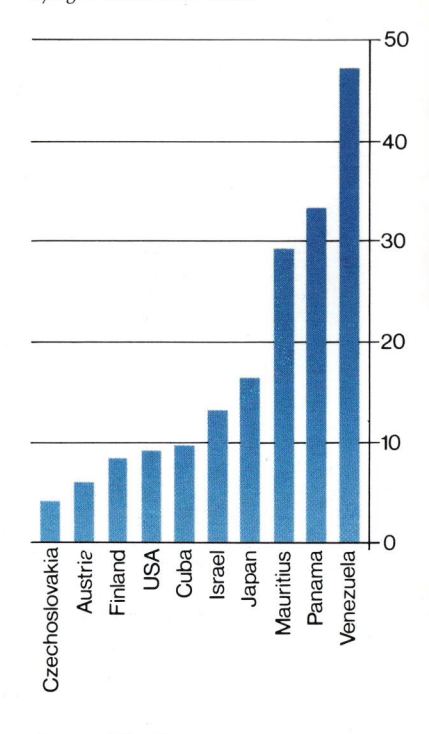

Cause of death
Comparison of developed and developing countries.

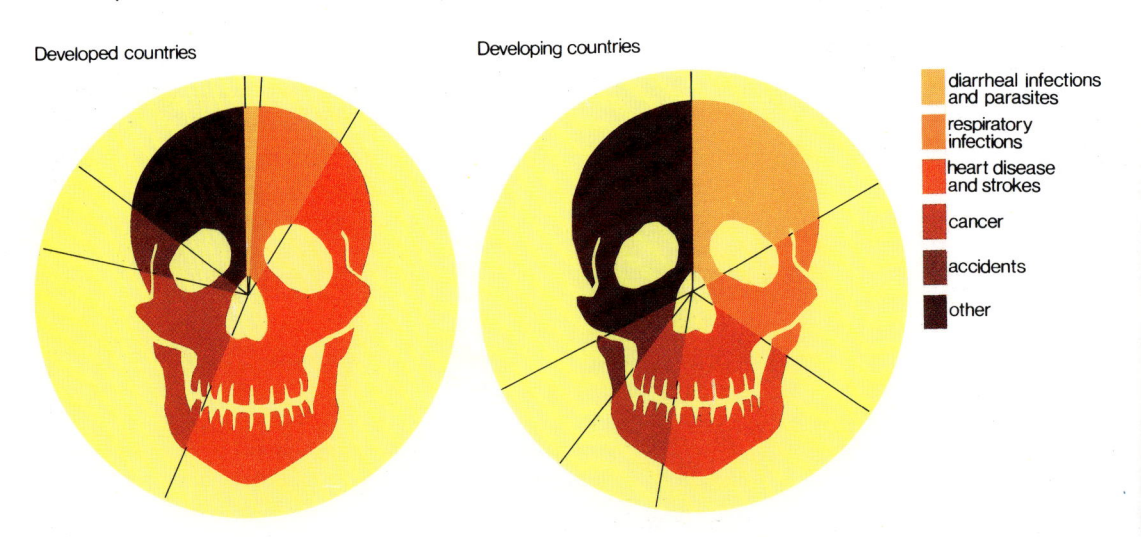

Developed countries

Developing countries

- diarrheal infections and parasites
- respiratory infections
- heart disease and strokes
- cancer
- accidents
- other

African epidemic

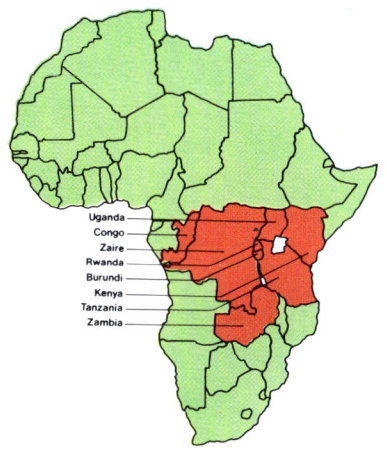

AIDS

In October 1986 Acquired Immune Deficiency Syndrome (AIDS) had struck in 69 countries around the globe. The WHO estimated that up to ten million people worldwide may have been infected by the virus. In central Africa, where many researchers suspect the disease originated, AIDS is taking on epidemic proportions (see above). An estimated 50,000 Africans were suffering from AIDS at the end of 1986, with a minimum of 10,000 new cases a year for the next five years. Some specialists suspect that the real figures may be several times higher.

In the United States and the UK the figures (see below) are relatively small, but in the UK the number of cases may be doubling every ten months. One fact that is not in doubt, however, is that AIDS kills. Governments are waking up to a severe problem; they are now putting money into public information and the international race to find an effective treatment.

By contrast, in the South — the Third World — the number of deaths resulting from cardiovascular diseases and cancer combined is only about one quarter of the total, due to low life expectancy. Diarrhoea and associated infections, in theory very simple to cure, are major killers, while in the North they are insignificant. According to one estimate, there are more deaths from diarrhoea in the Third World in one decade than the total number of deaths from plague in Europe throughout the Middle Ages. The victims are mainly children under the age of five.

Measles, whooping cough, polio, tuberculosis, tetanus and diptheria are major child-killers worldwide, accounting for about 5 million deaths a year. Yet immunization is possible against all of them, and practically all the deaths occur in Third World countries where on average fewer than two out of ten children receive immunization. One bright spot in this grim picture is the victory over smallpox, formerly a major killer. The World Health Organization announced the eradication of smallpox throughout the world in 1980. The fight against some diseases is prolonged when strains resistant to certain drugs appear. In the case of malaria the map shows areas where resistance to the drugs chloroquine and Fansidar occurs.

The WHO, which is largely occupied with prevention, has often pointed out that as an indication of health care the number of water taps available is better than the number of hospital beds (see WORLD HEALTH). Contracted from contaminated water supplies are the major infectious diseases associated with diarrhoea: cholera, dysentry and typhoid. Schistosomiasis and hookworm infestation are also associated with water in unsanitary conditions. Malaria and yellow fever are transmitted by mosquitoes breeding in stagnant water, and biting insects are also involved in filariasis, leishmaniasis, trypanosomiasis, as well as plague. Insufficient water supplies in contrast predispose to conjunctivitis, trachoma, leprosy and scabies.

AIDS

UK	Estimated number September 1986	Predicted number end 1990
CARRIERS	30,000	650,000
CASES	512	11,060
DEATHS	250	5,400

USA	Estimated number September 1986	Predicted number end 1990
CARRIERS	1.5 million	
CASES	23,000	270,000
DEATHS	18,000	150,000

Reported cases, June 1986

Canada	529
27 European countries	2,442
Australia	209
New Zealand	11
Soviet Union	12

FOREIGN AID

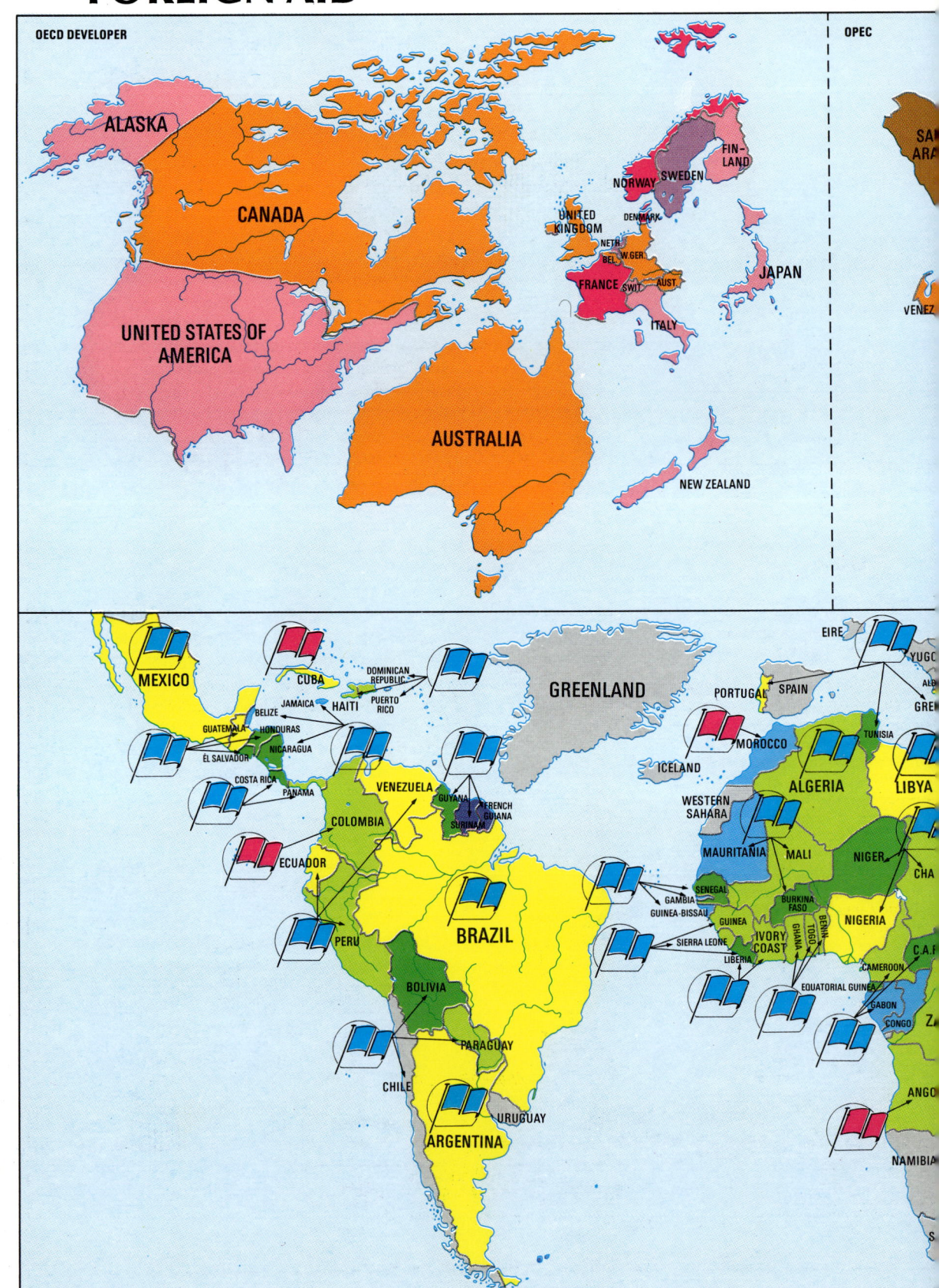

ECONOMIC AID DONORS
Donations 1982 as % of GNP

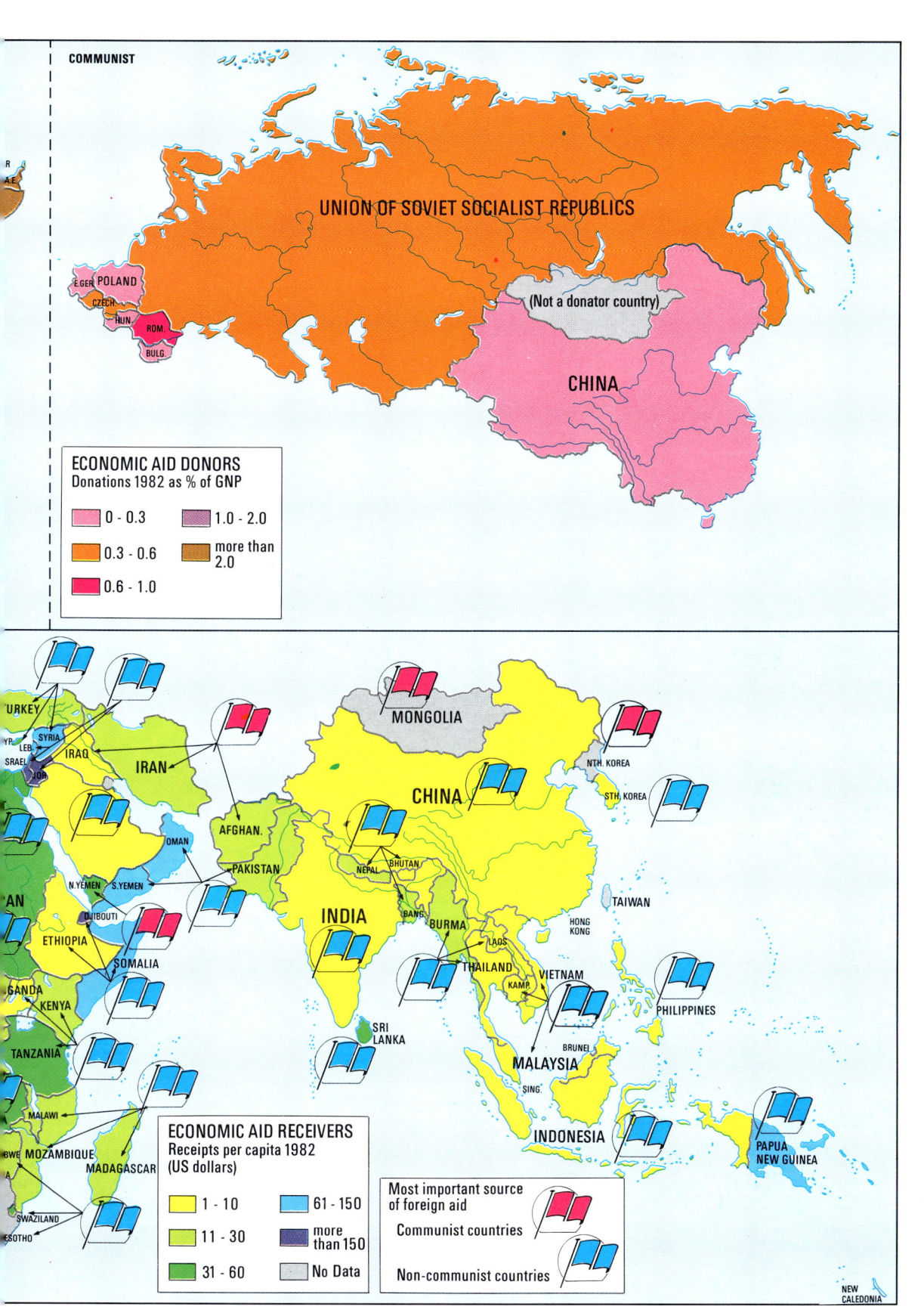

- 0 - 0.3
- 0.3 - 0.6
- 0.6 - 1.0
- 1.0 - 2.0
- more than 2.0

ECONOMIC AID RECEIVERS
Receipts per capita 1982 (US dollars)

- 1 - 10
- 11 - 30
- 31 - 60
- 61 - 150
- more than 150
- No Data

Most important source of foreign aid:
- Communist countries
- Non-communist countries

79

FOREIGN AID

This term covers a multitude of arrangements of which few, if any, can be characterized as examples of undiluted international generosity. Although it would be too cynical to suggest that this motive is entirely absent, most foreign economic aid takes the form of loans, credits or grants which involve some form of reciprocation by the grantee — such as the purchase of equipment or services from the grantor.

The main problem with foreign aid, however, is that it is insufficient. Rich people may be prepared to help poor people, but seldom to a degree which would seriously affect their own comfort. Besides, there are still plenty of poor people in even the richest country in the world.

The map is based on statistics compiled by the Organization for Economic Co-operation and Development and is concerned with aid to the "developing" nations of the Third World flowing from the rich industrialized countries which make up OECD membership, (North America, Western Europe plus Japan, Australia and New Zealand), countries of the Soviet bloc and some oil-producing nations that have become important donors in the last 15 years or so.

Some countries are in the apparently anomalous position of both giving and receiving aid. In the cases of Saudi Arabia and Venezuela, aid received may be reciprocated by cheap oil. China has set itself up as a sort of champion of the Third World, so that while the country still receives foreign aid it also donates a smaller quantity to less developed countries.

Principal aid-reliant developing ▶ countries
Net development aid receipts in 1982/83 shown as percentage of GNP.

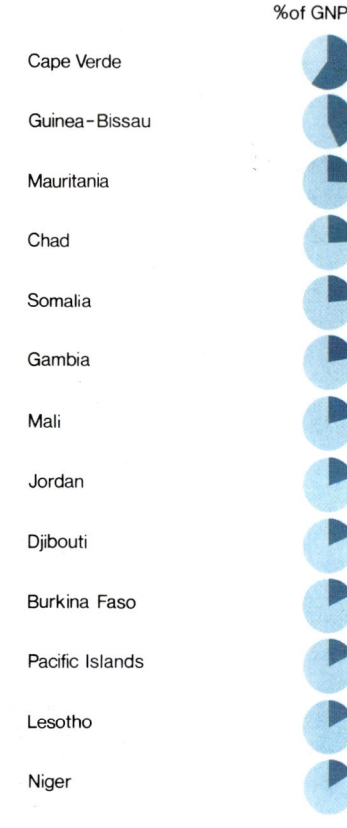

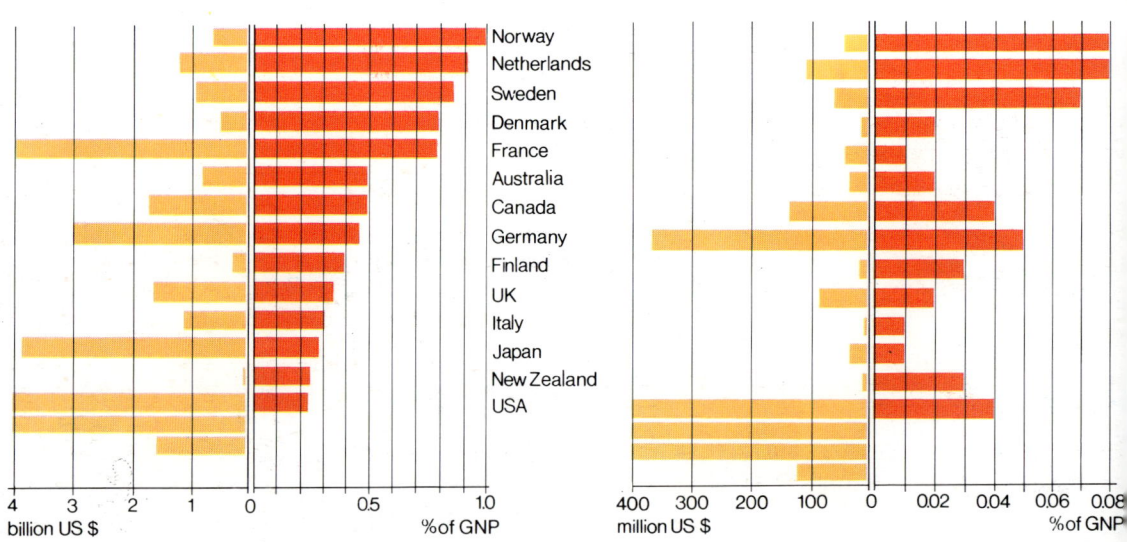

% of GNP

Cape Verde
Guinea-Bissau
Mauritania
Chad
Somalia
Gambia
Mali
Jordan
Djibouti
Burkina Faso
Pacific Islands
Lesotho
Niger

Norway
Netherlands
Sweden
Denmark
France
Australia
Canada
Germany
Finland
UK
Italy
Japan
New Zealand
USA

Overseas development aid from OECD countries, 1985

Overseas development and relief aid from non-governmental agencies, 1983

Overseas development aid from major OPEC countries and principal recipients, 1985
Just three of 13 OPEC members are major aid donors, thus the total aid as per cent of GNP for all OPEC countries is apparently small, though still larger than for all OECD or Soviet bloc countries.

recipients

Syria	19%
Jordan	14%
Bahrain	5%
N. Yemen	4%
Sudan	3%

Overseas development aid from major Soviet bloc countries and percentage of total aid to each of the principal recipients, 1985

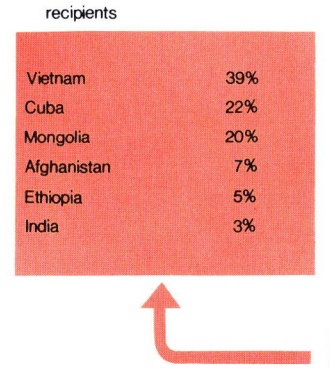

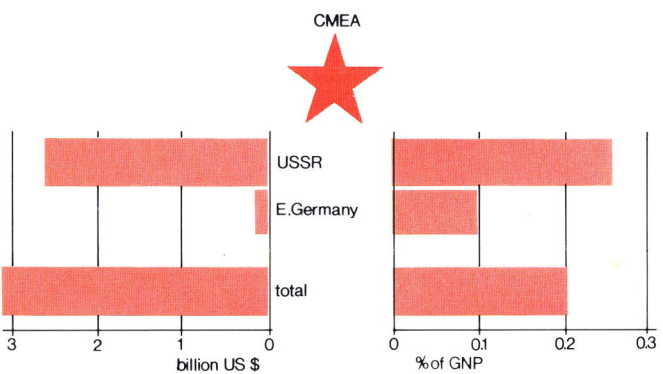

recipients

Vietnam	39%
Cuba	22%
Mongolia	20%
Afghanistan	7%
Ethiopia	5%
India	3%

Government aid can be broadly divided into two categories: bilateral arrangements, including grants, loans, technical assistance; and contributions to multilateral agencies such as UN agencies.

Most governments also encourage private investment in developing countries, for instance by the provision of government insurance and tax relief, and an important contribution is made by private voluntary organizations (see opposite) such as OXFAM which may be best known for relief work but is also engaged in economic development, education and health.

The diagram below far left shows the total contributions in government foreign aid, excluding military aid, by member states of the OECD Development Assistance Committee. The United States is by far the largest contributor, providing more than twice as much as any other nation. However, when these figures are expressed as a percentage of GNP a rather different picture emerges. The most generous donors in these terms are some of the OPEC countries (see above).

MINERAL WEALTH

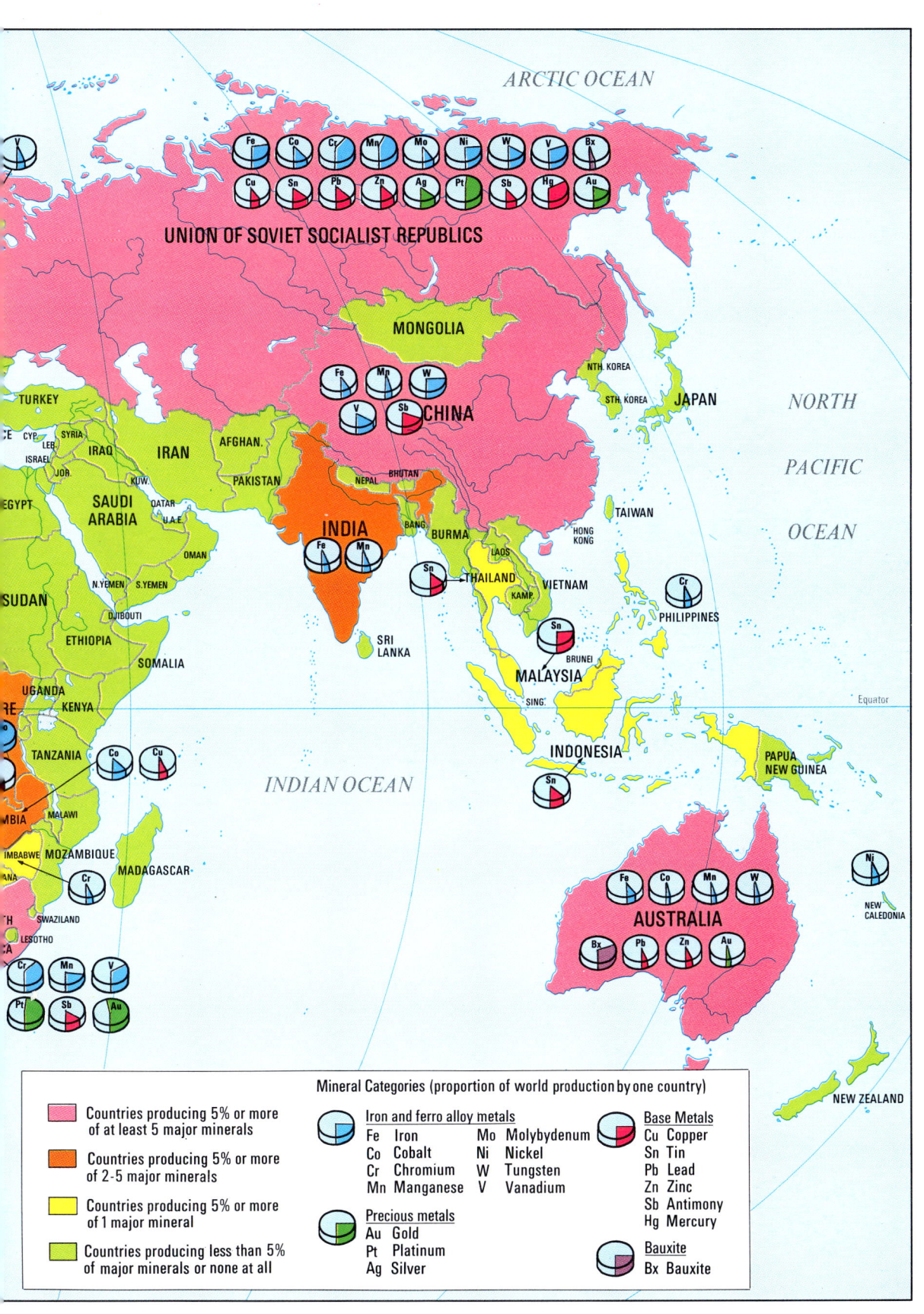

Mineral Categories (proportion of world production by one country)

Legend (colour key):
- Countries producing 5% or more of at least 5 major minerals
- Countries producing 5% or more of 2-5 major minerals
- Countries producing 5% or more of 1 major mineral
- Countries producing less than 5% of major minerals or none at all

Iron and ferro alloy metals
- Fe Iron
- Co Cobalt
- Cr Chromium
- Mn Manganese
- Mo Molybdenum
- Ni Nickel
- W Tungsten
- V Vanadium

Precious metals
- Au Gold
- Pt Platinum
- Ag Silver

Base Metals
- Cu Copper
- Sn Tin
- Pb Lead
- Zn Zinc
- Sb Antimony
- Hg Mercury

Bauxite
- Bx Bauxite

MINERAL WEALTH

The map is concerned with world production of the most important minerals excluding fuels and other non-metallic minerals such as building materials.

Mineral resources are, very largely, a lottery. Certain states, otherwise poorly endowed with natural resources, happen to have large deposits of one or more major mineral ores. This is not always an unmixed blessing however. A country largely dependent for foreign earnings on a particular mineral is vulnerable to fluctuations of the world price, which is notoriously unstable in this area. It is economically healthier to have moderate supplies of several minerals than a large supply of a single one, unless it happens to be a mineral with an assured market and limited producers (such as chromium). The collapse of the price of tin in the mid–1980s, due largely to its phasing-out in the canning industry, had dire effects for producers from Bolivia to Cornwall.

Profits from minerals, however, do not go exclusively to the miners. Processing is often more important, and many Third World countries are handicapped by the lack of plants to process their minerals. A large part is played by big international corporations, financially often more powerful than the countries in which they operate, in both the mining and processing of minerals.

Modern industrial society is dependent on about 80 minerals (only the major ones are shown on the map), and the question of supply can have important political connotations. The United States, for example, the world's largest consumer of "strategic" minerals, is for a number of them almost totally dependent on imports, mainly from Third World countries. To guard against possible interruptions in supply, the United States and other industrialized countries have tended to build up stocks of strategic minerals, such as manganese, cobalt, chromium and platinum. The United States's stockpiles of bauxite — aluminium ore — amount to the approximate equivalent of 600kg per head of the population. One incidental effect of stockpiling has been to moderate the sharp fluctuations in world prices.

There is, however, no potential shortage of these minerals. The diagram above right illustrates the approximate period for which reserves of selected minerals will last at the current rate of

Gold producers
Gold has long been important to the world economy, it is the one mineral that everybody wants. Its potential as an economic weapon is great. South Africa could exploit its position as the Western world's largest supplier by restricting exports, sending the price soaring and undermining Western economies. Many countries hoard massive stocks, however, and if Western banks started to sell reserves, creating a collapse in the world prices, the South African economy would be threatened in a way which no economic sanctions could ever achieve.

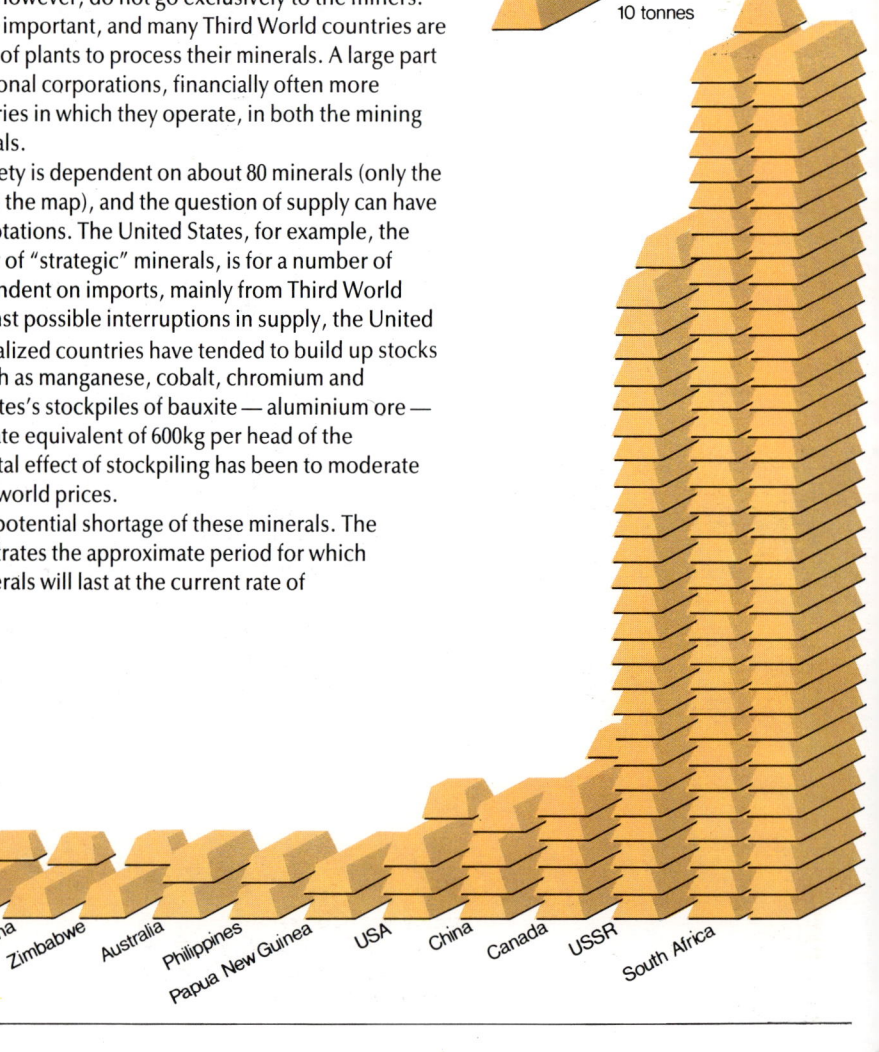

10 tonnes

Brazil, Colombia, Dominican Rep., Ghana, Zimbabwe, Australia, Philippines, Papua New Guinea, USA, China, Canada, USSR, South Africa

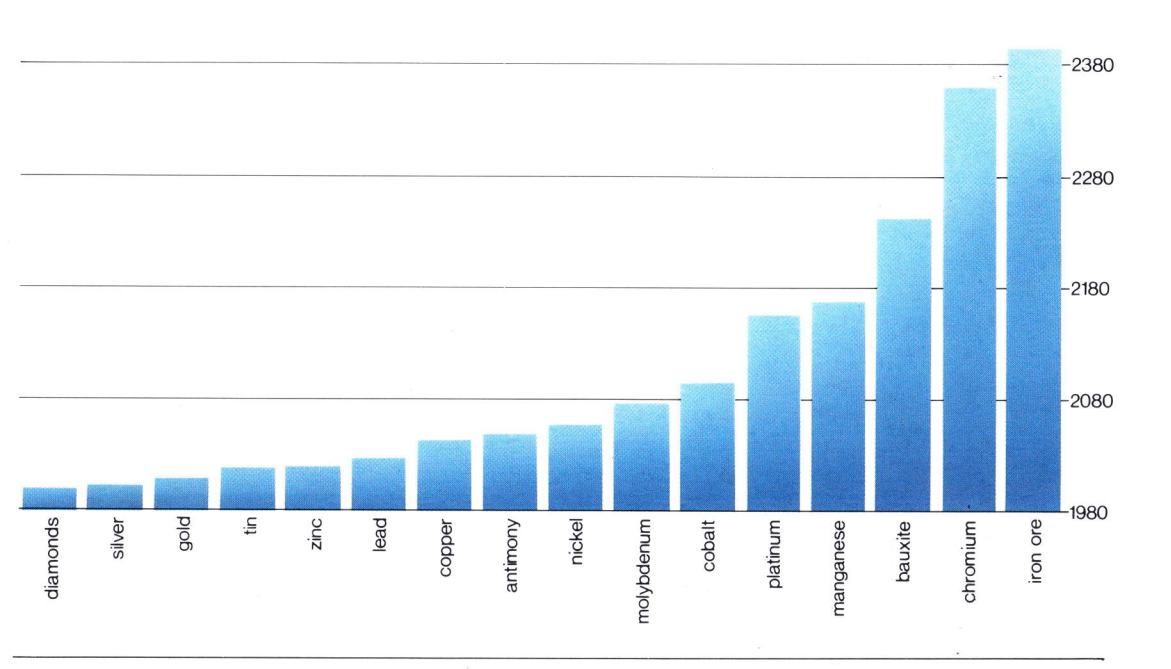

World mineral reserves
Years until exhaustion at 1981 consumption rates.

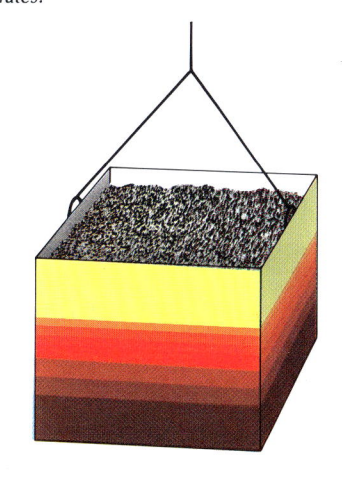

consumption. Clearly, these figures will alter as more reserves are discovered (or exploited), as greater proportions are obtained by recycling, as substitutes are introduced, and for other causes. For the majority of minerals, there is no immediate reason to panic — they should nearly all last longer than, for instance, oil.

The main producers of iron ore are shown at left. It is the most common and most widely distributed mineral ore, with reserves for about 400 years. This is fortunate, as it is still the basis of most large-scale industrial production.

Gold is a special case as, apart from industrial and manufacturing use, it is also, roughly speaking, the only form of "money" that can be trusted. Most countries hold part of their monetary reserves in gold which, while it does not gain interest, does not lose its value through inflation. Private holdings are also considerable — no one can guess how large. Much the largest gold producer is South Africa, with half the world total. The Soviet Union produces about one-fifth, and nearly all the remainder comes from just six other main producers.

Leading iron ore producers
- others
- Canada
- USA
- India
- China
- Brazil
- Australia
- USSR

Iron ore producers
The world's leading producers of iron ore, still the key mineral for many industrial and manufacturing activities.

85

WORLD TOURISM

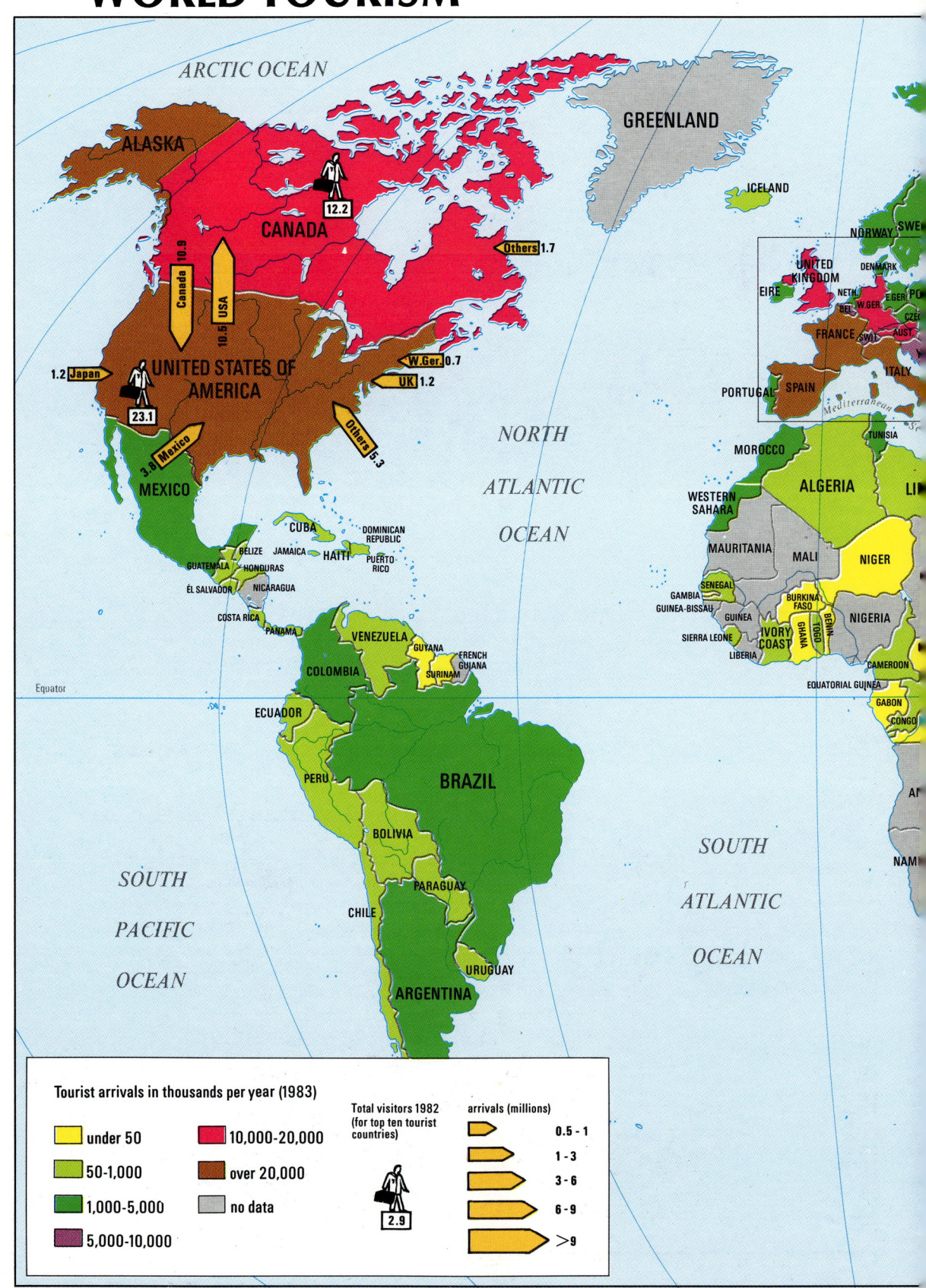

Tourist arrivals in thousands per year (1983)
- under 50
- 50-1,000
- 1,000-5,000
- 5,000-10,000
- 10,000-20,000
- over 20,000
- no data

Total visitors 1982 (for top ten tourist countries): 2.9

arrivals (millions)
- 0.5 - 1
- 1 - 3
- 3 - 6
- 6 - 9
- >9

Canada: 12.2
Others: 1.7
Canada 10.9
USA 10.5
Japan 1.2
USA: 23.1
W.Ger. 0.7
UK 1.2
Mexico 3.8
Others 5.3

86

ARCTIC OCEAN

UNION OF SOVIET SOCIALIST REPUBLICS

MONGOLIA

NTH. KOREA
STH. KOREA
JAPAN

CHINA

TURKEY
CYP
SYRIA
LEB
ISRAEL
JOR
IRAQ
IRAN
AFGHAN.
PAKISTAN
NEPAL
BHUTAN
KUW
SAUDI ARABIA
QATAR
U.A.E
OMAN
EGYPT
N.YEMEN
S.YEMEN
DJIBOUTI
INDIA
BANG
BURMA
LAOS
THAILAND
KAMP
VIETNAM
TAIWAN
HONG KONG
PHILIPPINES

SUDAN
ETHIOPIA
SOMALIA
UGANDA
KENYA
SRI LANKA
MALAYSIA
BRUNEI
SING.

TANZANIA

NORTH PACIFIC OCEAN

INDONESIA
PAPUA NEW GUINEA

MALAWI
MOZAMBIQUE
MADAGASCAR
ZIMBABWE
SWAZILAND
LESOTHO

INDIAN OCEAN

Equator

NEW CALEDONIA

NEW ZEALAND

Austria	A
Belgium	B
Czechoslovakia	CS
Denmark	DK
France	F
Germany East	DDR
Germany West	D
Greece	GR
Ireland	IRL
Italy	I
Netherlands	NA
Poland	PL
Portugal	P
Spain	E
Ex pat Spanish	Ex
Sweden	S
Switzerland	CH
UK	GB
USA	USA
Yugoslavia	YU
Others	OT

WORLD TOURISM

The expansion of tourism since 1950 is related to other rapid advances in communications and transport. Most people like to travel, and many of us do travel increasingly, for business or pleasure. Foreign holidays are no longer exotic luxuries but normal means of recreation. Tourism has become a profitable and highly competitive business, and there is a constant search for attractive and unexploited locations. The rise of tourism has been assisted by rising affluence and multiplying means of transport, from the jumbo jet to the collapsible bike. Despite a dip in the figures during the early 1980s, due to the world recession, all evidence suggests continued growth in the tourist industry.

It hardly needs saying that all this applies almost exclusively to the affluent West — North America, Western Europe, Australasia and Japan. Europe is the Mecca of tourism and accounts for about 85 per cent of the world total. Except for a few places which are statistically insignificant on a world scale tourism has little influence in Third World countries, and in most Communist countries, despite their governments' hunger for hard currency, foreign travel is restricted.

Satisfactory figures on tourism are notoriously hard to compile. The map is based on national returns for foreign visitors, which include business people, sometimes making several visits in the same year, and no doubt drug-smugglers and terrorists as well as others, who remain in the country for at least 24 hours.

The breakdown of foreign tourists by national origin in the main European countries also reveals some obvious anomalies. Thus, the figure for French visitors to Spain, clearly inflated by comparison with the number of German or British visitors in even more urgent need of

European tourism, 1984
Nights spent by tourists in accommodation of various types in selected European countries.

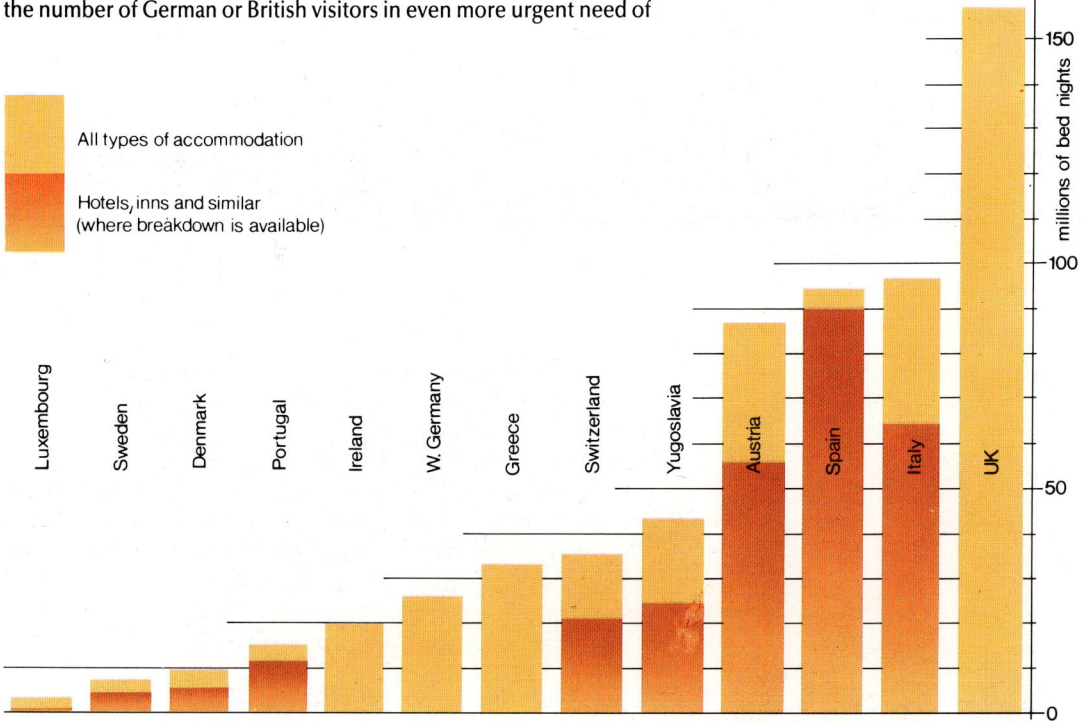

sun, is partly explained no doubt by local movements, such as visits to the shops, across the border.

A better way of calculating numbers of tourists is by counting bed/nights, which is the number of nights spent by foreign tourists in hotels and other accommodation. Unfortunately, figures are not always available, but the diagram opposite gives the figures for countries reporting in 1985, in terms of (a) hotels and similar establishments and (b) all types of accommodation (including tents and caravans).

The main tourist-generating countries are Britain, France, West Germany and the United States. In France, tourism represents over 12 per cent of household consumption. It accounts for nearly 9 per cent of the GDP (Gross Domestic Product) and contributes to the employment directly or indirectly, seasonally or full-time, of about 1.7 million people. Britain receives annually about 14 million overseas visitors who spend over £4 billion, but British residents make 22 million trips abroad and spend nearly £5 billion; London contains 52 foreign tourist offices and over 6,000 travel agents. In the United States, 10 million people travel abroad annually, half to Europe, and spend about $16 billion.

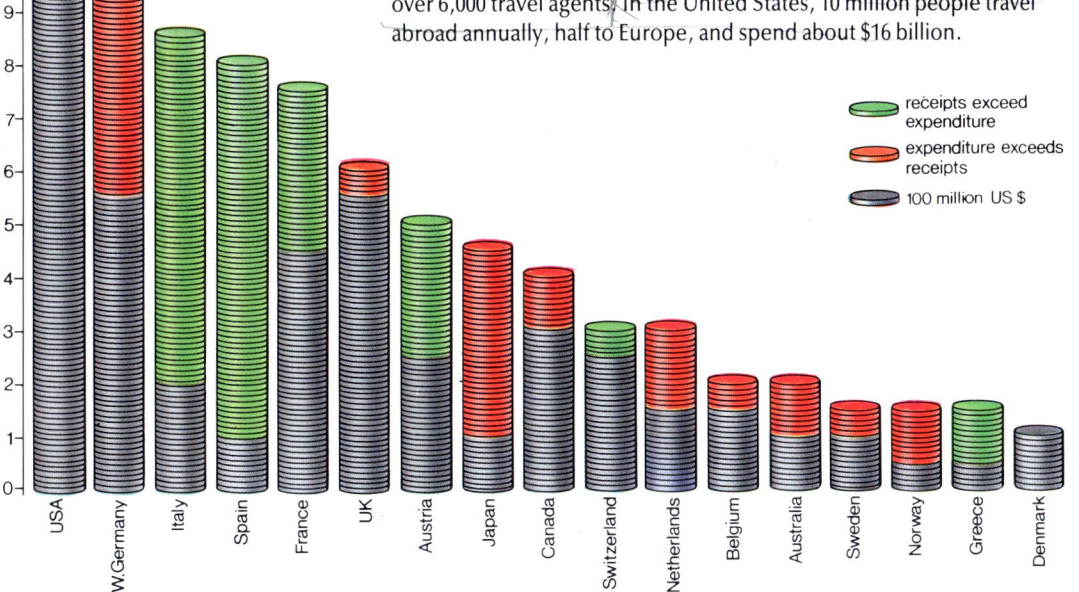

Tourist spending, 1984
Tourist accounts for a selection of countries. National receipts from foreign tourists and the expenditure of a country's travellers overseas.

Internal tourism is particularly significant in the United States. For example, tourism is far the largest industry in Florida, which attracts about 25 million visitors annually who spend about $7 billion.

In Europe, the largest movement of tourists is from the cool north to the warm south, making tourism especially important to relatively poor (poor by EEC standards, that is) countries such as Spain and Greece, all of whom enjoy a large balance of tourism receipts over expenditure (see diagram above).

WORLD ENERGY PRODUCTION

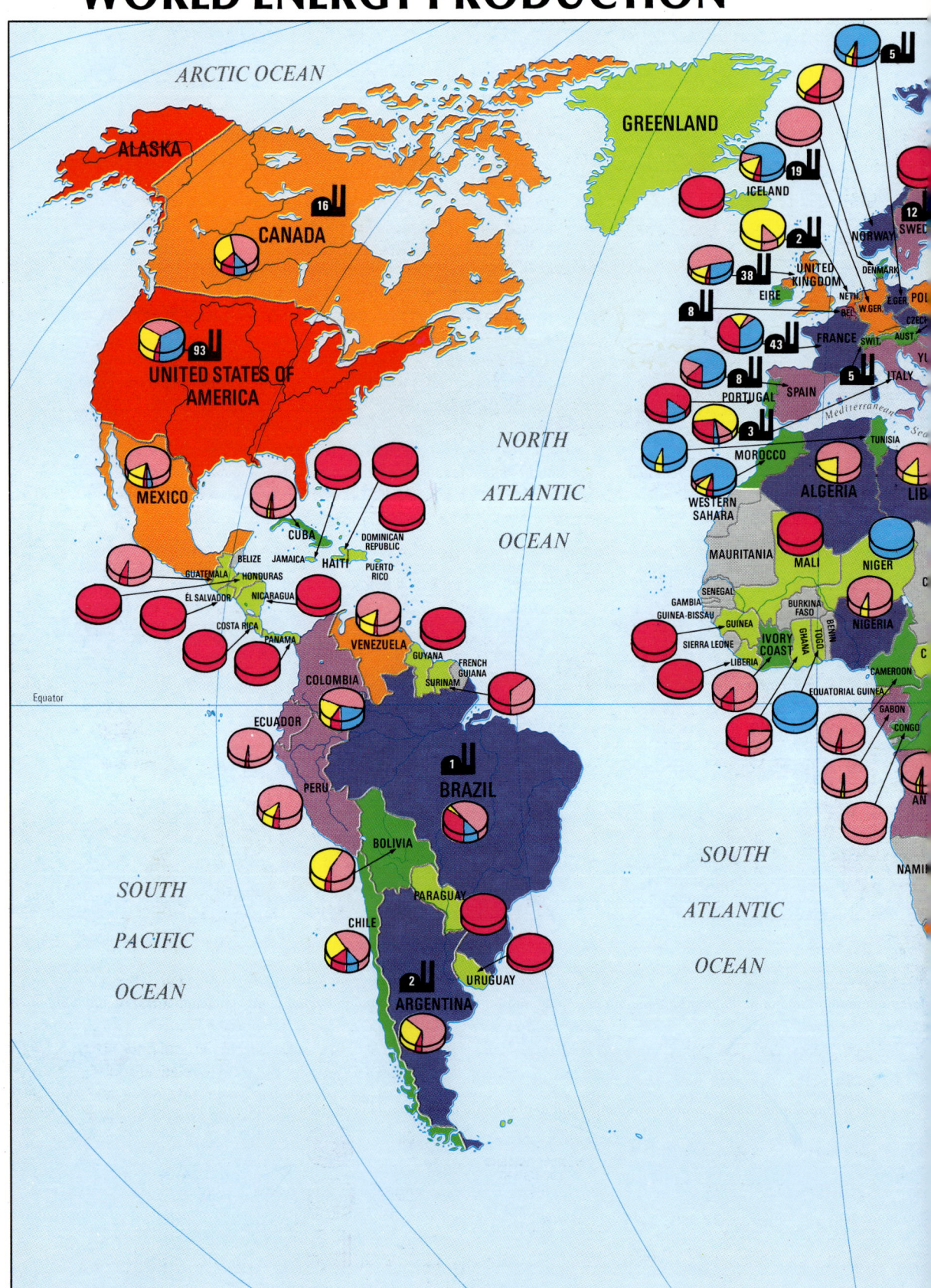

TOTAL ENERGY PRODUCTION

Million metric tons coal equivalent (1983)

- no data
- less than 1
- 1–10
- 10–50
- 50–100
- 100–500
- 500–1,000
- more than 1,000

Nuclear reactors in operation 1985

Major minerals (proportion of national energy production by fuel)
- Coal
- Oil
- Gas
- Other (Nuclear, Hydro-electric and Geothermal)

91

WORLD ENERGY PRODUCTION

Approximately 96 per cent of the world's commercial production of energy is derived from fossil fuels — coal, oil and natural gas — which are non-renewable resources. In the 1970s, rather late in the day, it dawned upon the world that the extinction of these resources, on which practically all human activity, from cooking the breakfast to making a space rocket, depends, would occur in the none too distant future. The reality of this impending deprivation was rammed home by the oil crisis precipitated by OPEC (Oil Producing and Exporting Countries) which resulted in the world price of oil tripling in a year (1973–74) and tripling again in the next five years. Oil being the largest source of energy, the crisis induced a world recession, the hardest-hit being Third World countries without oil. This resulted in lower energy consumption, exploitation of new oil reserves and consequent reduction in the price.

The relatively stable situation of the mid 1980s is obviously temporary. Oil reserves at the current rate of consumption will last only about 30 years, though new discoveries and techniques may extend the period perhaps another 30 years — even longer if oil is phased out more gradually. Of the other two main sources, natural gas will run out sooner than oil. Coal is plentiful, with reserves at current consumption for about 250 years, but there are powerful environmental objections to increased use of this fuel in current conditions.

The remaining 4 per cent of world energy production is electricity generated by hydro-, geothermal and nuclear power stations. Hydroelectric power has some potential in limited areas, but the most obvious candidate for expansion is nuclear power. The terrifying hazards of this source of energy, dramatically illustrated by the fire at the Chernobyl reactor in the Soviet Union in 1986, make this a questionable solution.

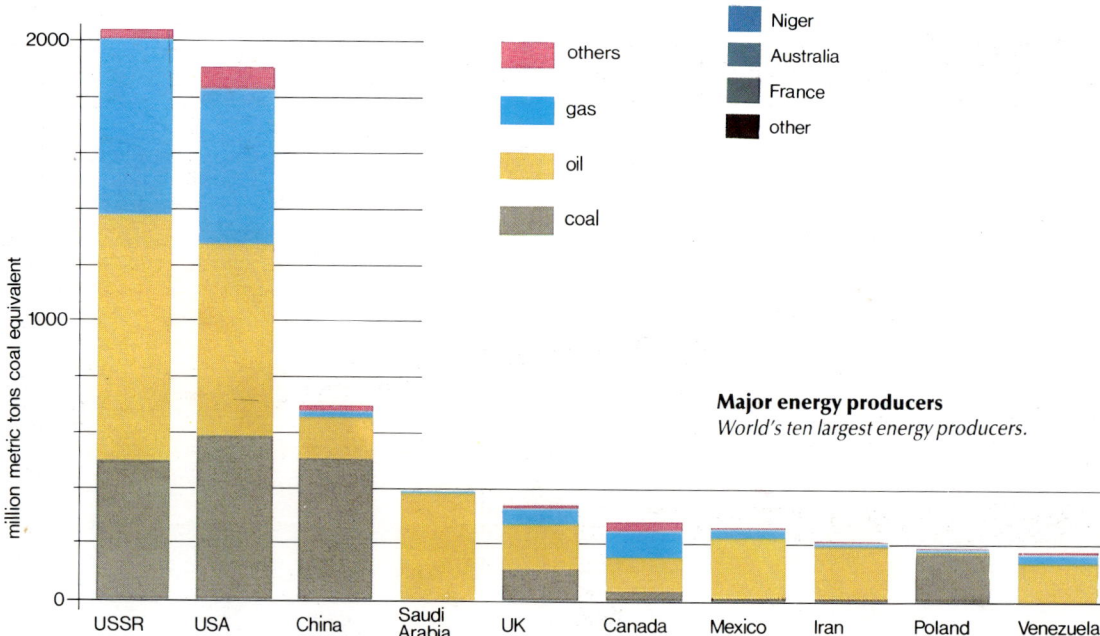

Uranium producers
World production of the nuclear fuel, 1983.

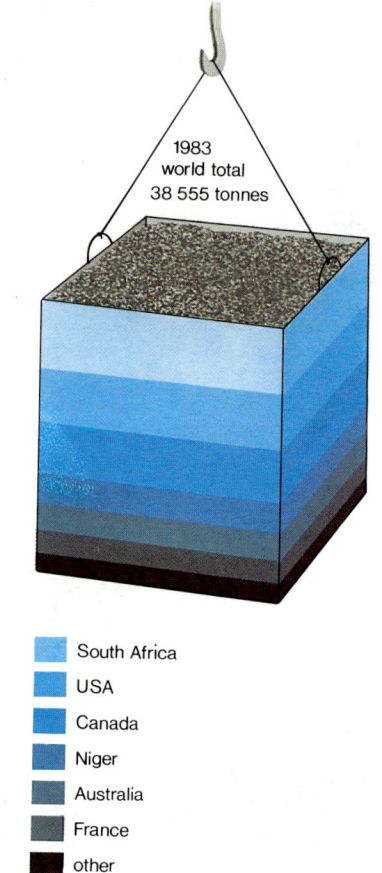

1983 world total 38 555 tonnes

- South Africa
- USA
- Canada
- Niger
- Australia
- France
- other

Major energy producers
World's ten largest energy producers.

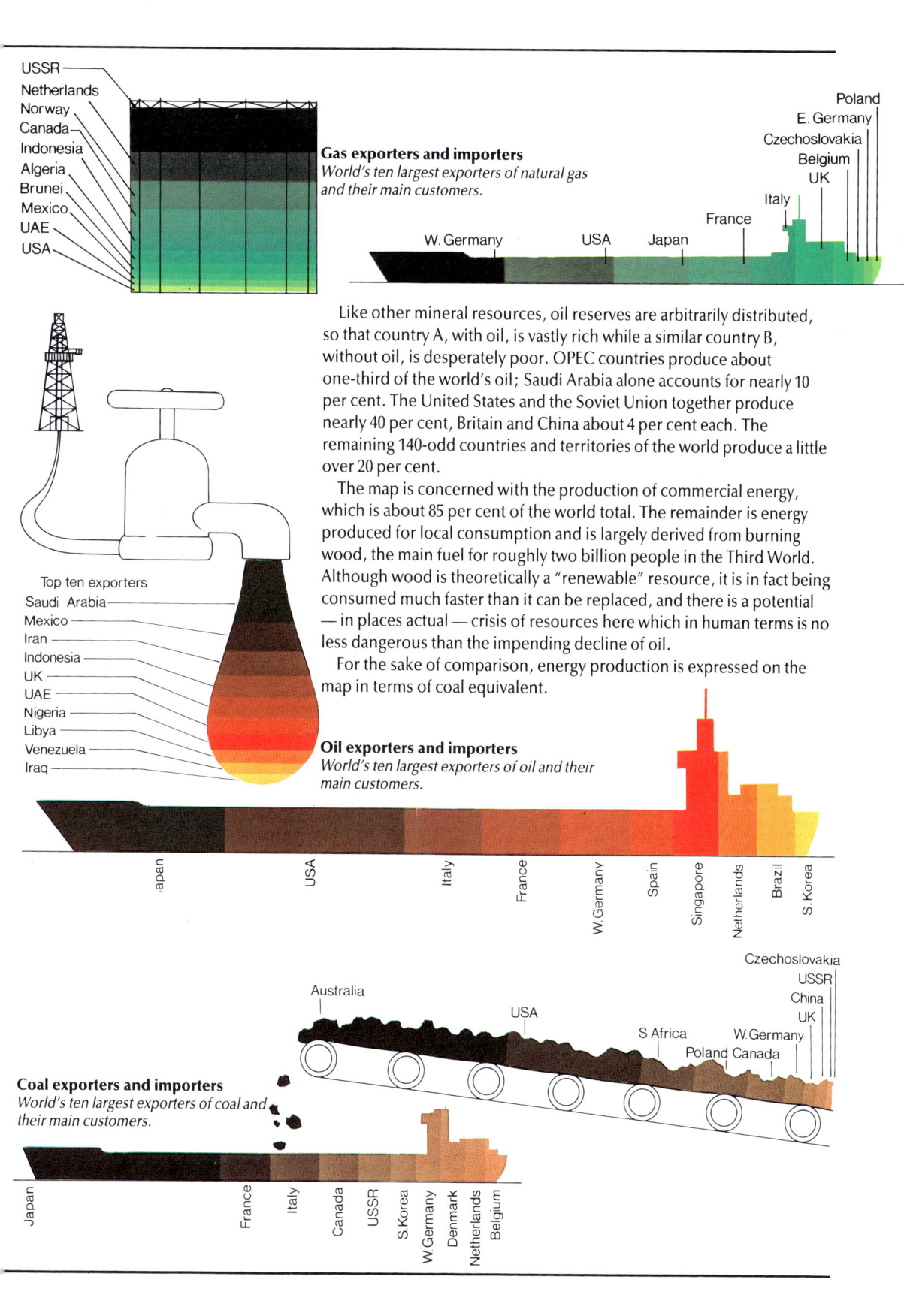

Gas exporters and importers
World's ten largest exporters of natural gas and their main customers.

Exporters: USSR, Netherlands, Norway, Canada, Indonesia, Algeria, Brunei, Mexico, UAE, USA

Customers: W. Germany, USA, Japan, France, Italy, UK, Belgium, Czechoslovakia, E. Germany, Poland

Like other mineral resources, oil reserves are arbitrarily distributed, so that country A, with oil, is vastly rich while a similar country B, without oil, is desperately poor. OPEC countries produce about one-third of the world's oil; Saudi Arabia alone accounts for nearly 10 per cent. The United States and the Soviet Union together produce nearly 40 per cent, Britain and China about 4 per cent each. The remaining 140-odd countries and territories of the world produce a little over 20 per cent.

The map is concerned with the production of commercial energy, which is about 85 per cent of the world total. The remainder is energy produced for local consumption and is largely derived from burning wood, the main fuel for roughly two billion people in the Third World. Although wood is theoretically a "renewable" resource, it is in fact being consumed much faster than it can be replaced, and there is a potential — in places actual — crisis of resources here which in human terms is no less dangerous than the impending decline of oil.

For the sake of comparison, energy production is expressed on the map in terms of coal equivalent.

Top ten exporters: Saudi Arabia, Mexico, Iran, Indonesia, UK, UAE, Nigeria, Libya, Venezuela, Iraq

Oil exporters and importers
World's ten largest exporters of oil and their main customers.

Customers: Japan, USA, Italy, France, W. Germany, Spain, Singapore, Netherlands, Brazil, S. Korea

Coal exporters and importers
World's ten largest exporters of coal and their main customers.

Exporters: Australia, USA, S Africa, Poland, Canada, W. Germany, UK, China, USSR, Czechoslovakia

Customers: Japan, France, Italy, Canada, USSR, S. Korea, W. Germany, Denmark, Netherlands, Belgium

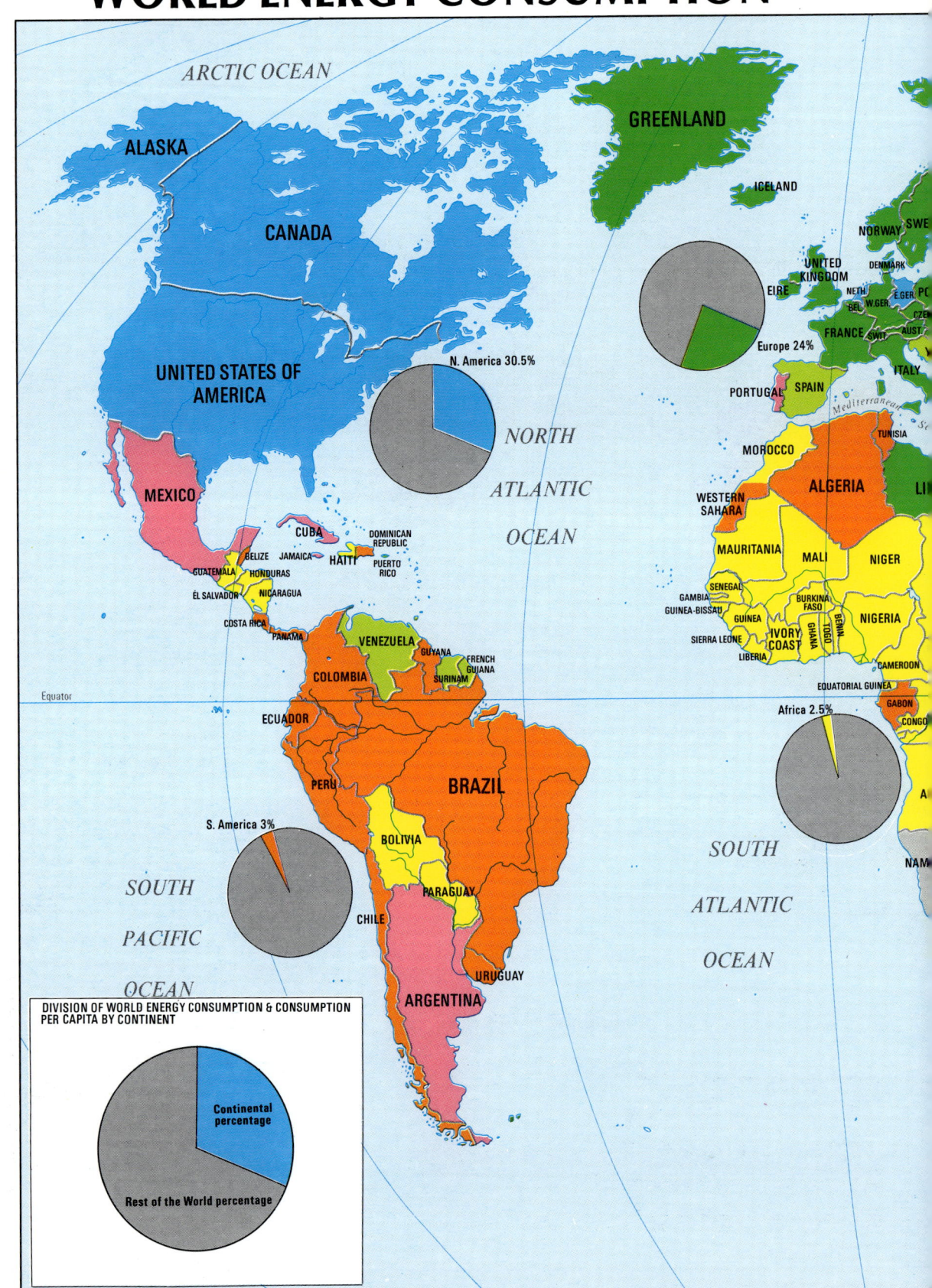

WORLD ENERGY CONSUMPTION

N. America 30.5%

Europe 24%

Africa 2.5%

S. America 3%

DIVISION OF WORLD ENERGY CONSUMPTION & CONSUMPTION PER CAPITA BY CONTINENT

Continental percentage

Rest of the World percentage

ARCTIC OCEAN
ALASKA
CANADA
UNITED STATES OF AMERICA
MEXICO
CUBA
BELIZE JAMAICA
GUATEMALA
HONDURAS
EL SALVADOR NICARAGUA
COSTA RICA
PANAMA
HAITI
DOMINICAN REPUBLIC
PUERTO RICO
VENEZUELA
COLOMBIA
GUYANA
SURINAM
FRENCH GUIANA
ECUADOR
PERU
BRAZIL
BOLIVIA
PARAGUAY
CHILE
URUGUAY
ARGENTINA
Equator

NORTH ATLANTIC OCEAN
SOUTH PACIFIC OCEAN
SOUTH ATLANTIC OCEAN

GREENLAND
ICELAND
NORWAY SWE
DENMARK
UNITED KINGDOM
EIRE
NETH
BEL
W.GER
E.GER
PO
CZE
FRANCE
SWI
AUST
PORTUGAL SPAIN
ITALY
Mediterranean Se
MOROCCO
TUNISIA
ALGERIA
LI
WESTERN SAHARA
MAURITANIA
MALI
NIGER
GAMBIA SENEGAL
GUINEA-BISSAU
GUINEA
BURKINA FASO
BENIN
NIGERIA
SIERRA LEONE
IVORY COAST
GHANA
TOGO
LIBERIA
CAMEROON
EQUATORIAL GUINEA
GABON
CONGO
A
NAM

94

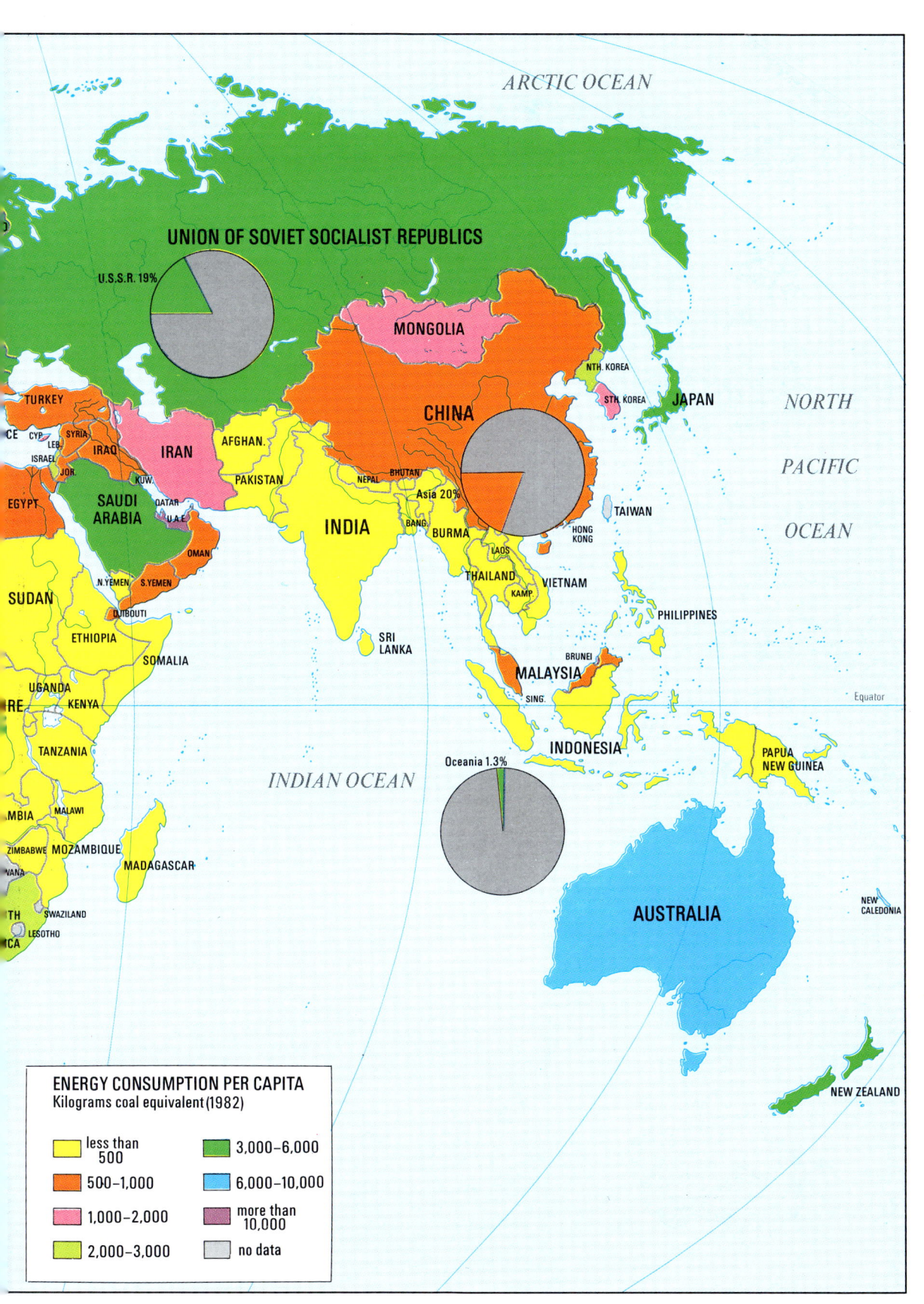

ENERGY CONSUMPTION PER CAPITA
Kilograms coal equivalent (1982)

- less than 500
- 500–1,000
- 1,000–2,000
- 2,000–3,000
- 3,000–6,000
- 6,000–10,000
- more than 10,000
- no data

U.S.S.R. 19%
Asia 20%
Oceania 1.3%

WORLD ENERGY CONSUMPTION

Commercial energy is derived from several sources, chiefly oil, coal and natural gas. As these have different calorific values, weight for weight, the figures for total energy are expressed in coal equivalent.

Not surprisingly, the biggest consumers of energy are generally among the biggest producers (see WORLD ENERGY PRODUCTION), although there are some exceptions, such as Japan, a high consumer but low producer, or Nigeria, where the situation is reversed. Energy consumption reflects industrial capacity; hence the high consumption of Japan and the low consumption of Nigeria.

The international variations in energy consumption are still more remarkable when expressed in terms of consumption per capita, with industrialized Western countries, led again by the United States, consuming over one hundred times as much as the majority of Third World countries. United States consumption per capita, for example, was nearly 10,000 kg (coal equivalent) per head in 1983. In Bangladesh it was 48 kg per head. In the Soviet Union the figure was nearly 6,000 kg per head. In China it was 600 (see below).

The diagram below compares consumption and production of energy in the main energy-consuming nations. Among other matters, this makes clear what appears to be — considered in isolation — the profligate energy policies of the superpowers. In 1950 the United States produced slightly more energy than it consumed, but by 1960 consumption exceeded production, and thereafter the gap widened steadily until interrupted by the oil crisis of 1973–74 and the ensuing

Energy consumption and production
World's ten largest energy consumers compared with their production.

Energy consumption, 1970–83
The pattern of per capita energy consumption, shown here in kilograms coal equivalent, has been affected by the World oil price. Major oil-producing nations such as Qatar and Kuwait are amongst the largest per capita energy consumers. The OPEC oil price rises in 1973 are reflected in minor decreases in consumption in countries such as the United States and UK in the mid–1970s. Further oil price increases in the early 1980s have caused a more significant decline in consumption in these countries. The Soviet Union, more self-sufficient in energy production, shows less reliance on international oil prices.

recession. United States oil imports increased by a factor of six between 1960 and 1976, although by 1983 the latter quantity had been halved. Meanwhile, reserves of oil and natural gas which together made up more than two-thirds of total energy consumption in 1983 are shrinking fast. The position of the Soviet Union is no better. At present it is a major exporter of oil, chiefly to industrialized Eastern European countries, but at current rates — and assuming no major new reserves are discovered — it will soon become an importer of oil like the United States.

The "energy crisis" which began with OPEC's restriction in 1973 led to some sharp changes in energy consumption. The rate of increase was considerably retarded and in some countries reversed. The diagram below indicates the trend in certain countries.

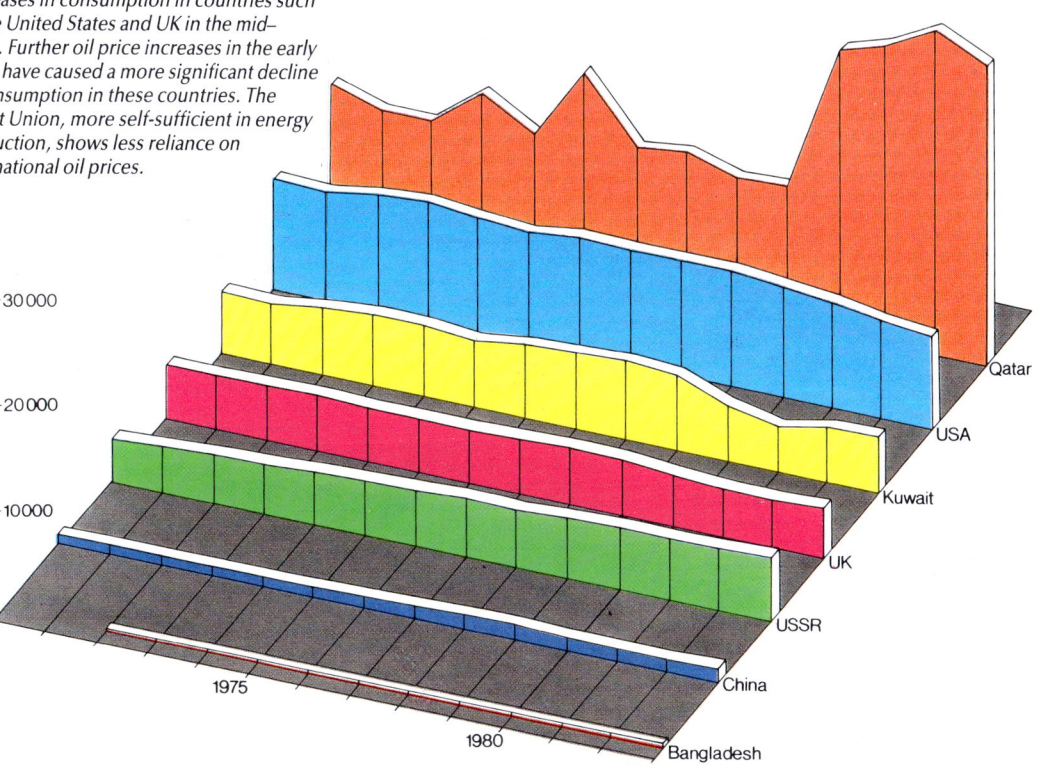

Energy consumption alone gives no reliable indication of industrial productivity. However, significant facts emerge from a comparison of energy consumption with GNP. It is notable that those industrial countries displaying the greatest economic health in this period are also those which were most successful in restraining energy consumption in relation to the rise in industrial productivity. Thus, in West Germany between 1973 and 1980, GNP increased by 17.5 per cent while energy consumption rose by only 3.1 per cent. In Japan, GNP increased by 35 per cent but energy consumption rose by only 15 per cent.

WORLD MANUFACTURING

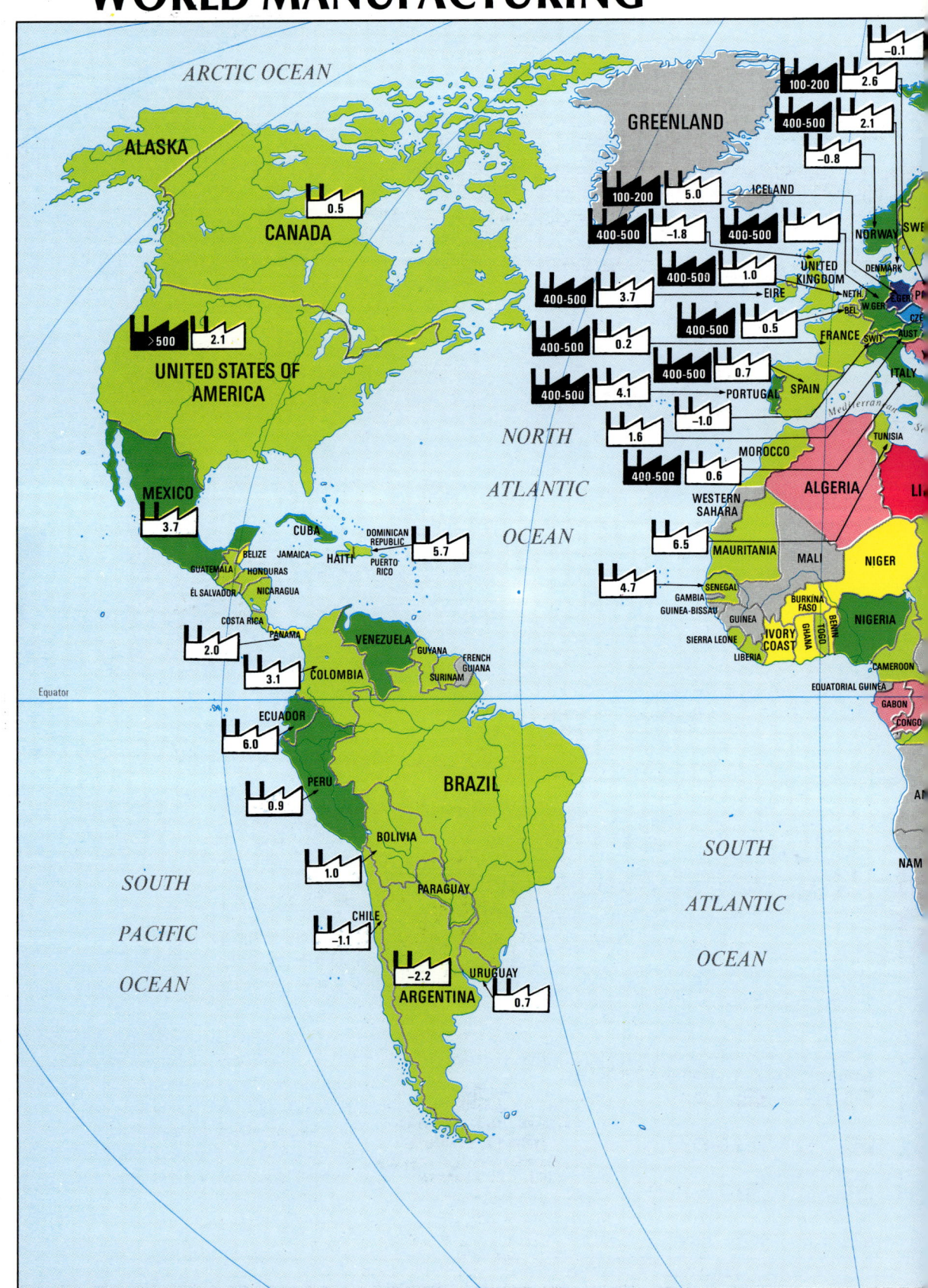

Asia and Oceania: Industrial Activity

Total industrial activity as percentage of GDP (1983)
- 0–15 (yellow)
- 16–30 (light green)
- 31–40 (dark green)
- 41–50 (pink)
- 51–60 (red)
- 61–70 (blue)
- more than 70 (dark blue)
- no data (grey)

Value of manufactured goods 1984 (Billions of US dollars) — Only countries with value more than 100 US dollars shown

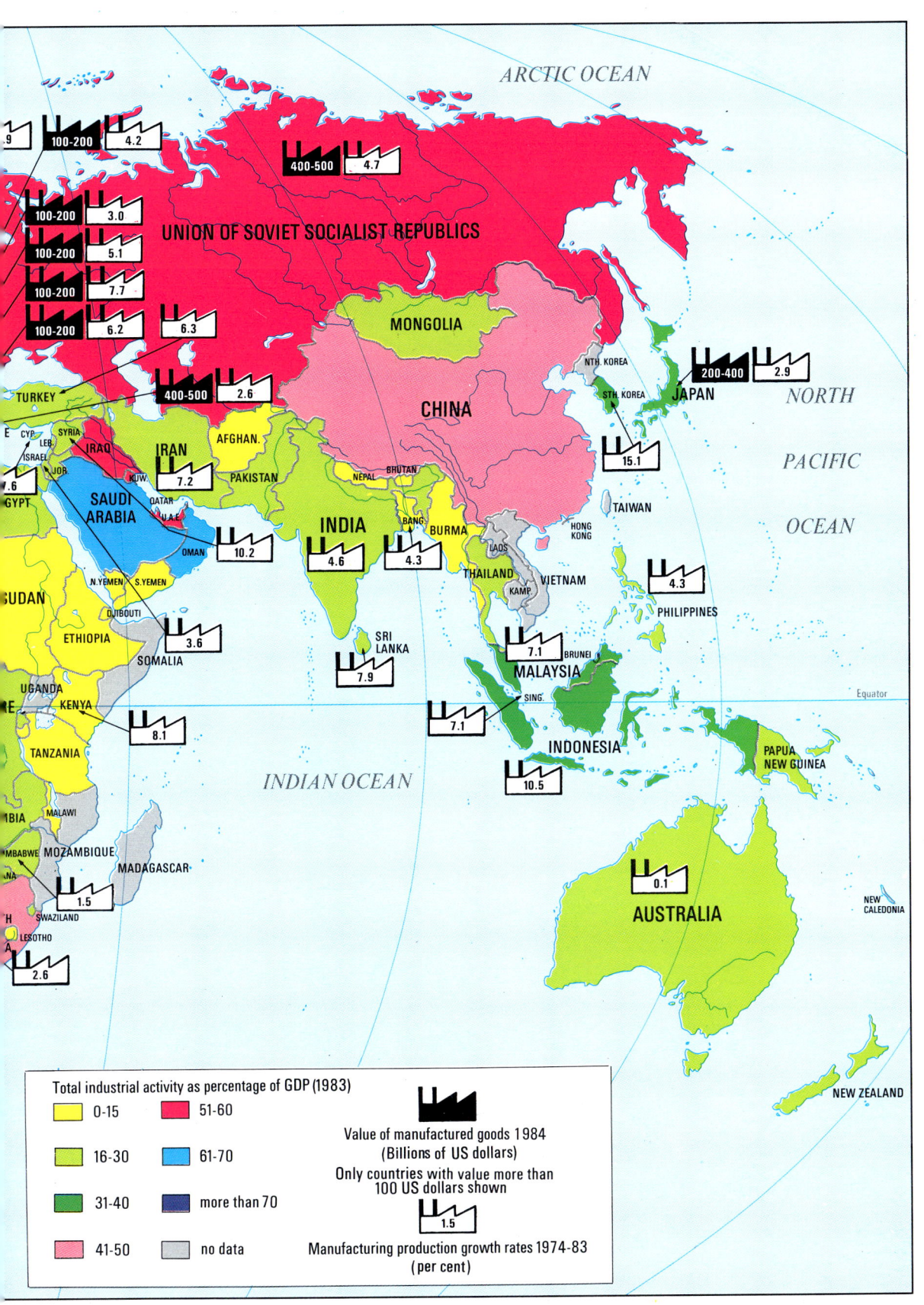

Manufacturing production growth rates 1974–83 (per cent)

Selected values shown on map:

- USSR: 400–500 / 4.7; 100–200 / 3.0; 100–200 / 5.1; 100–200 / 7.7; 100–200 / 6.2; 6.3; 400–500 / 2.6
- Turkey area: 100–200 / 4.2
- Japan: 200–400 / 2.9
- South Korea: 15.1
- Iran: 7.2
- Saudi Arabia: 10.2
- India: 4.6
- Bangladesh/Burma: 4.3
- Sri Lanka: 7.9
- Philippines: 4.3
- Malaysia: 7.1
- Singapore: 7.1
- Indonesia: 10.5
- Somalia area: 3.6
- Kenya: 8.1
- South Africa area: 1.5
- 2.6
- Australia: 0.1

WORLD MANUFACTURING

Since the amazing success of Great Britain, the first modern industrial nation, in the 19th century, manufacturing has been regarded as the key to economic prosperity. In the industrial boom after the Second World War, which lasted with ups and downs into the 1970s, this doctrine led to some unfortunate results, notably in certain Third World countries which neglected basic agricultural reforms in favour of large industrial projects. Nevertheless, the extraordinary advances in industrial production in that period had highly beneficial results which were not entirely confined to the major industrial nations themselves, although the belief that rapidly expanding production in those countries would raise living standards proportionately in the poorer countries has proved unfounded.

Since the 1970s, the scene has changed, largely because of a general awareness that booming growth based on non-renewable resources cannot last, that environmental pollution is insidiously destroying the planet, and that the miracles of modern technology and production have failed to alleviate poverty and sickness.

As the map illustrates, the major manufacturing nations in terms of value are the United States, the Soviet Union, Japan and the EEC. Few economic indicators provide a more dramatic picture of "haves" and "have-nots": over 80 per cent of total world production comes from just ten countries.

Nevertheless, industry in general is less important, as a proportion of the national domestic wage packet (GDP) in western Europe and North America than it is in some other countries. In the countries of the Eastern bloc, where a strong industrial sector is the ideological basis of the Communist system, industry represents a higher proportion of national wealth. The large majority of Third World nations, by contrast, are heavily reliant on agricultural produce and raw materials (see WORLD DEVELOPMENT).

Unit labour costs, 1981–85 (in US dollars)
The percentage change in unit labour costs reflects wage settlements, output and productivity growth and the strength of the dollar. These forces dramatically reduced disparities between the United States and its major trading partners in 1984.

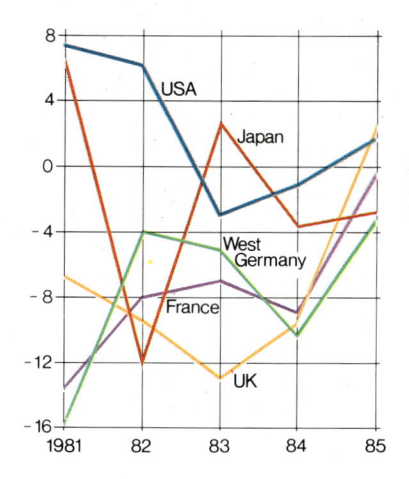

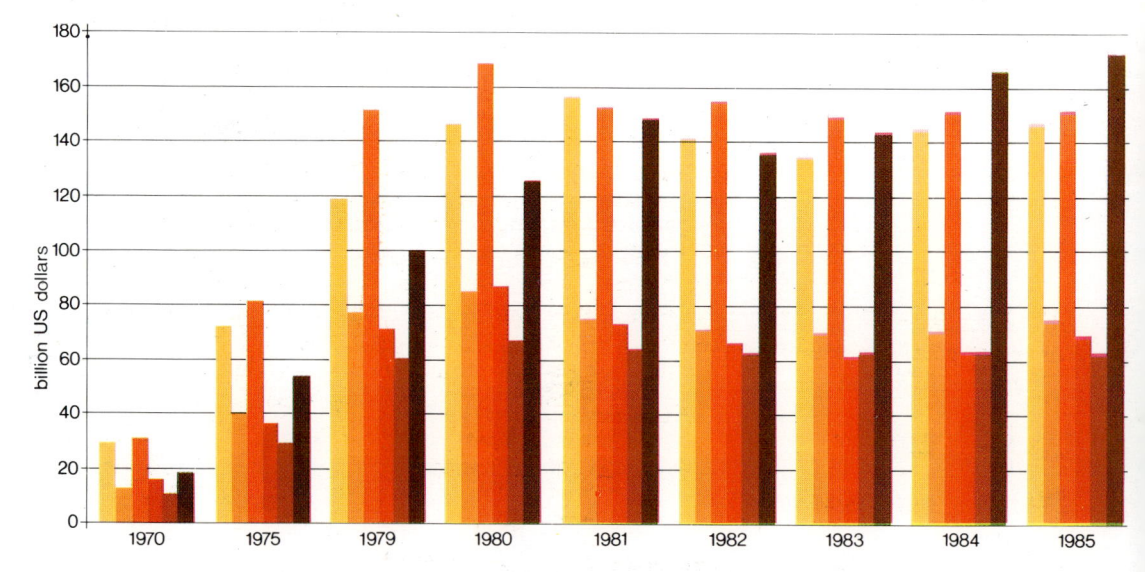

Manufactured goods exports, 1970–85

- USA
- France
- W Germany
- UK
- Italy
- Japan

100

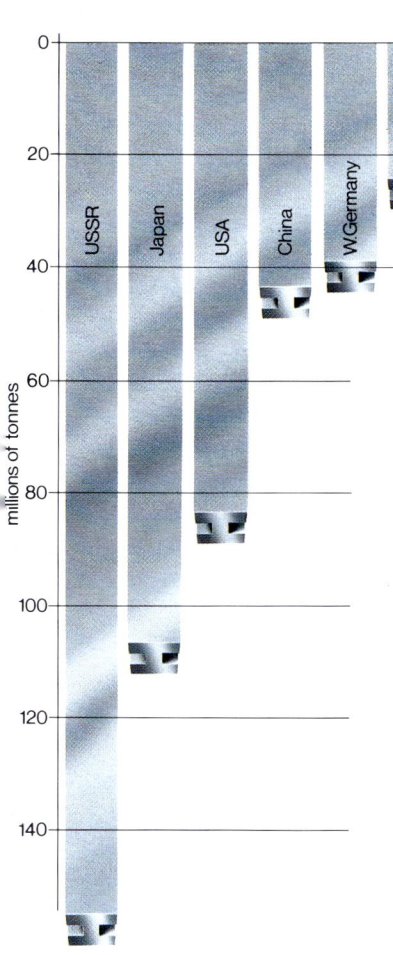

Principal steel producers, 1984

The expansion of the manufacturing sector in developing countries is hampered by a number of factors. The management of resources in the Third World is all too often controlled, either directly or indirectly, by large Western companies. Since many of these resources, both mineral and agricultural, provide the raw materials for manufacturing in the developed world, such companies are reluctant to allow the growth of local processing and manufacture.

Tariff barriers and trade control may also impede the sale of manufactured products from developing countries on international markets. The less developed countries have generally low labour costs, however, and in recent years some smaller nations such as South Korea, following the example of Japan, have rapidly increased their manufacturing output and successfully competed in world markets. Larger Third World nations, such as Indonesia and India, have huge domestic markets for their goods, and both these countries have considerably expanded their manufacturing industries. The poorer countries generally are finding their feet in the international market place; between 1975 and 1980 export earnings from manufactures in the developing countries increased at well over twice the rate of the industrialized countries.

The relative performance of the leading industrial countries has also changed considerably. Manufacturing production growth rates in the ten years 1974 to 1983 were relatively low in the developed world, with some countries such as the United Kingdom and Norway showing declines. The diagram opposite illustrates the dramatic rise of Japan and West Germany in the export sector since 1970, while the United Kingdom, France and Italy have been sluggish.

In the past, steel production (see diagram above) has been treated as a key index of industrial performance, although with the world recession in this industry and the rise of "high-technology" industries such as electronics it is probably a less reliable guide today. There are advantages in selecting a single product for comparison: it avoids many of the problems that arise in converting a huge number of quite different products, quantified in different ways by different people under different governments, to a simple measure of value.

INTERNATIONAL TRADE

Value of exports in billions of US dollars (1983)

- less than 1
- 1-5
- 5-15
- 15-50
- 50-100
- more than 100
- no data

Countries with large imbalance of trade (+/- 10 billion US dollars) 1983

- Trade deficit (−)
- Trade surplus (+)

Countries with more than half of all export income from three products or fewer

INTERNATIONAL TRADE

The extent to which nations are engaged in foreign trade varies enormously. Broadly, the larger the country, the smaller its role (in relation to its size) in international trade, since large countries naturally have more resources of their own. This is true even of the United States, whose total exports and imports are each equivalent to less than 10 per cent of Gross National Product (GNP), while in the case of the Soviet Union the figure is still lower. By contrast, in a country such as the Netherlands, total exports and total imports each approach 50 per cent of GNP. The United States is still the world's greatest trading nation, but this is merely a reflection of its immense GNP. The Soviet Union is not a major trading nation, in spite of occasional forays into the grain market during years of poor harvest, but its role has been increasing in recent years while that of the United States has been decreasing.

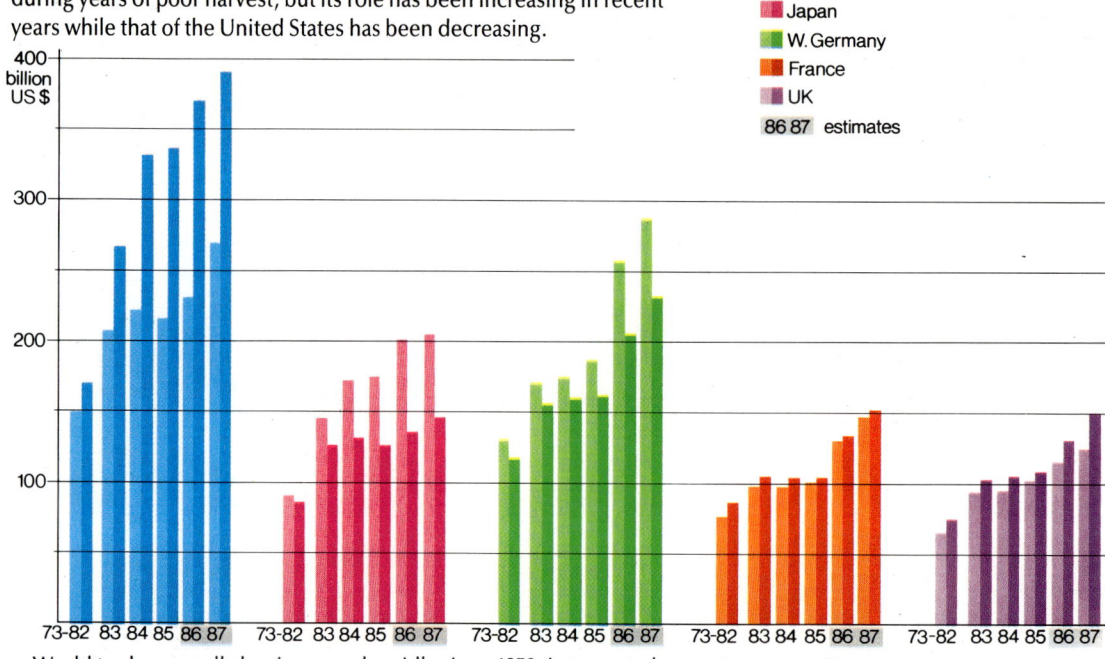

Exports
Imports
- USA
- Japan
- W. Germany
- France
- UK

86 87 estimates

World trade generally has increased rapidly since 1950, interrupted only by the recession of the late 1970s, but not all nations have benefited equally. A major source of controversy is the relationship between manufacturing nations, mainly the United States and the EEC, and primary producers in the Third World. In theory there are obvious advantages to both sides when manufactures are exchanged for raw materials, but in practice the greatest growth in markets for manufacturers has been among manufacturing nations themselves. Developing nations dependent on the export of a small number of primary products labour under several disadvantages. The world price of crops such as sugar or cocoa and of minerals such as copper or tin is subject to large fluctuations due to changing demand and supply, a drawback to which manufacturers are less liable. Many attempts have been made to unite primary producers with the aim of stabilizing prices and output, but with the partial exception of OPEC (oil producers) they have had little success.

Exports and imports
The role of the United States as the world's largest consumer has been reflected in its increasing trade imbalance during the 1980s, an imbalance that is likely to continue. The Japanese trade surplus is expected to peak in 1986, while West Germany is projected to have an increasing surplus.

In the market economies, chiefly Western Europe and North America, lip service is paid to the ideal of free trade, and there was a general lowering of tariffs between the 1950s and 1970s. There are, however, other barriers, including political ones, to trade, and the recession of the 1970s has resulted in moves towards greater protection, by tariffs or other means, of domestic industry. A particular source of controversy is the flooding of "high-wage" markets, such as the United States, with goods from "low-wage" producers, such as South Korea.

Japanese economic policies, stimulating high exports and low imports, also irritate its chief industrial trading partners. A country's trading position in relation to the rest of the world is reflected in its balance of payments — the relationship between exports and imports. Ideally, no nation should run a persistent surplus or a persistent deficit, and if it does it should take steps to rectify the situation, for example by introducing deflationary policies to combat a persistent deficit. However, political or other factors may make this impracticable. In the early 1980s the US balance of payments deficit has been steadily growing (see left), a situation that would have been unthinkable a few years earlier.

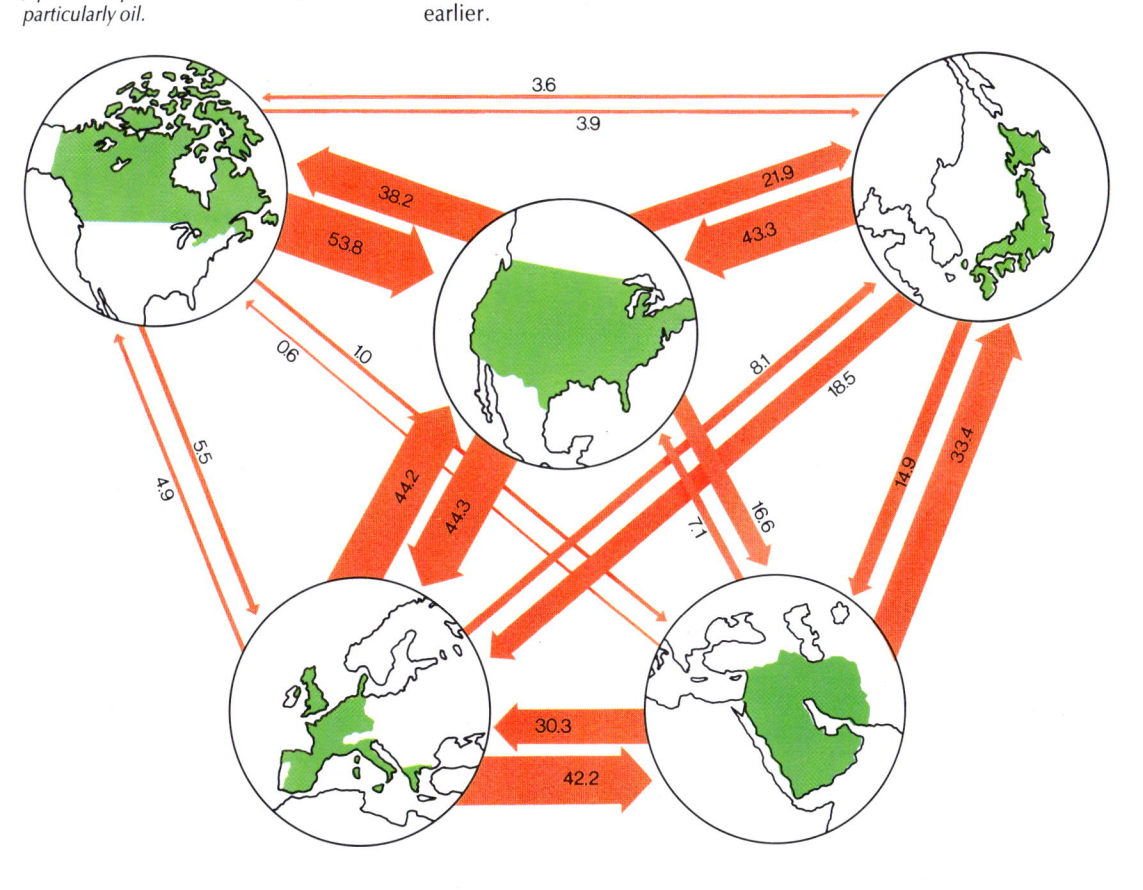

International trade by major partners, 1983
Figures in billions of US dollars.
The imbalance between Japan and the United States and EEC reflects large volumes of manufactured goods, while that between Japan and the Middle East reflects large Japanese imports of raw materials, particularly oil.

FOREIGN INVESTMENT

Rank	Company	Headquarters	Sales
1.	General Motors	Detroit	96.37
2.	Exxon	New York	86.67
3.	Royal Dutch/Shell Group	The Hague/London	81.74
4.	Mobil	New York	55.96
5.	British Petroleum	London	53.10
6.	Ford Motor	Dearborn, Mich.	52.77
7.	International Business Machines	Armonk, N.Y.	50.05
8.	Texaco	Harrison, N.Y.	46.29
9.	Chevron	San Francisco	41.74
10.	American Tel & Tel	New York	34.90
11.	E.I. du Pont de Nemours	Wilmington, Del.	29.48
12.	General Electric	Fairfield, Conn.	28.28
13.	Standard Oil (Ind.)	Chicago	27.21
14.	IRI	Rome	26.75
15.	Toyota Motor	Toyota City	26.04
16.	ENI	Rome	24.46
17.	Atlantic Richfield	Los Angeles	22.35
18.	Unilever	Rotterdam/London	21.62
19.	Chrysler	Highland Park, Mich.	21.25
20.	Matsushita Electric Industrial	Osaka	20.74
21.	Hitachi	Tokyo	20.52
22.	Pemex (Petróleos Mexicanos)	Mexico City	20.38
23.	Shell Oil	Houston	20.30
24.	Elf-Aquitaine	Paris	20.10
25.	Française des Pétroles	Paris	19.26
26.	U.S. Steel	Pittsburgh	18.42
27.	Nissan Motor	Yokohama	18.22
28.	Philips' Gloeilampenfabrieken	Eindhoven	18.07
29.	Siemens	Munich	17.83
30.	Volkswagen	Wolfsburg	17.83

TOP 30 LARGEST INDUSTRIAL CORPORATIONS

Legend

Total monetary reserves (including gold) in millions of Special Drawing Rights (SDRs) with the IMF (1985)

- more than 20,000
- 10,000 – 20,000
- 5,000 – 10,000
- 2,500 – 5,000
- 500 – 2,500
- 100 – 500
- less than 100
- no data

Top 30 largest industrial corporations ranked by sales in billion US dollars (1985) Rank numbers refer to table at left.

- 15 – 25
- 25 – 50
- 50 – 75
- 75 – 100

Ten most heavily indebted countries (1985).

- 51 Total debt – billion US dollars
- 20 Debt service

FOREIGN INVESTMENT

Money makes money: capital is attracted to sources of potential profit. The bulk of foreign investment therefore flows between the major industrialized nations (excluding the Soviet bloc). About two-thirds of the total United States direct investment abroad is in Canada and the EEC, while the flow of private investment from EEC countries is predominantly to their European partners and to North America. The Netherlands, for example, had direct private investments in the United States amounting to a colossal $29 billion in 1983, over $2,000 per head of the Dutch population.

The ability of a country to attract foreign investment depends not on need but on economic performance, political stability and government policy. The map is coloured to show each country's total monetary reserves expressed in Special Drawing Rights (SDRs). The SDR is the unit of account for the International Monetary Fund (IMF). It is indicative of the economic power of a country and is used for a range of international financial transactions including the settlement of financial obligations, the making of donations and the extension of loans. For poor countries, requiring capital for economic development, there is a double bind. They need investment to strengthen their economy, but because their economy is weak they find it difficult to attract investment.

During the 1970s the commercial banks held a surfeit of capital resulting from the vast profits of oil producers, and they were eager to invest in Third World countries whose credit looked good. Then came the world recession and sharply rising interest rates. The funds dried up, while poor nations found themselves with debts on which they were unable to pay the interest let alone repay the capital.

The logical outcome of such a situation is bankruptcy, but as this is deleterious to all parties, it is avoided by renegotiation of loans or by other more drastic means. For example, the government of Peru declared unilaterally in the mid 1980s that it would limit debt-service payments (interest on loans, etc.) to 25 per cent of its export earnings. Peru's debts in 1986 amounted to about $5 billion, nearly two and a half times her total export earnings (see below). As a result, Peru paid less than 10 per cent of payments due in the year ending June 1986.

Borrowers

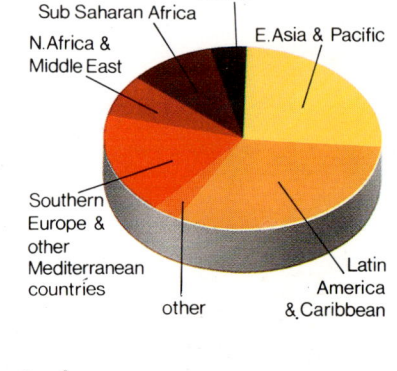

Lenders

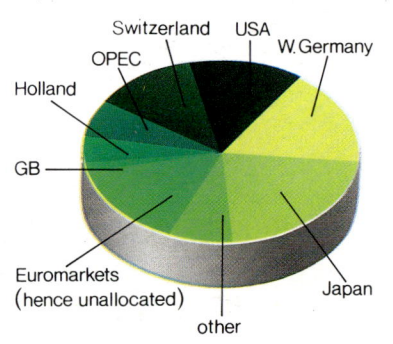

World Bank's borrowers and lenders
The World Bank acts to bridge the financial gap between North and South, directing capital from the developed countries to the developing. Although this money is lent to the world's poorest states, most of the projects backed by the World Bank are commercially viable and borrowers are charged a market rate of interest on the majority of loans.

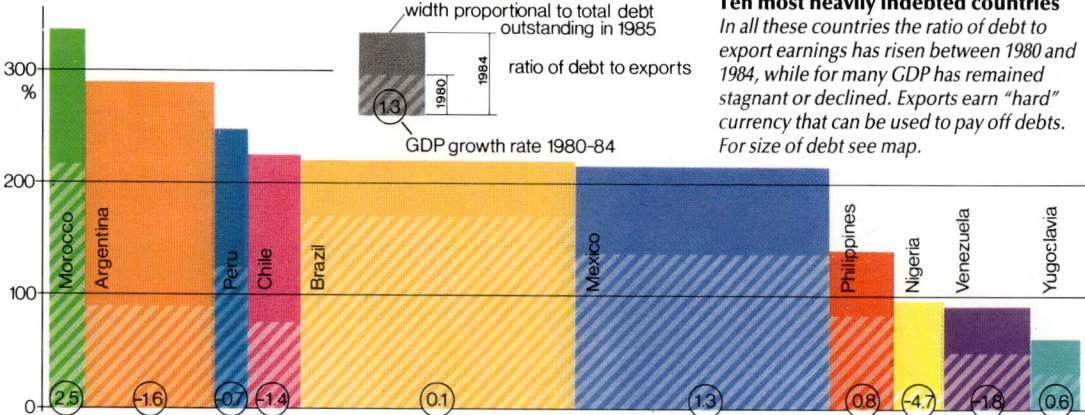

Ten most heavily indebted countries
In all these countries the ratio of debt to export earnings has risen between 1980 and 1984, while for many GDP has remained stagnant or declined. Exports earn "hard" currency that can be used to pay off debts. For size of debt see map.

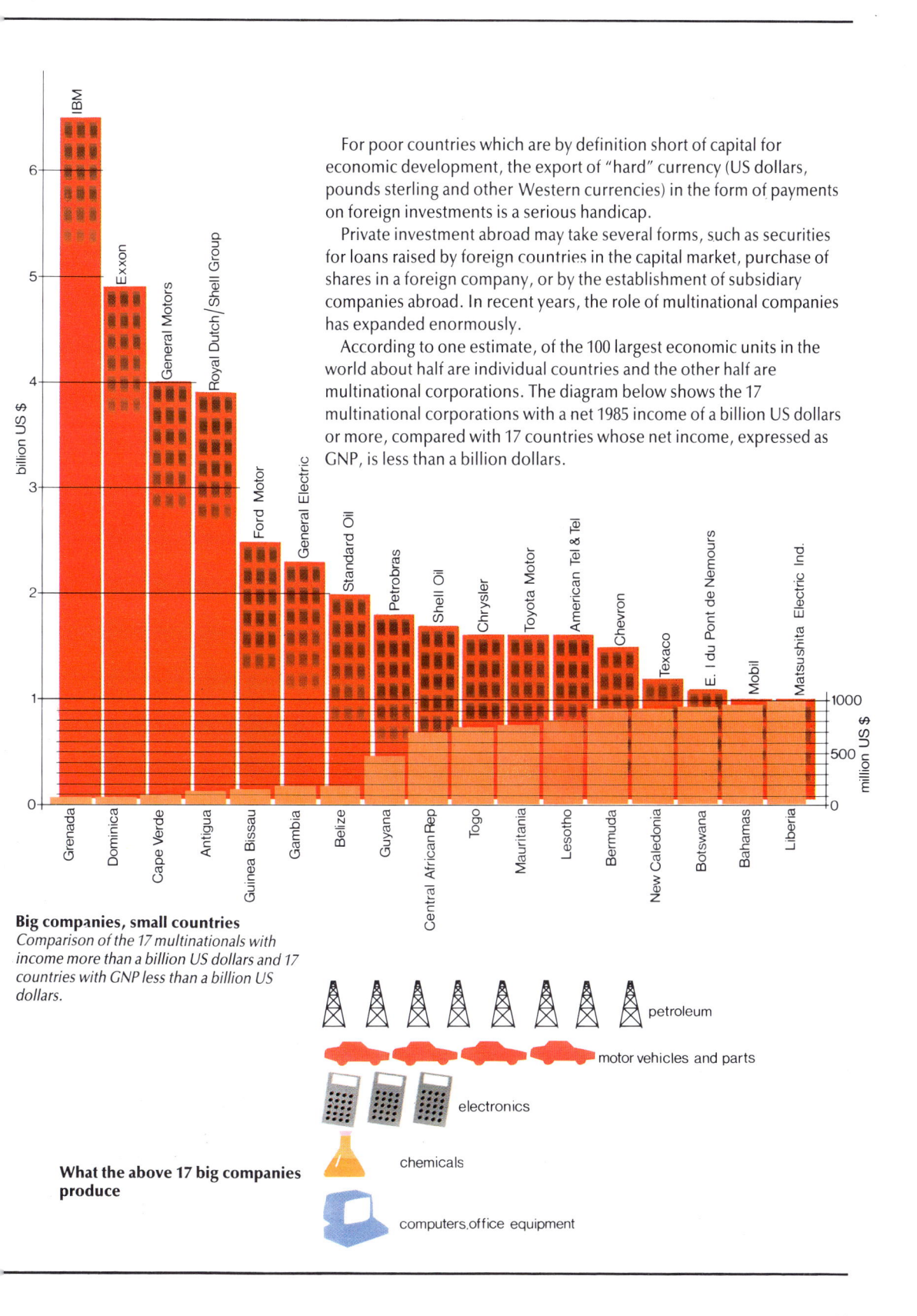

For poor countries which are by definition short of capital for economic development, the export of "hard" currency (US dollars, pounds sterling and other Western currencies) in the form of payments on foreign investments is a serious handicap.

Private investment abroad may take several forms, such as securities for loans raised by foreign countries in the capital market, purchase of shares in a foreign company, or by the establishment of subsidiary companies abroad. In recent years, the role of multinational companies has expanded enormously.

According to one estimate, of the 100 largest economic units in the world about half are individual countries and the other half are multinational corporations. The diagram below shows the 17 multinational corporations with a net 1985 income of a billion US dollars or more, compared with 17 countries whose net income, expressed as GNP, is less than a billion dollars.

Big companies, small countries
Comparison of the 17 multinationals with income more than a billion US dollars and 17 countries with GNP less than a billion US dollars.

What the above 17 big companies produce

- petroleum
- motor vehicles and parts
- electronics
- chemicals
- computers, office equipment

EXCHANGE RATES

Asia & Oceania — National Currencies

Map labels

Oceans: Arctic Ocean · North Pacific Ocean · Indian Ocean

Countries and currencies:
- Union of Soviet Socialist Republics — roubles
- Mongolia — tughrik
- China — yuan renminbi
- Nth. Korea — won
- Sth. Korea — won
- Japan — yen
- Taiwan — new yuan
- Hong Kong
- Philippines — pesos
- Vietnam — dong
- Kamp. (Kampuchea) — no data
- Laos — no data
- Thailand — baht
- Burma — kyats
- Bangladesh — taka
- Bhutan
- Nepal
- India — rupees
- Sri Lanka — rupees
- Pakistan — rupees
- Afghanistan — afghanis
- Iran — rials
- Iraq — dinars
- Turkey — liras
- Cyprus
- Syria
- Lebanon
- Israel — shekels
- Jordan
- Saudi Arabia — riyals
- Kuwait
- Qatar
- U.A.E.
- Oman — rials Omani
- N. Yemen
- S. Yemen
- Djibouti
- Ethiopia — birr
- Somalia — shillings
- Sudan — pounds
- Egypt — pounds
- Uganda
- Kenya
- Tanzania
- Malawi — kwacha
- Mozambique — meticals
- Madagascar — francs
- Zimbabwe — dollars
- Zambia
- Swaziland
- Lesotho
- South Africa — rand
- Malaysia — ringgit
- Brunei
- Singapore
- Indonesia — rupiahs
- Papua New Guinea — kina
- Australia — dollars
- New Caledonia
- New Zealand — dollars
- Finland — markkaa
- Deutsche marks
- Zlotych
- Marks

Legend

Percentage movement of national currencies against the US dollar (1980–85)

- increase 0–10%
- no change
- decrease 0–10%
- decrease 10–25%
- decrease 25–50%
- decrease 50–100%
- decrease 100–500%
- decrease 500–2000%
- decrease over 2000%
- no data

National currency — dollars

111

EXCHANGE RATES

Payments from one country to another in the course of trade or tourism, for example, require the exchange of one country's currency for another's. The exchange rate is the price of a country's currency in terms of another's — for example, the amount in United States dollars that can be purchased with £1 sterling.

Reasonably stable exchange rates are vital to international commerce, and in the 20th century numerous attempts have been made to establish a reliable system. None has been entirely satisfactory.

Exchange rates fluctuate according to normal market forces of supply and demand. However, monetary authorities, such as governments and central banks, have ways of controlling them, for example by buying or selling their own currency in the international market in order to raise or lower its value.

A currency which can be freely exchanged for any other currency, or for gold, at the standard rate of exchange is called a convertible currency. In practice, convertibility is to some extent relative: governments have various ways of restricting it in order, for example, to prevent a sudden rush of selling which would dangerously reduce national reserves.

In the 1920s international currencies generally belonged to the gold standard, which meant that exchange rates were fixed by the value of the currency in gold. This system was abandoned during the Great Depression, but gold still plays an important part in the international monetary system. In the 1960s central banks bought and sold gold at a fixed price, which for many years remained about US $35 an ounce, and imbalances were settled by exchanges of gold bullion. In the 1970s prevailing conditions — expanding world trade, inability to expand gold production sufficiently and rampant inflation, leading to rocketing gold prices which touched US $850 an ounce in 1980 — highlighted the inadequacy of gold as a form of international currency. One notable drawback was that those who benefited most were countries with large gold reserves, which did not need help, and international speculators who did not deserve it.

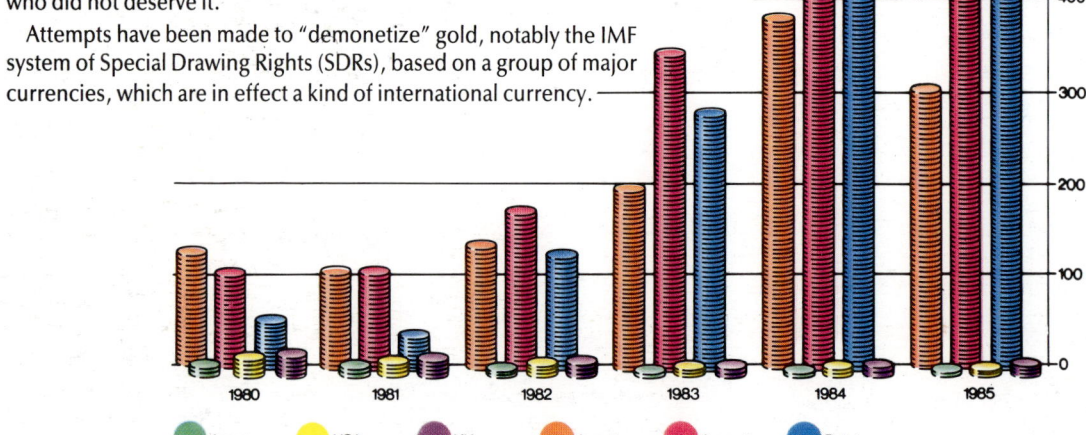

Attempts have been made to "demonetize" gold, notably the IMF system of Special Drawing Rights (SDRs), based on a group of major currencies, which are in effect a kind of international currency.

Consumer price inflation rates (%), 1980–85

The victims of runaway inflation in the 1980s include many of the South American states with heavy international debt burdens, weakened economies and political instability. In 1986, however, Argentina, Bolivia and Israel have all managed to bring down their inflation rates to well below 100 percent. In Japan, the United States and the United Kingdom inflation has been reduced after the high rates of the 1970s; in some countries, notably the UK, this has been at the expense of high unemployment.

US dollar against major currencies, 1980–85

Percentage increase in the value of the US dollar against selected major currencies. Since its peak in February 1985, the dollar has lost ground to these currencies, most particularly to the Japanese yen.

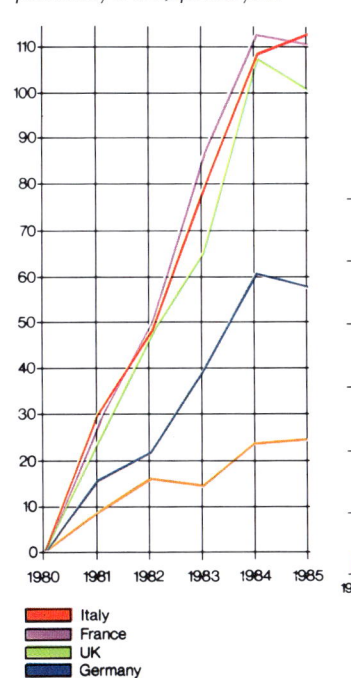

- Italy
- France
- UK
- Germany
- Japan

The IMF has been the chief agency for regulating foreign exchange rates since the Bretton Woods agreement of 1944. Members then agreed to make their currencies convertible at fixed exchange rates, though minor deviations were permitted. Members who run into balance-of-payments difficulties may borrow foreign currencies from the Fund, to which all members contribute a "quota" based on national income and other economic indicators.

The Bretton Woods system collapsed in the 1970s as a result of speculation against the United States dollar (the US balance-of-payments deficit having encouraged expectation of a dollar devaluation). A new IMF agreement in 1978 introduced more flexible or "floating" exchange rates and abolished the — unrealistic — official price of gold. Floating exchange rates have avoided the problems caused by large devaluations of a particular currency, but they are no panacea. They have been held responsible for contributing to inflation and for large, destabilizing movements of capital across international boundaries. They were envisaged as temporary; however, the oil crisis and ensuing world recession have made a return to fixed rates impracticable (notwithstanding the European "snake", a fixed-rate system among most EEC countries).

The currencies most widely employed in international payments are the US $ and the £ sterling. However, all currencies of OECD members (North America, Western Europe, Japan) may be regarded as "hard" currencies, that is generally convertible.

The currencies of COMECON members (The Soviet Union and its allies) are not "hard" and therefore not traded internationally. For foreign purchases these countries depend on credits and hard currency earned through exports.

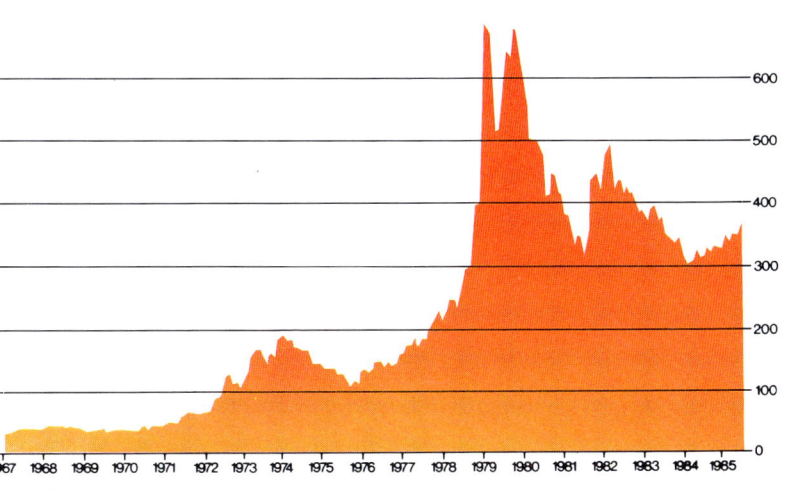

Gold price, 1967–86
Monthly average price in US dollars per ounce to August 1986.

WORLD ROAD AND RAIL TRANSPORT

Legend

Road passenger vehicles in use per 1,000 population (1983)

- more than 500
- 300–500
- 100–300
- 50–100
- 10–50
- less than 10
- no data

Rail passenger – kilometres (1982)
- more than 100 billion
- 20–100 billion
- 10–20 billion
- 1–10 billion
- less than 1 billion

Rail cargo tonne – kilometres (1982)
- more than 1,000 billion
- 100–1,000 billion
- 10–100 billion
- less than 10 billion

WORLD ROAD AND RAIL TRANSPORT

Passenger vehicles provide yet another rough guide to general prosperity. It is no surprise that the greatest numbers of cars and buses in relation to population are to be found in North America, Western Europe and Australasia, with the United States (fewer than two persons per vehicle) leading the way and the People's Republic of China (about 5,000 persons per vehicle) bringing up the rear. It is noticeable that for a number of African countries no figures are available. In most of those countries, this reflects the fact that, except for a tiny urban elite, cars are hardly more common than spaceships, and similarly irrelevant to most people's needs.

Nevertheless, there is no simple equation between passenger vehicles and individual prosperity. All sorts of other factors are involved, such as the existence, or nonexistence, of suitable roads or the priorities of the political regime. In Communist countries cars are relatively scarce, largely due to lack of emphasis on production of consumer goods, but partly, no doubt, to ideological motives also — public transport being politically more commendable. The total number of motor vehicles in the Soviet Union is about the same as in Britain, but whereas in Britain cars make up about 90 per cent of the total, in the Soviet Union they make up little more than 50 per cent.

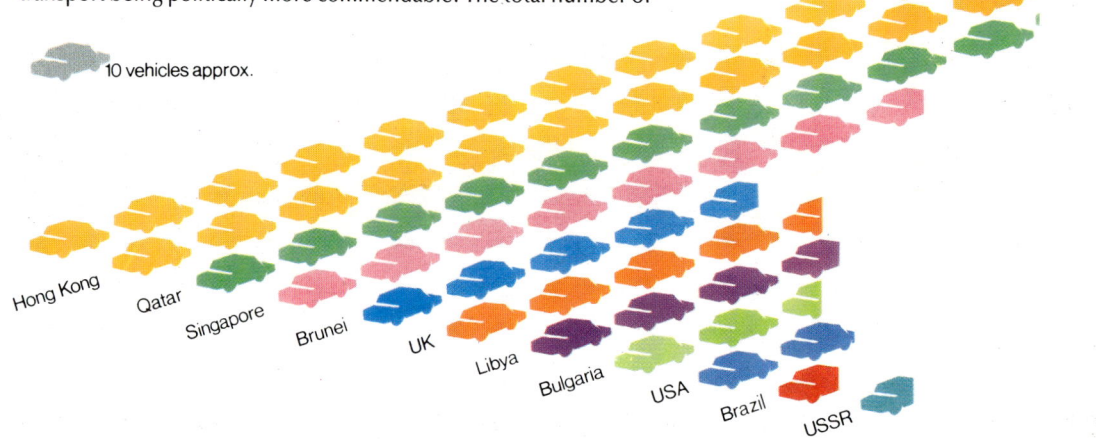

Statistics on world transport, as on other matters, are complicated by the variations, not to say errors, involved in their compilation. One obvious example: the number of cars reported is the number officially registered; in many countries the true figure would be somewhat higher. Differences in methods of classification and calculation raise an even greater number of problems in rail transport: when are parcels "cargo"? When are troops "passengers"? In general the figures given on the map refer to public railways, excluding local transport, industrial or cable railways; "cargo" excludes mail and official goods and personal luggage; "passengers" means persons paying a fare, which generally excludes government personnel (including troops).

Cars per kilometre of national road length (selected countries)
In some Western countries, and particularly small but prosperous states, if every car took to the road at once the entire system would probably seize up. In Hong Kong there is one vehicle for every 4.1 metres of road. In larger countries road congestion is highly localized in major cities, sometimes requiring extreme measures. The traffic chaos in Lagos, Nigeria, for example, has necessitated a restrictive law based on vehicle number plates: cars with even numbers are allowed on the roads on Mondays, Wednesdays and Fridays and odd numbers on Tuesdays, Thursdays and Saturdays.

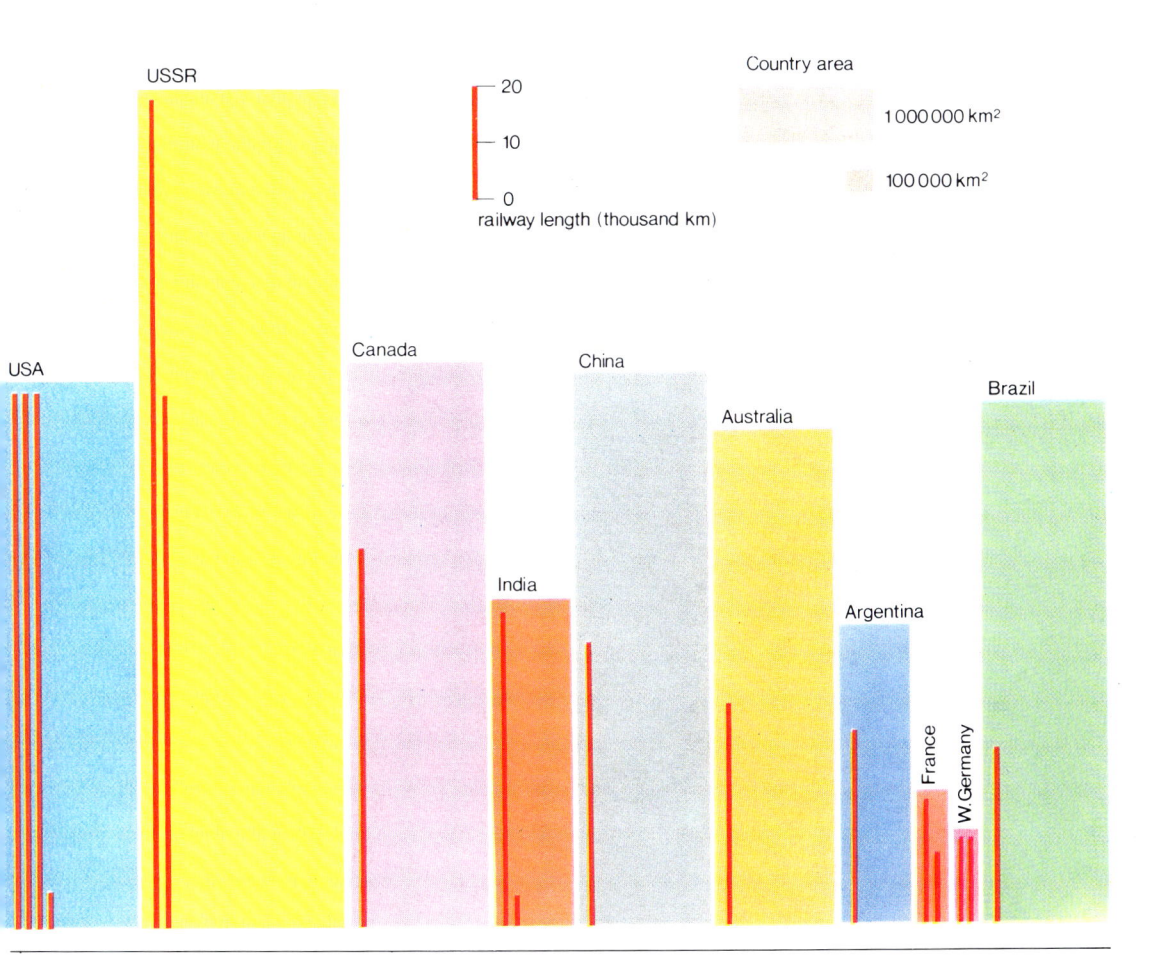

Rail networks
The ten countries are those with the largest rail networks overall, shown in descending order of total length, which of course is not the same as the ten countries with the densest railway networks.

In general, the tendency in industrialized countries in recent years has been for a relative decrease in rail traffic as against road, although there are many exceptions. Perhaps surprisingly, the oil crisis of the 1970s appears to have had little effect on this general trend. Rail traffic is usually of greater importance in Communist states and in many countries of the Third World, especially in transport of goods. In the Soviet Union, for example, the quantity of rail freight, in tonne-kilometres, is roughly three times as much as the United States, and although the Soviet Union is much the larger in area, its rail network is in fact smaller than that of the United States.

The USSR is also the leading nation in rail passengers per kilometre, but it is closely followed by Japan, whose high position in this league is evidence of the generally greater mobility of the more prosperous, as well as Japan's strikingly efficient railway system.

WORLD AIR AND SEA TRANSPORT

Asia and Oceania: Transport

Air traffic: billion passenger kilometres (1982)
- more than 100
- 10–100
- 5–10
- 2–5
- 1–2
- less than 1

Countries handling more than 1 billion tonne-kilometres air cargo (1982)

Sea traffic: goods unloaded, million tonnes (1982)
- more than 100
- 50–100
- 10–50
- less than 10

Major sea lanes

WORLD AIR AND SEA TRANSPORT

Since commercial air travel began, traffic has grown enormously, especially since World War II. The world's largest airline, Aeroflot, the state airline of the Soviet Union, carried 229 passengers in the first year of operation (1923). In 1940 it carried 400,000, in 1965 40 million, in 1984 112 million. Annual air travel in passenger-kms in the United States averages 1,700 km per head of the total population; Heathrow Airport, London, handles 30 million passengers a year.

In the industrialized countries air travel has become standard for long-distance journeys, internal as well as foreign. The figures, in passenger-kms, are obviously affected by the size of the country — average internal journeys being longer in larger countries — but that is not the decisive factor. Thus, the figure for little Japan is high, third in the world rankings, behind the United States and the Soviet Union. The diagram below shows the total distance flown by registered civil airlines (some figures are approximate).

The map also shows the average quantity of goods unloaded from merchant ships in tonnes. This might be regarded as a measure of exports and imports, but it is an unreliable indicator of trade volume, if

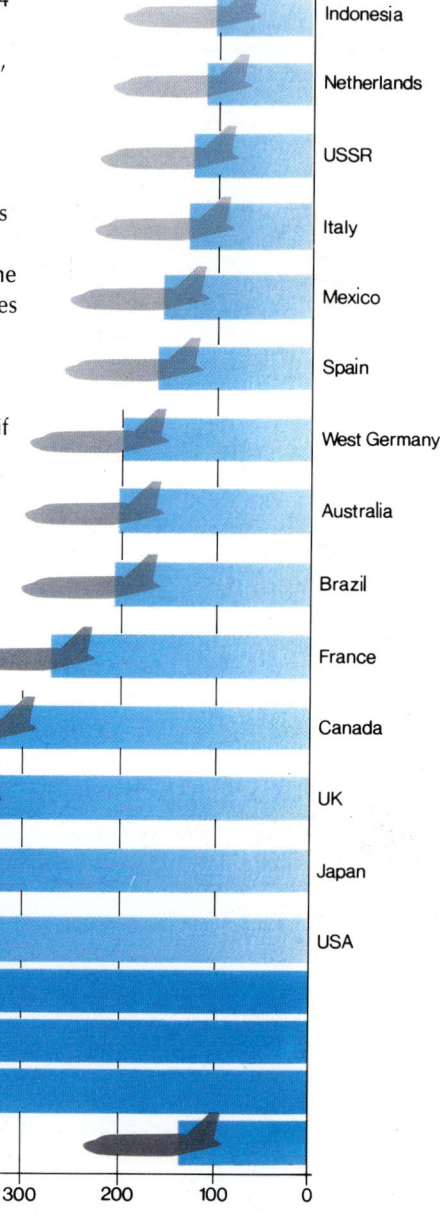

Distances flown by national civil airlines, 1982

Legend:
- Liberia
- Japan
- Greece
- Panama
- USSR
- UK
- Norway
- USA
- France
- Italy
- Rest of the world

10 million gross tons (1982)

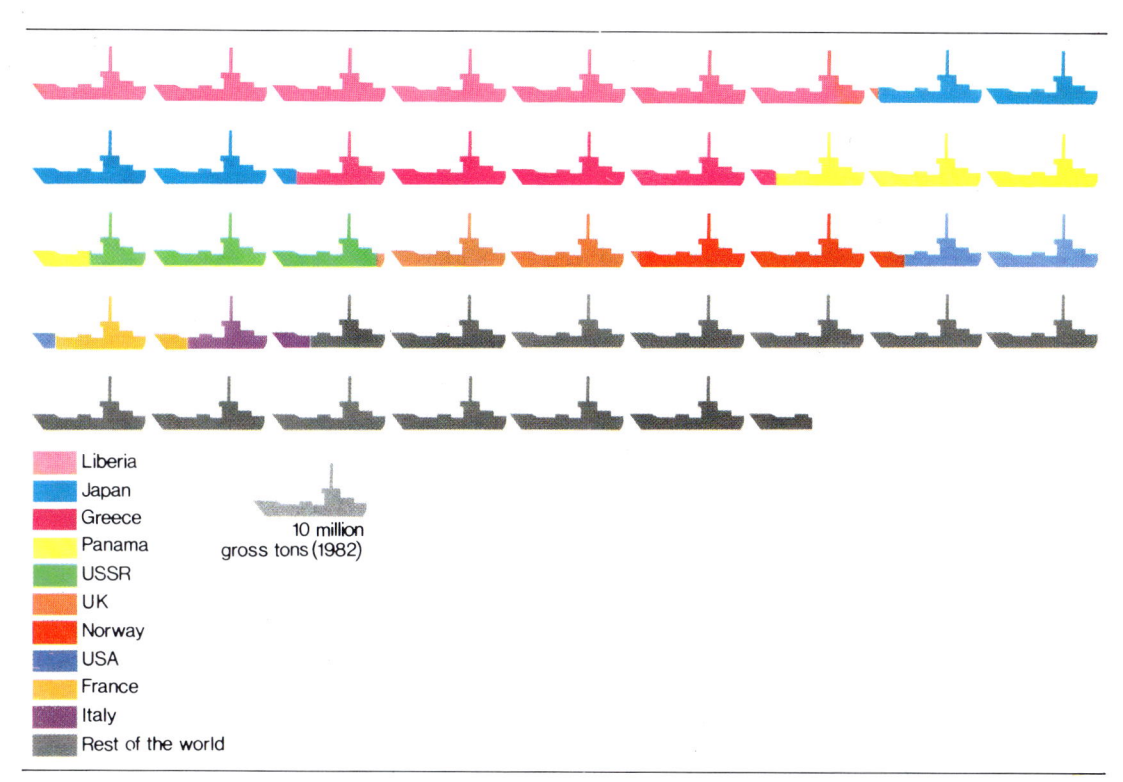

World's merchant shipping fleets

The world tonnage of merchant shipping has increased roughly five times in the period since the Second World War. However, the actual number of ships increased very little in that period. They have merely grown larger, oil tankers being the most noticeable examples of the trend. They have also grown faster, and the increase in ton-kilometres in that period was proportionately even greater than the increase in gross tonnage.

only because weight does not equal value. In the case of Japan, for example, goods loaded average about 7.5 tonnes per month and goods unloaded about 46 million tonnes, but appearances notwithstanding, Japan's trade balance is actually very healthy since it imports raw materials such as iron ore and fuels, with a low cost/weight ratio and exports manufactures such as electronic equipment with a high cost/weight ratio. The vast operations at Rotterdam and other Dutch ports reflect the Netherlands's role as an international entrepôt — handling other countries' goods — and oil refiner. The relatively low figure for West Germany results from the preponderance of road and rail transport of German goods.

The diagram above, illustrating the relative size of the world's largest merchant fleets in gross registered tons (gross tonnage is a measure of total capacity), also reveals some anomalies. Certain countries, such as Liberia and Panama, encourage registration of foreign-owned shipping under a "flag of convenience" by offering lower taxation and costs.

The large majority of new merchant ships are now built in the Far East. In 1984, 2,210 new merchant ships were completed, according to Lloyds Register of Shipping, representing just over 18 million gross tons. Just three countries accounted for 65 per cent of this gross tonnage: Japan, South Korea and Taiwan. Japan alone accounted for 9.7 million gross tons. West Germany and the United Kingdom combined produced 960,000 gross tons, by contrast.

WORLD COMMUNICATIONS

ARCTIC OCEAN
432
308
405
358
535
UNION OF SOVIET SOCIALIST REPUBLICS
6
100
34
71
44
78
55
55
15
3
7
MONGOLIA
NTH. KOREA
STH. KOREA
556
JAPAN
575
NORTH
PACIFIC
OCEAN
CHINA
TURKEY
CYP.
LEB.
SYRIA
ISRAEL
IRAQ
IRAN
AFGHAN.
JOR.
KUW.
PAKISTAN
NEPAL
BHUTAN
EGYPT
SAUDI
ARABIA
QATAR
U.A.E.
OMAN
254
12
14
INDIA
BANG.
BURMA
LAOS
TAIWAN
HONG
KONG
26
18
49
SUDAN
N.YEMEN
S.YEMEN
THAILAND
VIETNAM
KAMP.
PHILIPPINES
DJIBOUTI
5
ETHIOPIA
SOMALIA
3
SRI
LANKA
17
96
BRUNEI
MALAYSIA
SING.
1
21
UGANDA
KENYA
Equator
4
TANZANIA
11
INDONESIA
PAPUA
NEW GUINEA
INDIAN OCEAN
22
MALAWI
MOZAMBIQUE
ZIMBABWE
MADAGASCAR
8
6
423
336
AUSTRALIA
NEW
CALEDONIA
SWAZILAND
LESOTHO
NEW ZEALAND
288
325
RADIOS PER 1000 INHABITANTS (1983)
less than 50
50 -200
200 -400
400 -600
more than 600
no data
TELEVISION RECEIVERS
Per 1000 inhabitants (1983)
49
CIRCULATION OF DAILY NEWSPAPERS
Per 1000 inhabitants (1983)
91

WORLD COMMUNICATIONS

The "communications revolution" of the 20th century may turn out to have been as great an agent for change in human society as the Industrial Revolution of the 19th century. All the most striking developments of contemporary "high technology" lie in this field — computers, microelectronics, lasers, optical fibres, space satellites — and the results of our amazing new ability to store, analyse and transmit information on a massive scale cannot be foreseen. They ought to be immensely beneficial.

The trouble is that high technology is expensive. Although Indonesia, a country of islands, has established a national radio and telephonic system via satellite, Third World countries cannot normally afford satellite technology. Even less advanced means of communication are in short supply in the Third World, as the map shows.

Television has proved an enormous boon to education in rural areas, notably in India, yet India has only three TV sets for every thousand people, a minute proportion compared with the 300 to 400 sets common in the industrialized world. At present, 25 per cent of the world population possess 86 per cent of the total TV receivers. It is true that where TV sets are scarce they usually have a larger number of viewers, but that hardly compensates for the deficiency.

Overall, radio has probably had a greater effect than television in the Third World, being relatively cheap and able to reach larger audiences. It has the additional advantage over printed matter of being intelligible to people who are illiterate. Radios, like all consumer goods, are far less numerous in the Third World than in the industrialized countries, but

Consumption of printing and writing paper
Selected countries, consumption in tonnes per 1000 inhabitants, 1982

USA	62
W Germany	50
Norway	40
France	39
UK	32
New Zealand	21
Greece	8
Argentina	6
USSR	5
Romania	4
Philippines	1
Nigeria	0.7
Sudan	0.4
Bangladesh	0.3

Telephone communications

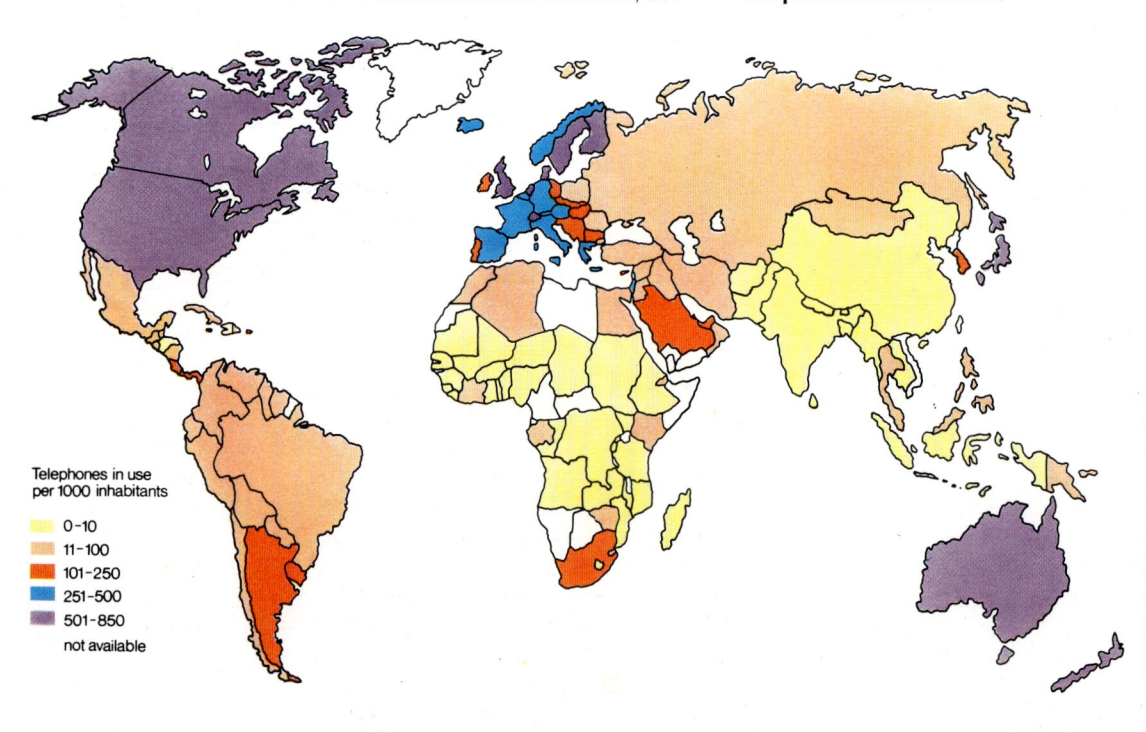

Telephones in use per 1000 inhabitants
- 0–10
- 11–100
- 101–250
- 251–500
- 501–850
- not available

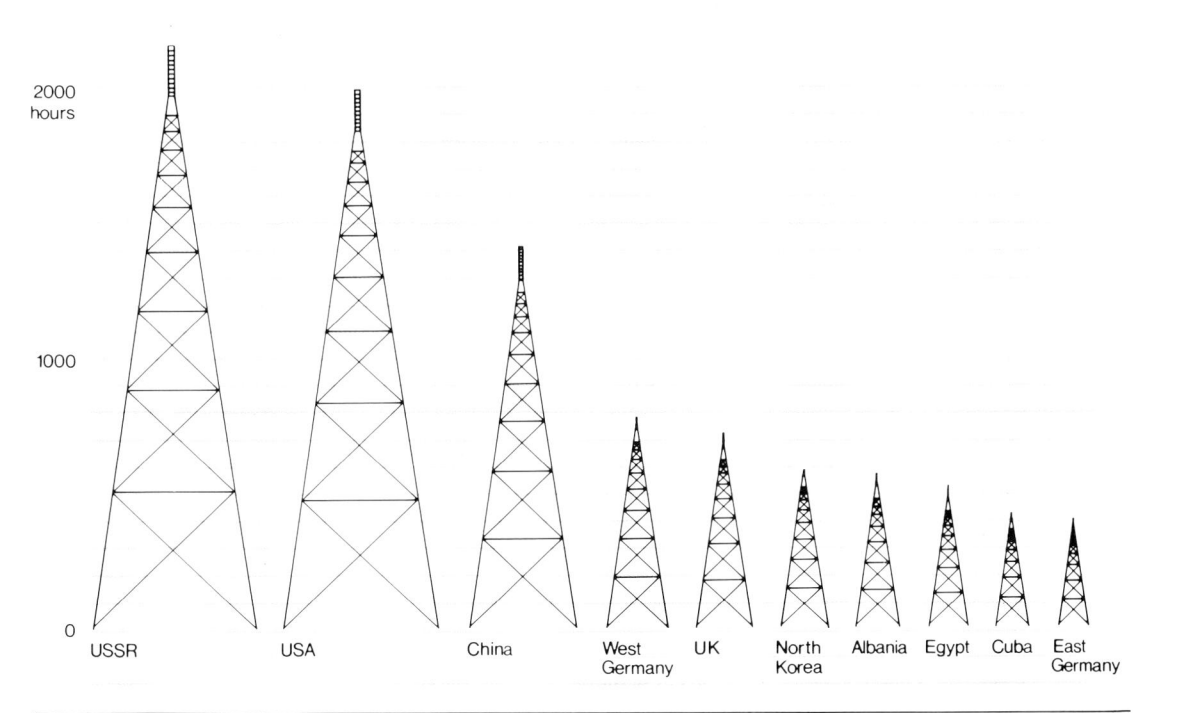

[Chart: External radio broadcasting hours per week, 1983 — USSR, USA, China, West Germany, UK, North Korea, Albania, Egypt, Cuba, East Germany; scale 0 to 2000 hours]

External radio broadcasting
Estimated total number of programme hours per week of some external broadcasters in 1983. Radio programmes broadcast for foreign listeners are used to communicate culture, news, views and propaganda. The Soviet Union figures include Radio Moscow, Radio Station Peace & Progress and regional stations; the United States includes Voice of America, Radio Free Europe and Radio Liberty; West Germany includes Deutsche Welle and Deutschlandfunk; the United Kingdom figures are for the BBC.

they are more common than TV sets. In India, for example, there are about 20 radios to every TV set. It is also likely that, especially where the estimates are based on the issue of licences, the true figure is larger than the official one.

The map also shows circulation of daily newspapers on the basis of copies distributed per thousand people. "Newspapers" is a broad category. The figures here refer to publications appearing at least four days a week and containing predominantly reports of current events. They may be as fat as the *New York Times* or they may consist of a single sheet. Clearly, no effort can be made to grade them qualitatively. The concept of "news" varies considerably and "freedom of the press" is limited to some degree in many countries. Control of the main international news agencies by the United States and other Western countries causes some resentment in the Third World.

The telephone, which first permitted instant two-way communication over long distances, has been the single most important advance in communications for people generally. Telephones remain relative rarities in many of the poorer countries, where the infrastructure is lacking. In some African countries especially, there are no published figures available, which in itself is evidence of the scarcity of telephone lines. In China and India the number of telephones per 100 people is much less than one, whereas in the United States it is about 80 (see diagram left).

LITERACY AND LEARNING

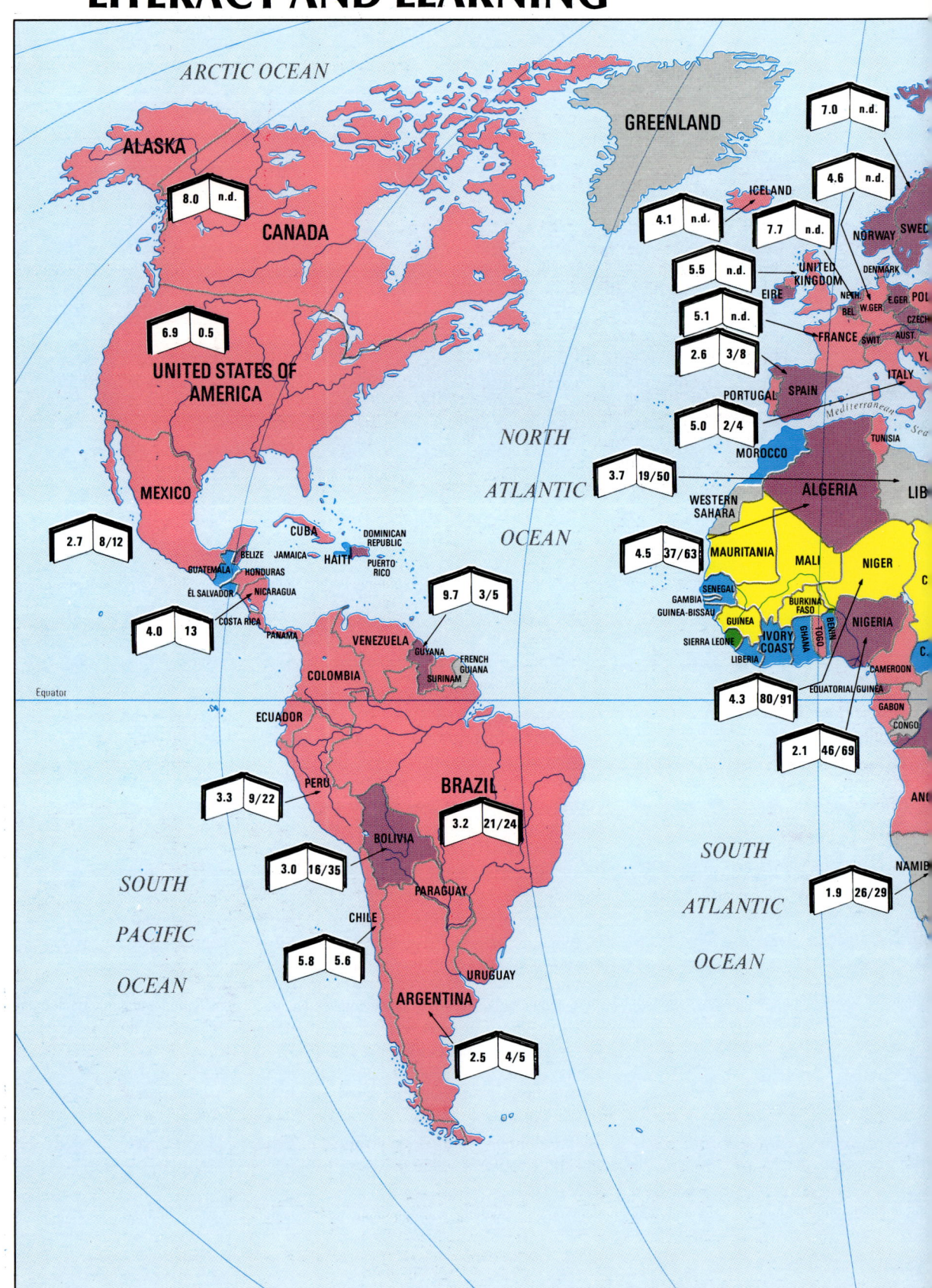

Asia & Oceania — Education

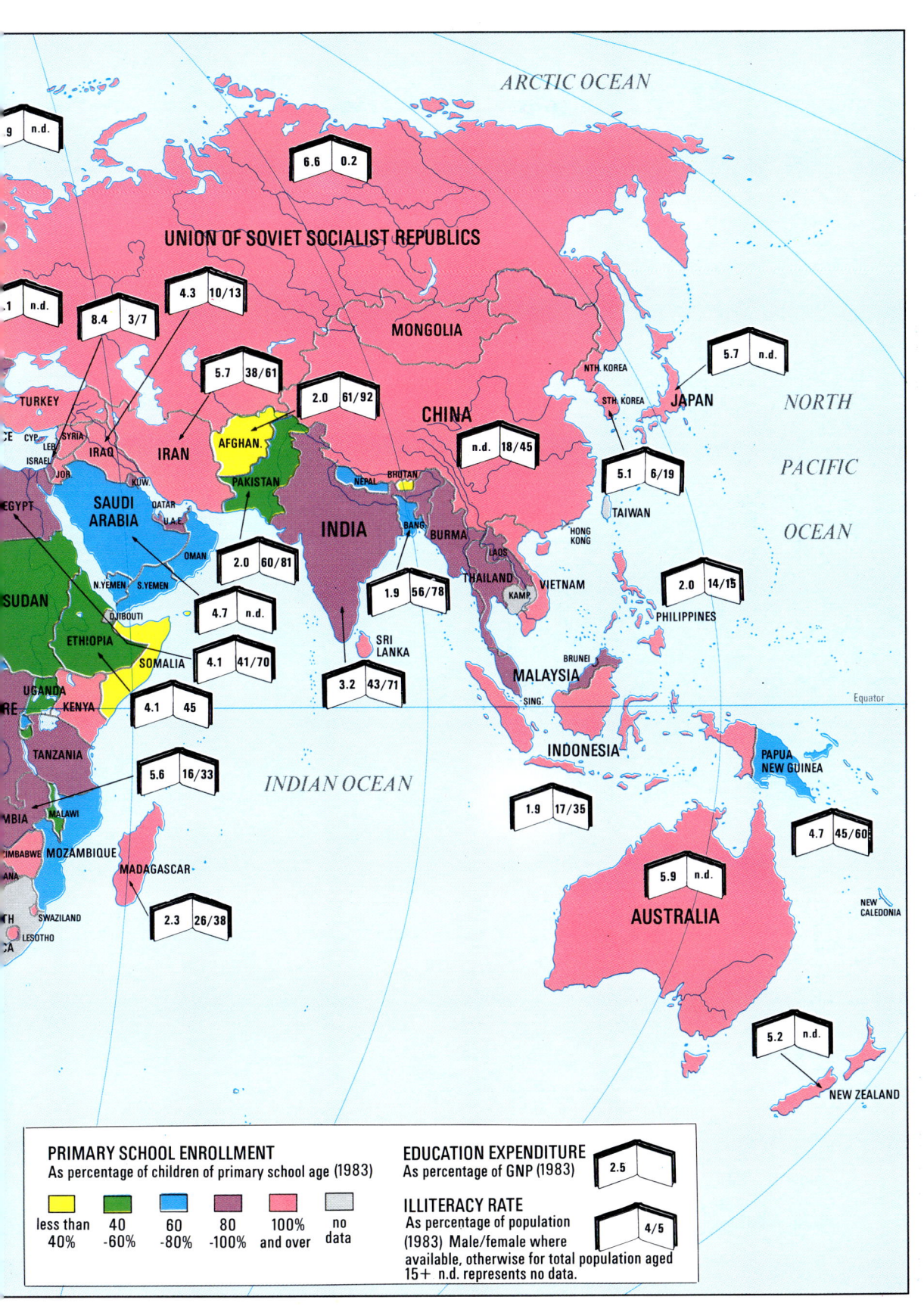

Map Data

Location	Education Expenditure (% GNP)	Illiteracy Rate (M/F)
(top left)	9	n.d.
USSR	6.6	0.2
(near Turkey)	.1	n.d.
Iraq/Syria area	8.4	3/7
(north of Iran)	4.3	10/13
Iran	5.7	38/61
China	2.0	61/92
China	n.d.	18/45
Japan	5.7	n.d.
Taiwan	5.1	6/19
Saudi Arabia / Pakistan region	2.0	60/81
N./S. Yemen area	4.7	n.d.
Philippines	2.0	14/15
Ethiopia/Somalia	4.1	41/70
India	1.9	56/78
Kenya	4.1	45
Sri Lanka	3.2	43/71
Tanzania/Malawi	5.6	16/33
Indonesia	1.9	17/35
Papua New Guinea	4.7	45/60
Madagascar	2.3	26/38
Australia	5.9	n.d.
New Zealand	5.2	n.d.

Legend

PRIMARY SCHOOL ENROLLMENT
As percentage of children of primary school age (1983)

- yellow: less than 40%
- green: 40–60%
- blue: 60–80%
- purple: 80–100%
- pink: 100% and over
- grey: no data

EDUCATION EXPENDITURE
As percentage of GNP (1983) — 2.5

ILLITERACY RATE
As percentage of population (1983) Male/female where available, otherwise for total population aged 15+. n.d. represents no data. — 4/5

127

LITERACY AND LEARNING

In the widest sense, education is the very basis of human society: children must learn in order to function as adults. Today it is less widely accepted that "education" in the narrower sense in which we usually think of it is quite such a solution to the problems of the world as earlier generations believed. The sort of education provided by schools may be less important than the "traditional" wisdom imbibed less formally from experience, especially in less specialized cultures than that of the industrialized world. A distinction is often made between "knowledge" and "wisdom". Many people would say that in the West too much emphasis has been placed on the former.

However, few would deny that the expansion of education is in general desirable, or that government expenditure on education is in general rather low (a comparison with MILITARY EXPENDITURE is depressing). The question, What kind of education?, is controversial; undoubtedly, too much schooling in the Third World is geared to inappropriate priorities and there is a danger of "wisdom" being swamped by the advance of "knowledge".

As the map shows, primary education is still far from universal, and in large areas of the poorest African countries there are simply no schools. This is naturally reflected in the rate of adult (age 15 and over) illiteracy, that is an inability to read and write. In Niger only one adult in seven can

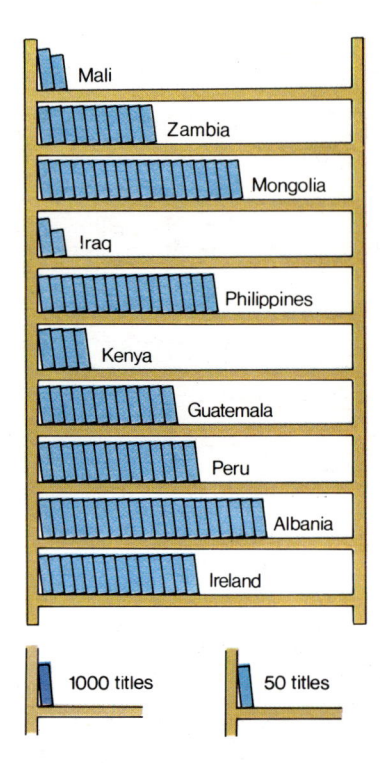

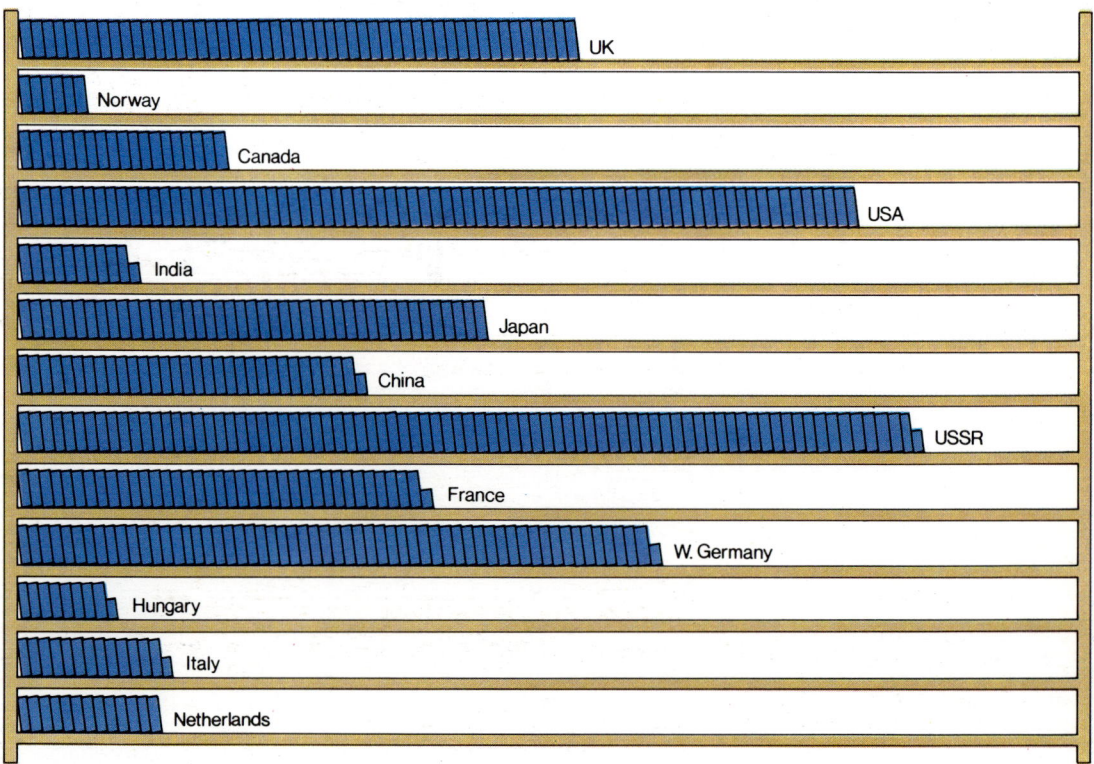

128

Pupil/teacher ratios, 1983

The average number of pupils in a teacher's classroom in a selection of countries.

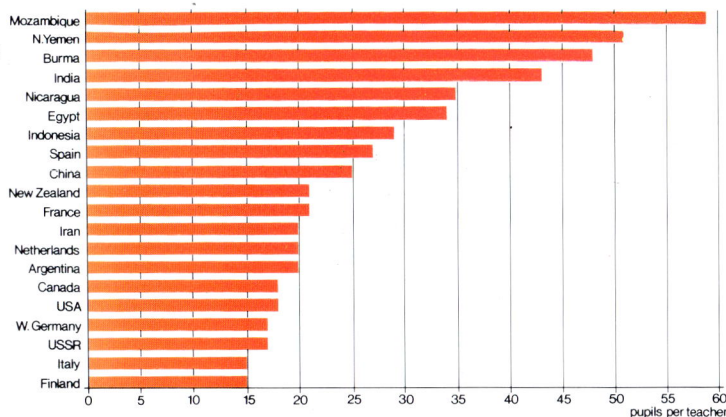

Country	Pupils per teacher
Mozambique	~59
N.Yemen	~51
Burma	~48
India	~43
Nicaragua	~35
Egypt	~34
Indonesia	~29
Spain	~27
China	~25
New Zealand	~21
France	~21
Iran	~20
Netherlands	~20
Argentina	~20
Canada	~18
USA	~17
W.Germany	~17
USSR	~17
Italy	~16
Finland	~15

◀ Number of book titles published, 1983

A selection of countries showing the vast differences in the number of books produced. Naturally these differences will be partly explained by population size, but compare, for example, the UK with the Philippines, two countries with about the same population but large differences in titles published and illiteracy rates. In many south east Asian and Latin American countries, however, many people avidly read large numbers of comic books that are not included in these figures.

Compulsory education

Duration (years)	Number of countries
4	1
5	12
6	37
7	7
8	33
9	33
10	35
11	5
12	4
NIL	27

In most countries education is compulsory, although the rule is often relaxed either temporarily (such as at harvest time) or permanently (no school within a reasonable distance).

read and write, and even in India about half the adult population is illiterate. Figures are based on estimates made by UNESCO, who do not include figures for many countries.

The data on which the map is based require some interpretation. The definition of primary education varies from one country to another, but usually means children aged 6–11. However, in many countries older and younger students are also receiving primary education and since the figures are based on total enrollment they are included, hence some countries appear to have over 100 per cent enrolment.

The data for education expenditure are also influenced by national differences, while the figures for the Soviet Union and East European countries are probably on the high side because they are a percentage of "Net Material Product" rather than GNP.

In spite of what is seen as the generally low level of educational expenditure, education has been expanding and illiteracy shrinking in recent years. Between 1960 and 1980 the *proportion* of children attending primary schools worldwide rose by nearly 20 per cent, a remarkable advance in view of the rocketing number of school-age children.

The educational boom of that period also encouraged secondary schooling and further education. The number of teachers in further education roughly tripled, for example. Proportionately, the rise was much greater in the Third World than elsewhere.

Of people aged 25 with some kind of further education, the estimated proportion in every country (with two or three exceptions) of South America, Africa and South Asia is less than 5 per cent, in many countries less than 1 per cent while in the United States the figure is over 30 per cent.

In those same regions, the proportion of people of 25 who have had some secondary education is (with two or three exceptions) less than 25 per cent.

WORLD DEVELOPMENT

Urban population as a percentage of total (1983)

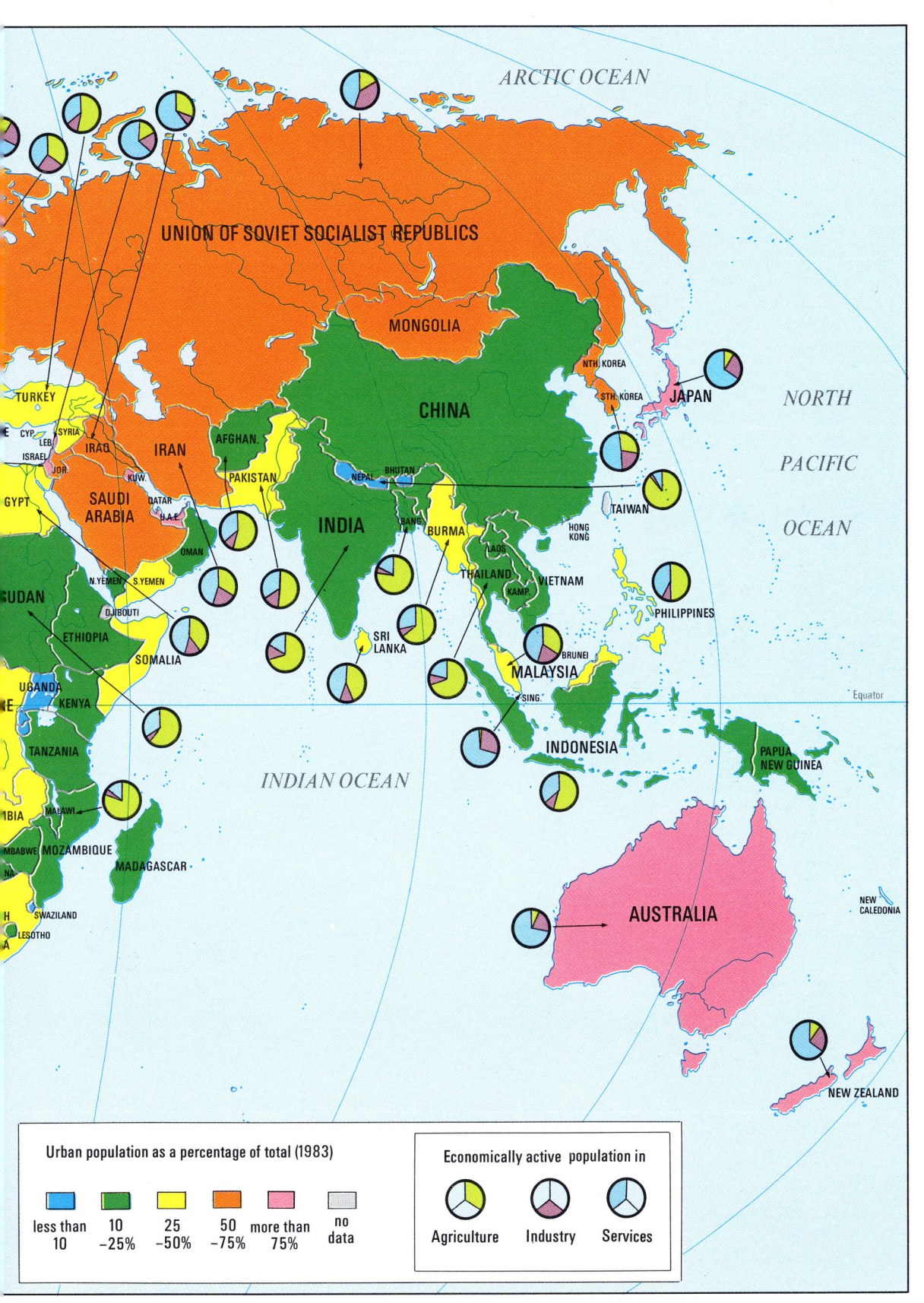

- less than 10
- 10–25%
- 25–50%
- 50–75%
- more than 75%
- no data

Economically active population in: Agriculture, Industry, Services

WORLD DEVELOPMENT

Before 1800 the great majority of people everywhere were largely occupied in producing food. Since the Industrial Revolution the parallel growth of manufacturing industry and urban society has often been taken as a rough measure of economic development. As the map shows, the rich nations of Europe and North America are today largely town-dwellers, while the poor nations of Asia and Africa are largely rural. Although many other factors have to be taken into account, such as area and natural resources, it is noticeable that among the rich countries even those noted for agricultural production (such as Denmark or New Zealand) have a predominantly urban population.

Cities were reshaped by the Industrial Revolution and later by the motor car. Today they are being reshaped again. Although the "inner city" is in decline, the suburbs are spreading like weeds. Many of the world's largest cities, swamped by penurious peasants, are close to being "ungovernable" (an adjective that has also been applied to New York, the archetypical modern city). But current figures suggest that the proportion of urban to rural dwellers will continue to increase. At the beginning of this century the ratio was about 1:7. By the end, it will be about even.

Three worlds

FIRST WORLD
Western Europe, North America, Japan, Australia, New Zealand

SECOND WORLD
Soviet Union and its Eastern European allies

THIRD WORLD
Latin America, Africa, other Asian countries

After World War II, in political terms the world was seen to be divided between, on the right, Western capitalist states led by the United States and, on the left, Communist States dominated by the Soviet Union. Shortly, however, with the abolition of European colonial empires, another group of countries, vociferous in the young UN Assembly, appeared on the scene. This group, whose economies were said to be "underdeveloped" or "developing", came to be known as the Third World — in contrast to the "developed", industrialized economies of the "First" and "Second" Worlds.

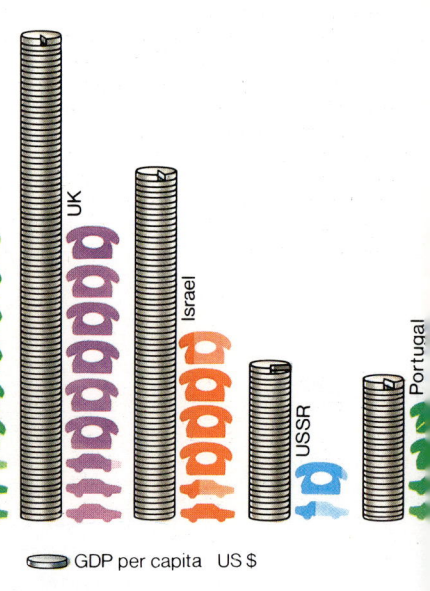

GDP per capita US $

100 telephones in use per 1000 population

100 passenger vehicles in use per 1000 population

Traditionally, "industry" has been popularly interpreted as the production of goods (manufacturing) and raw materials (mining), but in recent years the rich countries particularly have shown a rapid growth in "service" industries, a term which covers the vast range of economic activities not involved with material production. This sector, which is associated with the current decline of traditional heavy industries like steel or shipbuilding, is still growing. On the available figures (disregarding relative population) for 81 countries, the average national total for those employed in service industries is just under 50 per cent of the "economically active" (including unemployed and part-time workers) population. In the United States it is 74 per cent and in all Western European countries except Portugal over 60 per cent, while in India and Bangladesh it is under 20 per cent.

The diagram provides three additional indicators of general economic development for selected countries. Gross domestic product (GDP) per head is a fair measure of average individual prosperity in any country — remembering that the average of $99 and $1 is the same as the average of $51 and $49! Figures for GDP are not wholly reliable: different countries have different methods of compilation; some Third World figures may be too low because of the difficulty of calculating the value of a predominantly subsistence economy; in some countries there is an important "black economy" which does not feature in official returns. (See also GROSS NATIONAL PRODUCT)

The number of cars and telephones in use also suggests relative standards of material prosperity. Not surprisingly, the United States leads in all three categories. The number of cars is astonishing in view of the fact that about one-third of the US population are non-drivers, while the number of telephones exceeds the total population of those aged over 17.

These figures are of course affected by other factors. It is not surprising that cars are relatively much more numerous in Australia than in Japan; in Saudi Arabia, highly placed in terms of GDP per head, the figures for cars and telephones reveal a very different kind of society from that of Western Europe and North America.

Levels of development
Selected indicators for a range of countries showing the large disparities between the world's developed and developing nations. It should be remembered that while these figures indicate the average national level of development, inequalities within countries may be as great as those between different nation states. All too often the privileged few enjoy a standard of living far above that of the less well-off masses.

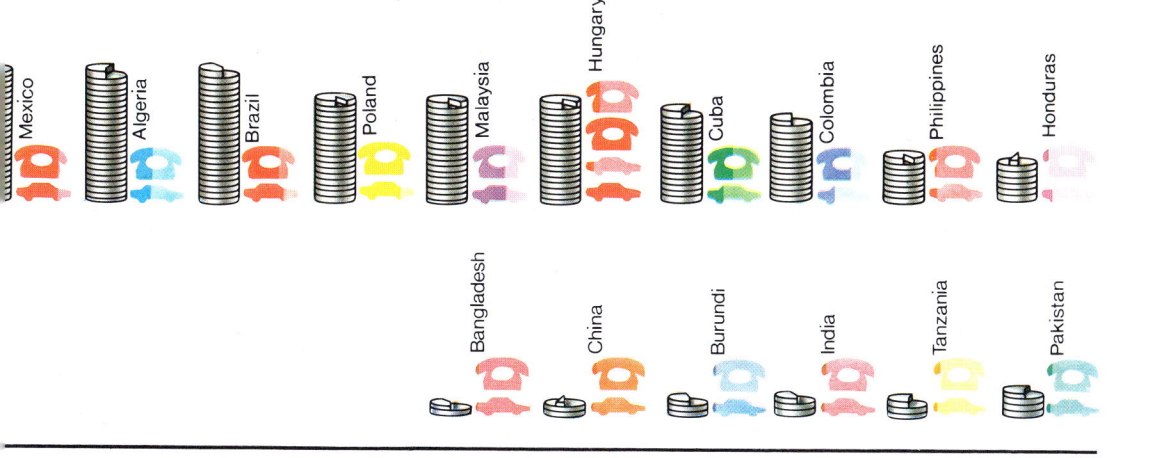

GOVERNMENTS IN POWER

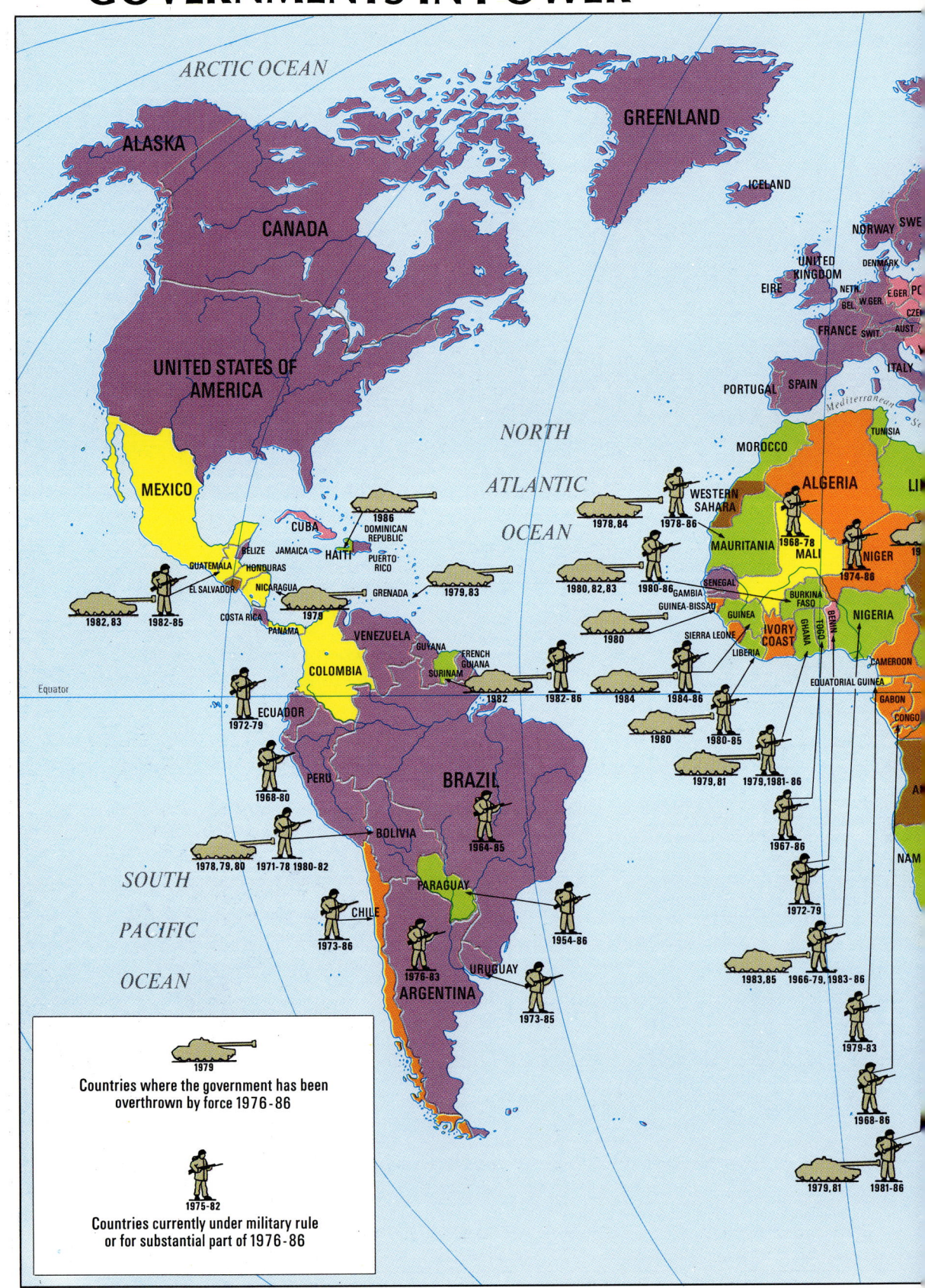

Legend

- **Communist states, elections but no free choice**
- **One party states, government largely autocratic**
- **Democratic elections with choice of parties**
- **Democratic elections & choice of parties but limitations favouring an elite**
- **Autocratic governments with or without some popular representation**
- **No government control over substantial area**

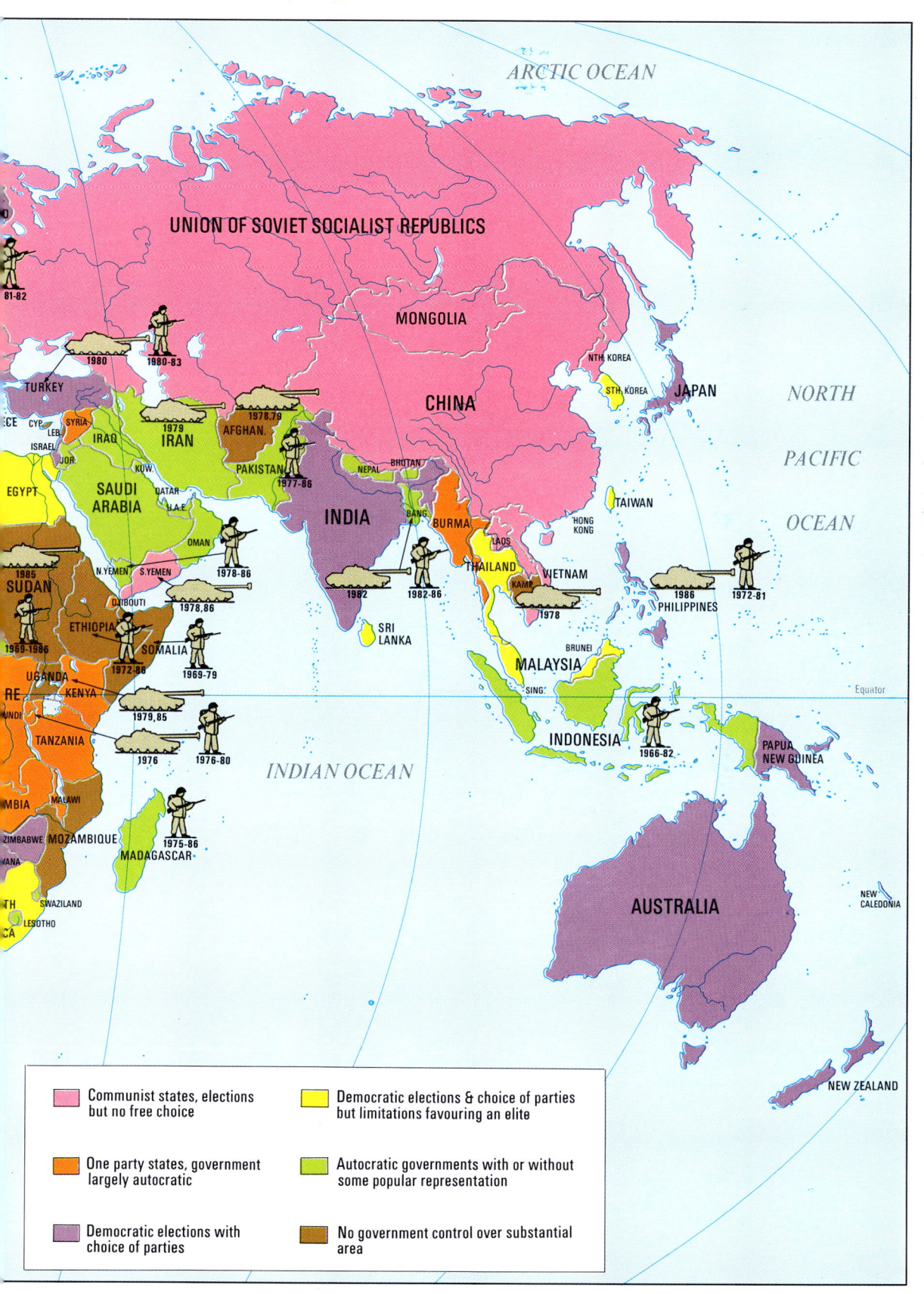

135

GOVERNMENTS IN POWER

All governments pay lip-service to certain principles, but most of them behave quite differently. It is unfortunately the case that the chief aim of governments is to stay in power, and while they may achieve this aim by good government, more often they do so by other means. To this extent governments, whatever their ideology or degree of popular consent, have much in common.

It is generally assumed in the West that the most desirable form of government is parliamentary democracy, with the government dependent on the freely given support of a majority of the voters, with a viable alternative offered by one or more other parties, and with civil rights such as freedom of speech upheld by an independent judiciary. The British bequeathed to their former colonies a form of government based closely on the Westminster model, complete with wigs, maces and paraphernalia, but the great majority of formerly British African countries have found this system inappropriate and have opted for one-party government. This is not in itself equivalent to a restriction of civil rights, though unfortunately that is a frequent corollary.

There is nothing sacred about Western-style democracy. It is a fairly recent development. Even in Britain, three generations ago half the adult population was excluded from the franchise. However, the principle of popular elections is almost universally acknowledged. With a few small exceptions, all governments either hold regular elections or provide some reason, such as national emergency, why they should be — temporarily — abandoned. In the majority of states, however, popular elections have little effect on the composition of the government as there is no choice of policies or, often, of candidates. Elections are merely a means of demonstrating popular approval of the status quo, whereas in Western-style democracies they may result in a change of government, albeit the change is usually somewhat limited in terms of practical policy.

Obviously, no two governments are exactly the same, and therfore any attempt to categorize the world's current political regimes must be a rough-and-ready exercise. No country other than South Africa, to take an extreme example, has a political system openly based on racial discrimination, but to create a separate category for every country demonstrating unique political aspects would reduce the whole attempt to

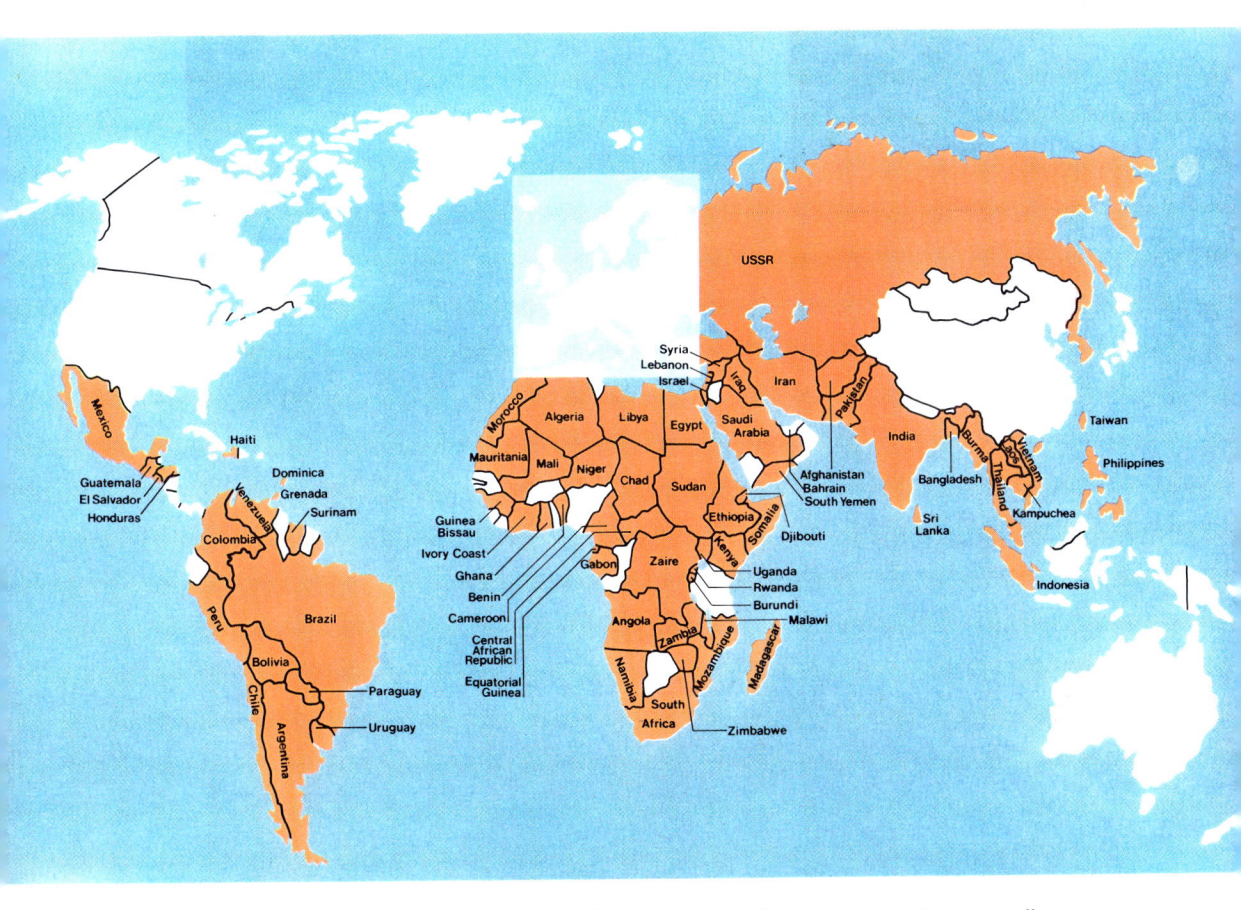

Human rights violations, 1980–86

Countries from which serious violations of human rights have been reported in the 1980s.

absurdity. Similarly, governments classed as autocratic are not all repressive, or at least, not repressive to the same degree.

The boundless hypocrisy of governments is harshly illustrated by the — inevitably incomplete — statistics on the employment of methods of oppression universally judged to be illegal, compiled by Amnesty International. The maps on these pages illustrate countries where mistreatment of prisoners, including secret execution and torture, was reported in 1980–86. It should be said that this map does not attempt to show the degree of mistreatment. There were, for example, no reported cases of physical torture of prisoners in countries such as the Soviet Union or Saudi Arabia, whereas in certain South American countries the murder of potentially troublesome citizens has been at times part of government policy. Also, some of the few countries which appear on the map in innocent white may owe it merely to the lack of reliable reports on violations of human rights within their borders.

ALLIANCES AND ASSOCIATIONS

ALLIANCES AND ASSOCIATIONS MEMBERSHIP

- European Economic Community
- European Free Trade Association
- Council for Mutual Economic Assistance (COMECON)
- Arab League
- Commonwealth
- Caricom
- Asean
- Organisation of American States
- North Atlantic Treaty Organisation
- Warsaw Treaty Organisation
- ANZUS
- Non members of major alliances

138

ARCTIC OCEAN
UNION OF SOVIET SOCIALIST REPUBLICS
MONGOLIA
CHINA
NTH. KOREA
STH. KOREA
JAPAN
NORTH
PACIFIC
OCEAN
TURKEY
CYP.
LEB.
SYRIA
ISRAEL
JOR.
IRAQ
IRAN
AFGHAN.
PAKISTAN
KUW.
QATAR
U.A.E.
SAUDI ARABIA
OMAN
EGYPT
N.YEMEN
S.YEMEN
SUDAN
DJIBOUTI
ETHIOPIA
SOMALIA
INDIA
NEPAL
BHUTAN
BANG.
BURMA
TAIWAN
HONG KONG
LAOS
THAILAND
KAMP.
VIETNAM
PHILIPPINES
SRI LANKA
BRUNEI
MALAYSIA
SING.
Equator
INDONESIA
PAPUA NEW GUINEA
UGANDA
KENYA
TANZANIA
INDIAN OCEAN
MALAWI
MBIA
ZIMBABWE
MOZAMBIQUE
MADAGASCAR
SWAZILAND
LESOTHO
AUSTRALIA
NEW CALEDONIA
NEW ZEALAND
CARIBBEAN COMMUNITY AND COMMON MARKET (CARICOM) MEMBERS
The Bahamas
Jamaica
Belize
St Kitts-Nevis
Antigua and Baruda
Montserrat
Dominica
St Lucia
St Vincent and the Grenadines
Barbados
Grenada
Trinidad and Tobago
Guyana

ALLIANCES AND ASSOCIATIONS

Nearly every independent country in the world belongs to the United Nations, founded in 1945. The UN provides a forum for international debate and its subsidiary organizations, such as the Food and Agriculture Organization (FAO), the UN Educational, Scientific and Cultural Organization (UNESCO) and the World Health Organization (WHO), are of great importance, especially in the Third World.

The main international military alliances reflect the situation created by the Second World War, which left two hostile "superpowers" dominating the world stage. The Warsaw Pact consists of the Soviet Union and its East European allies. The North Atlantic Treaty Organization (NATO) consists of the United States, Canada and most Western European nations. ANZUS (Australia, New Zealand, United States) plays a similar role in the Pacific region. Both superpowers also maintain a military presence in other, strategically located countries.

The major regional associations exist for a variety of purposes, economic, social and political. The European Economic Community (EEC) is potentially the largest economic unit in the world, with a larger "domestic" market than the United States, but political divisions plus certain economic factors make it inferior to the United States in terms of GNP. Some smaller Western European states are joined together in the European Free Trade Area (EFTA). The Warsaw Pact nations, together with certain other allies, or satellites, of the Soviet Union, are united in the Council for Mutual Economic Assistance (CMEA, better known as Comecon), which also includes Yugoslavia.

Other regional organizations include the Organization of American States (OAS), founded 1948 and for a long time dominated by the United States, though less so today; the Organization of African Unity (OAU), whose name has proved unduly optimistic; and the Association of South-East Asian Nations (ASEAN), founded 1967, which replaced the

The 59 non-sovereign territories of the world

 1 Midway Island (USA)
 2 Johnston and Sand Islands (USA)
 3 Tokelau (NZ)
 4 American Samoa
 5 Niue (NZ)
 6 Cook Islands (NZ)
 7 Cayman Islands (UK)
 8 Puerto Rico (USA)
 9 United States Virgin Islands
10 Netherlands Antilles
11 Monserrat (UK)
12 French Polynesia
13 Pitcairn Islands (UK)
14 Bermuda (UK)
15 Saint Pierre and Miquelon (France)
16 Turks and Caicos (UK)
17 British Virgin Islands
18 Anguilla (UK)
19 Guadeloupe (France)
20 Martinique (France)
21 French Guiana
22 Ascension (St Helena dependency)
23 St Helena (UK)
24 Tristan da Cunha (St Helena dependency)
25 Falkland Islands including South Georgia and South Sandwich Islands (UK)
26 Greenland (Kalaatllit Nunaat) (Denmark)
27 Svalbard and Jan Mayen Islands (Norway)
28 Faeroe Islands (Denmark)

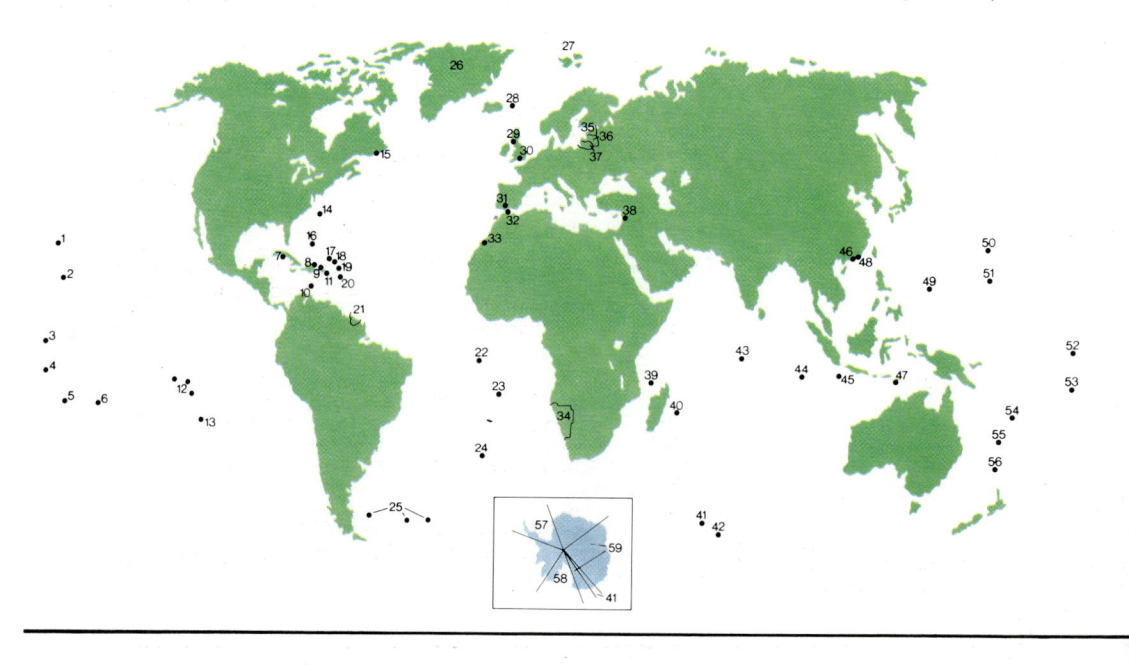

140

29 Isle of Man (UK)
30 Channel Islands (UK)
31 Gibraltar, City of (UK)
32 Spanish North Africa ((*de facto*)
33 Western Sahara (*de jure*) (*de facto*, Morocco)
34 Namibia (UN Trust Territory, *de facto* South Africa)
35 *Estonia (*de facto* non-sovereign USSR)
36 *Latvia (*de facto* non-sovereign USSR)
37 *Lithuania (*de facto* non-sovereign USSR)
38 Gaza Strip (*de jure*)
39 Mayotte (*de facto* Comoros)
40 Réunion (France)
41 French Southern and Antarctic Territories
42 Territory of Heard and McDonald Islands (Aust)
43 British Indian Ocean Territory
44 Cocos (Keeling) Islands (Aust)
45 Christmas Island (Aust)
46 Macao (Portugal)
47 East Timor (*de jure*) (*de facto* Indonesia)
48 Hong Kong (UK)
49 Guam (USA)
50 Wake Island (USA)
51 Pacific Islands
52 Canton and Endebury Island
53 Wallis and Futuna Islands (France)
54 Coral Sea Islands (Aust)
55 New Caledonia (France)
56 Norfolk Island (Aust)
57 British Antarctic Territory
58 Ross Dependency (NZ)
59 Australian Antarctica Territory

* Incorporation into USSR (June 1940) not internationally recognized.

OPEC

OPEC members
Algeria, Ecuador, Gabon, Indonesia, Iran, Iraq, Kuwait, Libya, Nigeria, Qatar, Saudi Arabia, UAE, Venezuela.

United States-dominated South-East Asia Treaty Organization. Such organizations have generally had little influence on the policy of member-states, though they have had occasional political successes. For example, ASEAN successfully resisted the appropriation of Kampuchea's UN seat by the puppet regime set up by the Vietnamese.

In other parts of the world numerous efforts have been made to achieve a degree of regional economic unification. The Latin America Integration Association (LAIA), founded 1980, is the latest of several such efforts in that region. The Caribbean Community (CARICOM), of former British colonies, was strengthened by the overthrow of a disruptive Marxist regime in Grenada, one of its members.

One form of international economic co-operation widely regarded as desirable, though difficult to achieve, is the association of producers of particular commodities. The one effective body of this kind has been the Organization of Petroleum Exporting Countries (OPEC), which succeeded in raising the world price of oil in the 1970s but at the cost of world recession and falling demand, which led to the virtual breakdown of OPEC's common policy in the 1980s.

The Arab League and the Commonwealth are examples of international associations which are largely cultural. The Arab League was formed in 1945 with, among its aims, co-ordination of policy among Arab states, but it has been more effective in less problematic areas. The Commonwealth, a distant echo of what was once the British Empire with the British monarch as its ceremonial head, preserves friendly contacts among countries sharing a British colonial heritage and endeavours to achieve a common policy on international issues of common concern.

Institutions of the UN

1 *General Assembly*. Main deliberative assembly. Equal representation for all members

2 *Security Council*. Concerned with international peace and security. Five permanent members (China, France, UK, USA, USSR) Ten additional members each elected for 2 years on a regional basis

3 *Economic & Social Council*. Responsible for UN functions regarding economic, social, cultural, health and other matters. 54 members, elected by percentage majority of General Assembly. Various economic/social commissions, standing committees

4 *Trusteeship Council*. Responsible for safeguarding the interests of non-selfgoverning territories' inhabitants, under Security Council

5 *International Court of Justice*. Members elected by General Assembly and Security Council

6 *Secretariat*. The Secretary-General & administrative staff.
About 17 independent agencies (IAEA, ILO, FAO, UNESCO, WHO, IMF etc.).
About 14 major programmes devoted to economic/social progress in the Third World.

Sovereign states which are non-members of UN:
Taiwan (China), Switzerland, Korea (North and South), plus various very small states

NATIONS IN TURMOIL

FREEDOM FIGHTERS/REVOLUTIONARIES CURRENTLY ACTIVE (1976–86)
1. Mujahaddin
2. UNITA
3. Fighting Communist Cells (CCC)
4. Karens
5. M-19 (April 19 Movement)
6. Left wingers (Farabundo Marti Liberation Front)
7. Eritrean People's Liberation Front (EPLF)
8. Action Directe/Corsican National Liberation Front
9. Sikhs [Punjab]
10. Free Papua Movement (OPM) [Irian Jaya]
11. PLO and other Arab groups
12. Khmer Rouge
13. Mozambique National Resistance Movement (MNRM)
14. Southwest African People's Organisation (SWAPO)
15. Contras (FDN and ARDE)
16. Sendero Luminoso
17. Communist and Muslim guerrilla groups
18. Somali National Movement (SNM)
19. ETA (Basque Separatists)
20. Tamil Separatists
21. Sudan People's Liberation Army (SPLA) [Southern Regions]
22. Irish Republican Army (IRA)
23. Polisario Front
24. African National Congress (ANC)

COUNTRIES OCCUPIED BY FOREIGN MILITARY PRESENCE (1976–86)
1. USSR 1979-86
2. Libya (N.Chad) since 1973
3. USA 1983
4. E. Timor 1975-86
5. Vietnam 1979-86
6. Israel 1982-86
7. S. Africa 1975-86
8. Morocco 1975-86

Casualties from Wars and Conflicts since 1945
- 1,000 to 10,000
- 10,000 to 100,000
- 100,000 to 1 million
- more than 1 million
- no data or less than 1,000

WARS WITH OTHER COUNTRIES (1976–86)
1. UK (Falklands) 1982
2. Iran 1980-86
3. Iraq 1980-86
4. Vietnam 1978-79
5. Syria 1976
6. W. Sahara 1975-86
7. S. Africa 1975-86
8. Lebanon 1976
9. Uganda 1979
10. Tanzania 1979
11. Kampuchea 1978-79
12. Morocco 1975-86

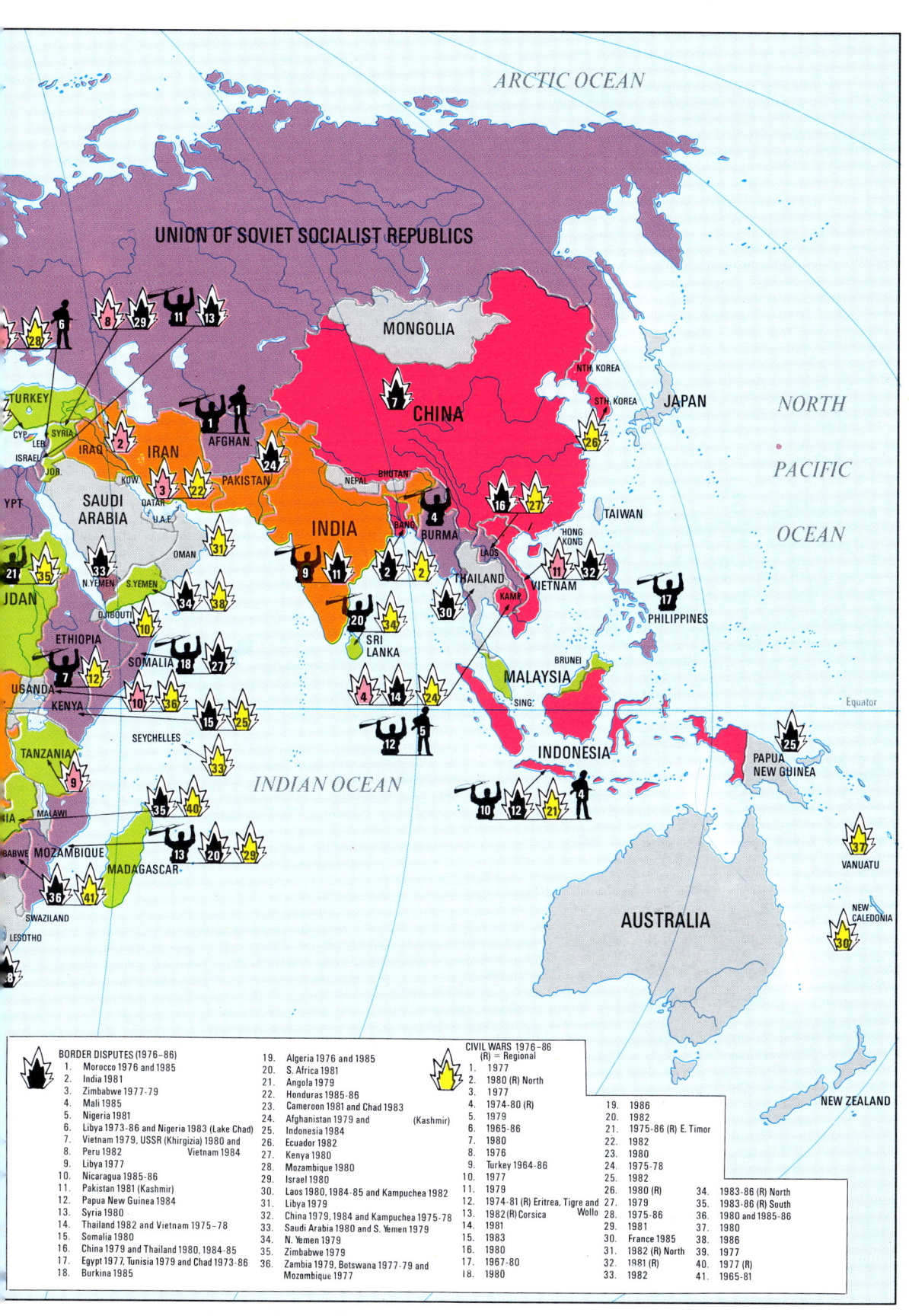

	BORDER DISPUTES (1976–86)			CIVIL WARS 1976–86		
	1. Morocco 1976 and 1985	19. Algeria 1976 and 1985		(R) = Regional		
	2. India 1981	20. S. Africa 1981		1. 1977		
	3. Zimbabwe 1977–79	21. Angola 1979		2. 1980 (R) North		
	4. Mali 1985	22. Honduras 1985–86		3. 1977		
	5. Nigeria 1981	23. Cameroon 1981 and Chad 1983		4. 1974–80 (R)	19. 1986	
	6. Libya 1973–86 and Nigeria 1983 (Lake Chad)	24. Afghanistan 1979 and (Kashmir)		5. 1979	20. 1982	
	7. Vietnam 1979, USSR (Khirgizia) 1980 and Vietnam 1984	25. Indonesia 1984		6. 1965–86	21. 1975–86 (R) E. Timor	
	8. Peru 1982	26. Ecuador 1982		7. 1980	22. 1982	
	9. Libya 1977	27. Kenya 1980		8. 1976	23. 1980	
	10. Nicaragua 1985–86	28. Mozambique 1980		9. Turkey 1964–86	24. 1975–78	
	11. Pakistan 1981 (Kashmir)	29. Israel 1980		10. 1977	25. 1982	
	12. Papua New Guinea 1984	30. Laos 1980, 1984–85 and Kampuchea 1982		11. 1979	26. 1980 (R)	
	13. Syria 1980	31. Libya 1979		12. 1974–81 (R) Eritrea, Tigre and Wollo	27. 1979	34. 1983–86 (R) North
	14. Thailand 1982 and Vietnam 1975–78	32. China 1979, 1984 and Kampuchea 1975–78		13. 1982 (R) Corsica	28. 1975–86	35. 1983–86 (R) South
	15. Somalia 1980	33. Saudi Arabia 1980 and S. Yemen 1979		14. 1981	29. 1981	36. 1980 and 1985–86
	16. China 1979 and Thailand 1980, 1984–85	34. N. Yemen 1979		15. 1983	30. France 1985	37. 1980
	17. Egypt 1977, Tunisia 1979 and Chad 1973–86	35. Zimbabwe 1979		16. 1980	31. 1982 (R) North	38. 1986
	18. Burkina 1985	36. Zambia 1979, Botswana 1977–79 and Mozambique 1977		17. 1967–80	32. 1981 (R)	39. 1977
				18. 1980	33. 1982	40. 1977 (R)
						41. 1965–81

143

NATIONS IN TURMOIL

Conflict appears to be inevitable in human society, and in the modern world conflicts are increasing. Since 1945 many more people have been killed by bombs and bullets than the total military casualties of the Second World War. Although full-scale war among the major powers has been avoided, so-called "limited" wars have burgeoned. If war is defined as a conflict involving the participation of regular armed forces, there have been over 150 wars, mostly in the Third World, since 1945, and their incidence is increasing. In the 1950s the average was about nine outbreaks a year; in the 1970s it was about 14. The map shows armed conflicts in the period 1976–86, divided into wars, border disputes and civil wars.

Whatever the underlying economic and social causes, the immediate motive for most outbreaks is political. More than half the armed conflicts since 1945 have originated in attempts to overthrow a current government. In the modern world, however, even civil wars cannot be fought in isolation. The interests of the superpowers run everywhere.

Or nearly everywhere. Civil conflicts tend to receive news coverage in the western world in proportion to their effect, actual or potential, on the interests of the United States and the Soviet Union and their allies. In terms of civilian deaths — and nowadays they usually exceed military casualties — probably the bloodiest episode since 1945 was not the Korean nor the Vietnam war (in which total casualties, military and civilian, were about 1,350,000) but the massacre of alleged Communists

United Nations peace-keeping forces

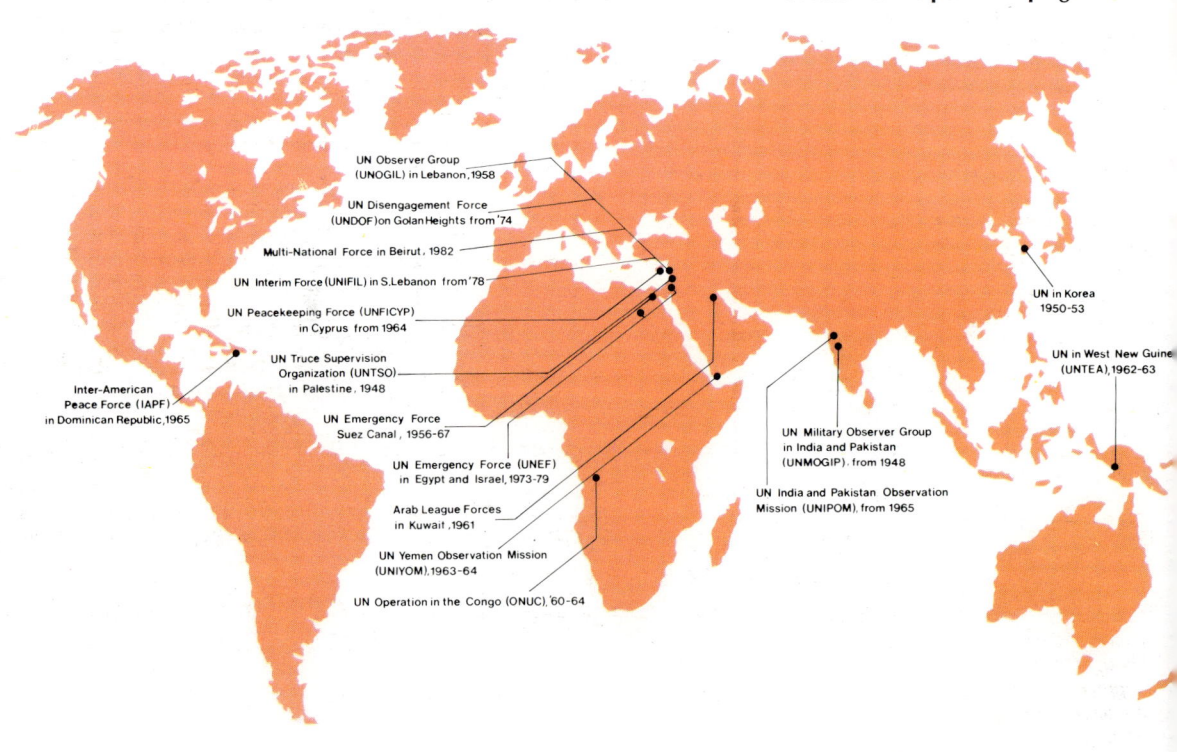

- UN Observer Group (UNOGIL) in Lebanon, 1958
- UN Disengagement Force (UNDOF) on Golan Heights from '74
- Multi-National Force in Beirut, 1982
- UN Interim Force (UNIFIL) in S.Lebanon from '78
- UN Peacekeeping Force (UNFICYP) in Cyprus from 1964
- UN Truce Supervision Organization (UNTSO) in Palestine, 1948
- Inter-American Peace Force (IAPF) in Dominican Republic, 1965
- UN Emergency Force Suez Canal, 1956-67
- UN Emergency Force (UNEF) in Egypt and Israel, 1973-79
- Arab League Forces in Kuwait, 1961
- UN Yemen Observation Mission (UNIYOM), 1963-64
- UN Operation in the Congo (ONUC), '60-64
- UN Military Observer Group in India and Pakistan (UNMOGIP), from 1948
- UN India and Pakistan Observation Mission (UNIPOM), from 1965
- UN in Korea 1950-53
- UN in West New Guinea (UNTEA), 1962-63

Hijacks
During the period 1980–86 there were 83 aircraft hijacks on domestic and international flights throughout the world, an average of one each month. The most affected airlines and the airports most often involved in terrorist embarkation in the 1980s are shown.

Totals (1980–86)		Airlines most affected		Airports most affected	
Domestic	60	LOT (Poland)	8	Miami	12
International	23	Eastern (US)	6	Teheran	4
		Delta (US)	6	Athens	3
		Iran Air	6	Atlanta	2
		Air Florida	5	Karachi	2
		Venezuelan	5	Frankfurt	2
		Aeroflot	4	Puerto Rico	2

and others, largely Chinese, in Indonesia in the 1960s. Yet it was only cursorily reported in the Western press.

The number of deaths in the anti-Communist operation, over one million according to estimates, cannot be known, nor can the number of Timorese who have died resisting the military government in the same country in the intervening period (probably about 100,000 — one in seven of the population). Thus the figures on which the map is based can only be approximate. True figures would in many cases be higher.

The main motive for the creation of the United Nations was to prevent international conflict. Its success in that role has been perhaps less negligible than is generally assumed, though it has frequently proved ineffective. UN peacekeeping forces have performed a thankless role in many of the world's troublespots (see below left), but without their presence civilian casualties would surely have been higher.

For the rich nations in particular, international terrorism has become a more immediate threat than international conflict: in the modern world the solitary saboteur can create immense damage. Since the 1960s the hijacking of civil aircraft has proved an attractive terrorist enterprise, aircraft being particularly vulnerable targets (see above).

State-sponsored terrorism
It is difficult to obtain an objective view of such acts: the independent observer is subject to conflicting information, disinformation and propaganda. One country's terrorism is often another country's legitimate action.

Many if not most acts of terrorism are sponsored, directly or indirectly, by governments, though the evidence may be concealed. In some cases, however, governments have made no bones about encouraging, or committing, terrorist acts against others (see below).

South Africa	Airstrike against suspected ANC bases, Mozambique	May 1983
Libya	Shooting from Libyan Embassy, London, UK	April 1984
South Africa	Raid on suspected ANC base, Gaborone, Botswana	June 1985
France	Blowing up "Rainbow Warrior" Greenpeace ship, Auckland, NZ	July 1985
South Africa	Raid on suspected SWAPO bases, Angola	September 1985
Libya	Bomb explosion in disco, Berlin, West Germany	April 1986
South Africa	Raids on suspected ANC bases Botswana, Zambia, Zimbabwe	May 1986

MILITARY EXPENDITURE

MILITARY EXPENDITURE
As percentage of GDP (1984)

- less than 1%
- 1-5%
- 5-10%
- 10-20%
- more than 20%
- no data

ACTUAL EXPENDITURE
Millions of US dollars (1984)

MILITARY EXPENDITURE

The huge amount spent on what governments prefer to call defence is a reproach to common sense. Reformers and others are fond of making odious comparisons: the world's annual military budget would fund all UN health and welfare programmes for a couple of centuries; Ethiopia maintains more than a hundred times as many soldiers as medical personnel; over one-third of total Soviet government expenditure (according to non-Soviet sources) is devoted to the military; the United States spends over $1,000 a year on each citizen to protect them from outside enemies, yet many of them dare not walk the streets at night.

It is difficult to arrive at reliable figures for military expenditure as there are many variables and governments are disinclined to report fully or accurately on this subject. Scientific research is one grey area: apparently innocent research often turns out to have military applications. The arms trade is another. Much of it is illicit: Iran, for example, has trouble finding national suppliers for its Gulf War weapons, but manages to get them all the same. With the possible exception of oil, the weapons industry is the world's largest business.

Governments spend as much on the military as they can afford, but their criteria for making that decision vary enormously. The Soviet government appears to have reached the conclusion that its vast burden of military expenditure cannot be sustained, hence its current interest in international disarmament. The map gives figures for total military expenditure and also expresses them as a proportion of Gross Domestic Product (equivalent to GNP less product originating abroad), a more meaningful comparison.

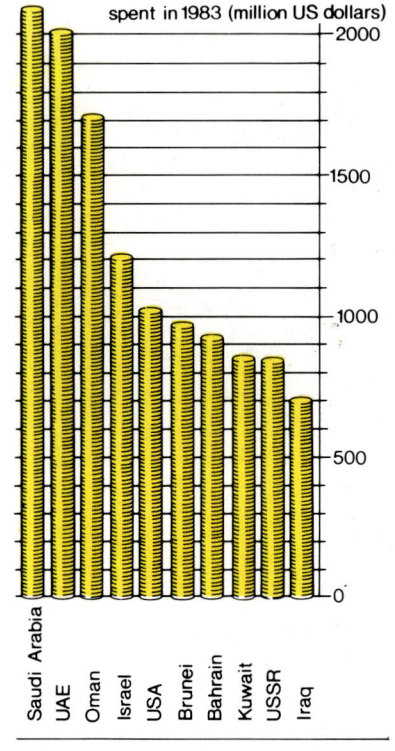

Major military spenders per capita

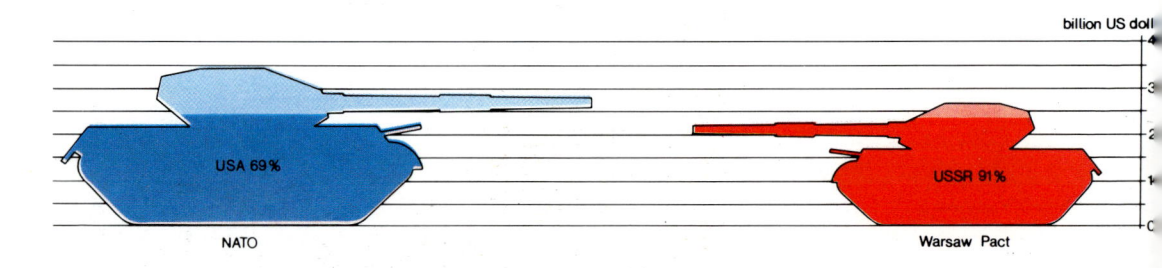

The ten highest per capita spenders (see above) are, with the exception of the two superpowers and Brunei, a small but rich oil state, all Middle Eastern countries. Except for Israel, they are not in fact the states most heavily involved in war in the recent era. Iraq only just gets on to the list; Iran and the "front-line" Arab states do not. Saudi Arabia's position may be explained by a combination of factors: a small population for a large area, ample cash and an antique regime fearful of revolutionary neighbours.

Six Arab countries plus Iran also appear among the ten largest arms importers (See right).

NATO v Warsaw Pact

Comparative military expenditure in 1983. The tank size represents total spending by NATO and the Warsaw Pact. The United States and the Soviet Union spent roughly equal amounts, but the Warsaw Pact relies more heavily on the USSR's military budget, whilst the USA's proportion of NATO spending is smaller.

The major exporters of weapons are the Soviet Union and the United States (see left). Among other industrialized countries who do particularly well out of this business are France and Italy (where restrictions on arms sales are relatively flexible). Among importers, the Middle Eastern countries are collectively the biggest buyers in terms of both population and area. That is not surprising, but the Third World in general is playing an increasing part in the arms trade. In the decade ending in 1985, the Third World's share of total world military spending almost doubled.

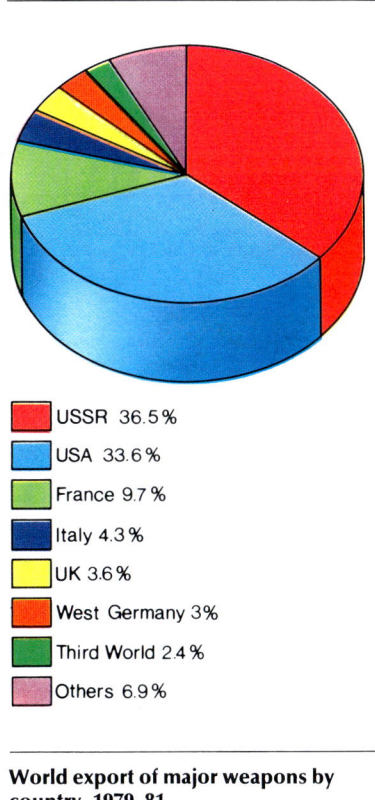

- USSR 36.5%
- USA 33.6%
- France 9.7%
- Italy 4.3%
- UK 3.6%
- West Germany 3%
- Third World 2.4%
- Others 6.9%

World export of major weapons by country, 1979–81

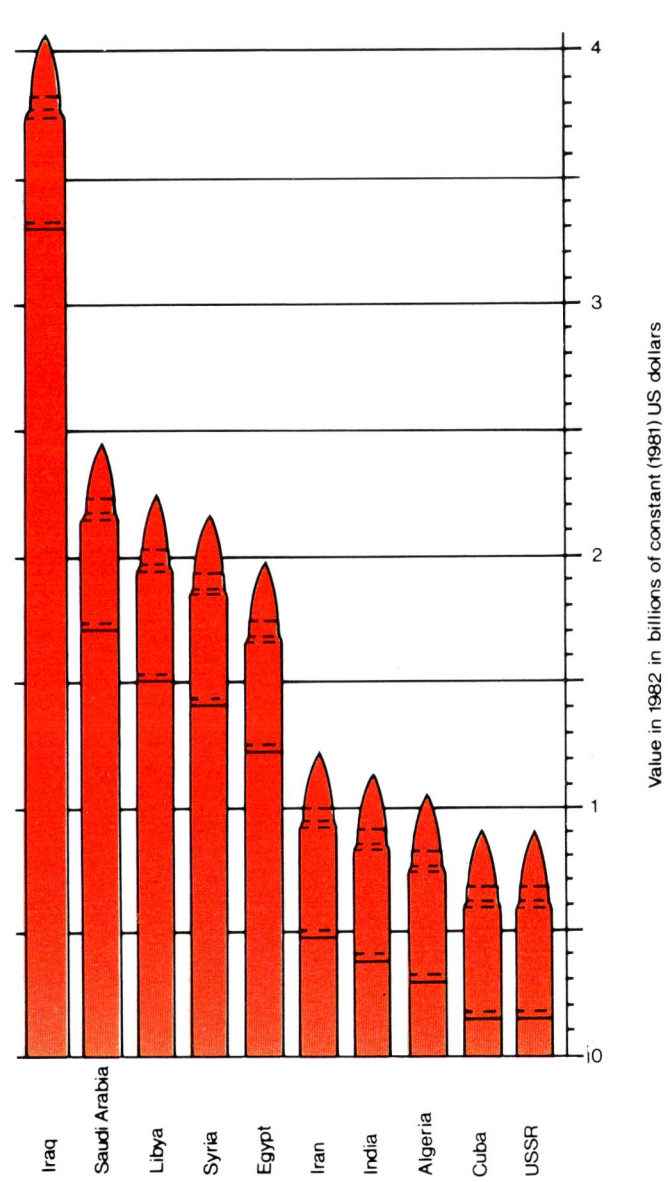

Major world arms importers

Value in 1982 in billions of constant (1981) US dollars

Iraq, Saudi Arabia, Libya, Syria, Egypt, Iran, India, Algeria, Cuba, USSR

149

MILITARY MIGHT

COMPARATIVE STRATEGIC NUCLEAR STRENGTHS
Launchers/warheads (1985)

STRATEGIC MISSILES

- Submarine-launched ballistic missiles (SLBMs)
- Land-based inter-continental ballistic missiles (ICBMs)

Figures shown on map:

- Canada: 83
- United States of America: 2,152; 616/5,536 (SLBM); 1,018/2,118 (ICBM)
- Mexico: 129
- Guatemala: 42
- Honduras: 17
- Nicaragua: 63
- Cuba: 162
- Venezuela: 49
- Colombia: 66
- Peru: 128
- Bolivia: 28
- Chile: 101
- Argentina: 108
- Uruguay: 32
- Brazil: 276
- Iceland: 106
- United Kingdom: 327; 64/192 (SLBM)
- Norway: 37
- Sweden: 66
- Denmark: 50
- France: 464; 80/80 (SLBM)
- Portugal: 320
- Spain: 385
- Italy: 170
- Tunisia: 73
- Algeria: 170
- Nigeria: 94
- Cameroon: 12
- Gabon: 48
- Angola: 50
- Namibia: 3
- (other): 106
- (Europe labels): 478 (W.GER area)

150

MILITARY PERSONNEL
Per thousand population (1985)

- less than 5
- 5 - 9.9
- 10 - 14.9
- 15 - 19.9
- more than 20
- no data

ACTUAL NUMBER OF MILITARY PERSONNEL
Thousands (1985)

MILITARY MIGHT

The results of the massive expenditure detailed in the previous section are awesome. Of all the remarkable scientific and technological advances made in the past generation, nothing exceeds the power of destruction. A single Trident submarine carries eight times as much firepower as was expended during the whole of the Second World War. At the touch of a button or two, all life on earth could be permanently extinguished in a matter of hours. There's progress for you!

The vast majority of the world's nuclear weapons belong to the two superpowers, the United States and the Soviet Union, although some of them are located on the territory of their allies in, respectively, NATO and the Warsaw Pact. A number of other countries possess their own nuclear weapons and, given the destructive potential of even a single nuclear explosion, the relatively small number of these weapons is small comfort. Moreover, membership of the "nuclear club" is growing.

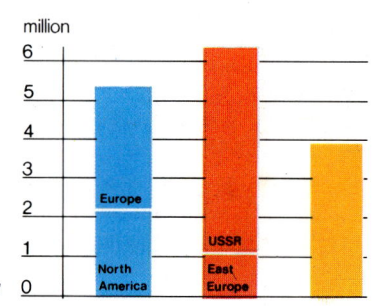

Military manpower

Production of nuclear weapons is imminent in at least a dozen "non-nuclear" states, including both participants in the Gulf War, in which poison gas has already been used. One or two states, such as Israel and South Africa, may already possess such weapons. Many others have the capacity to produce them and in a different political climate would presumably do so. It is quite easy to make a nuclear bomb. Delivery systems are another matter. The number of existing warheads is much greater than the number of launch vehicles — figures for both appear on the map — and recent research has concentrated on means of delivery rather than actual explosives. Claims that an ICBM can be directed on to a single building 4,000 miles away might or might not prove justified; what matters is that they are believed.

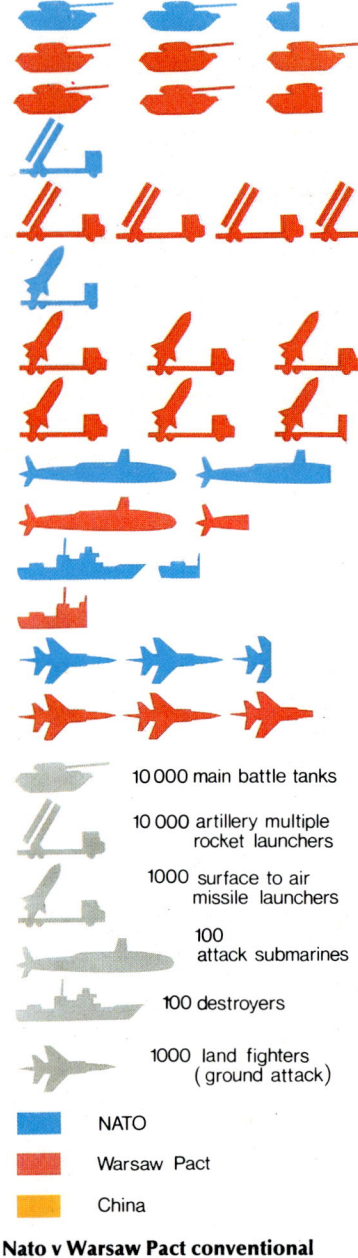

10 000 main battle tanks
10 000 artillery multiple rocket launchers
1000 surface to air missile launchers
100 attack submarines
100 destroyers
1000 land fighters (ground attack)

NATO
Warsaw Pact
China

Nato v Warsaw Pact conventional forces

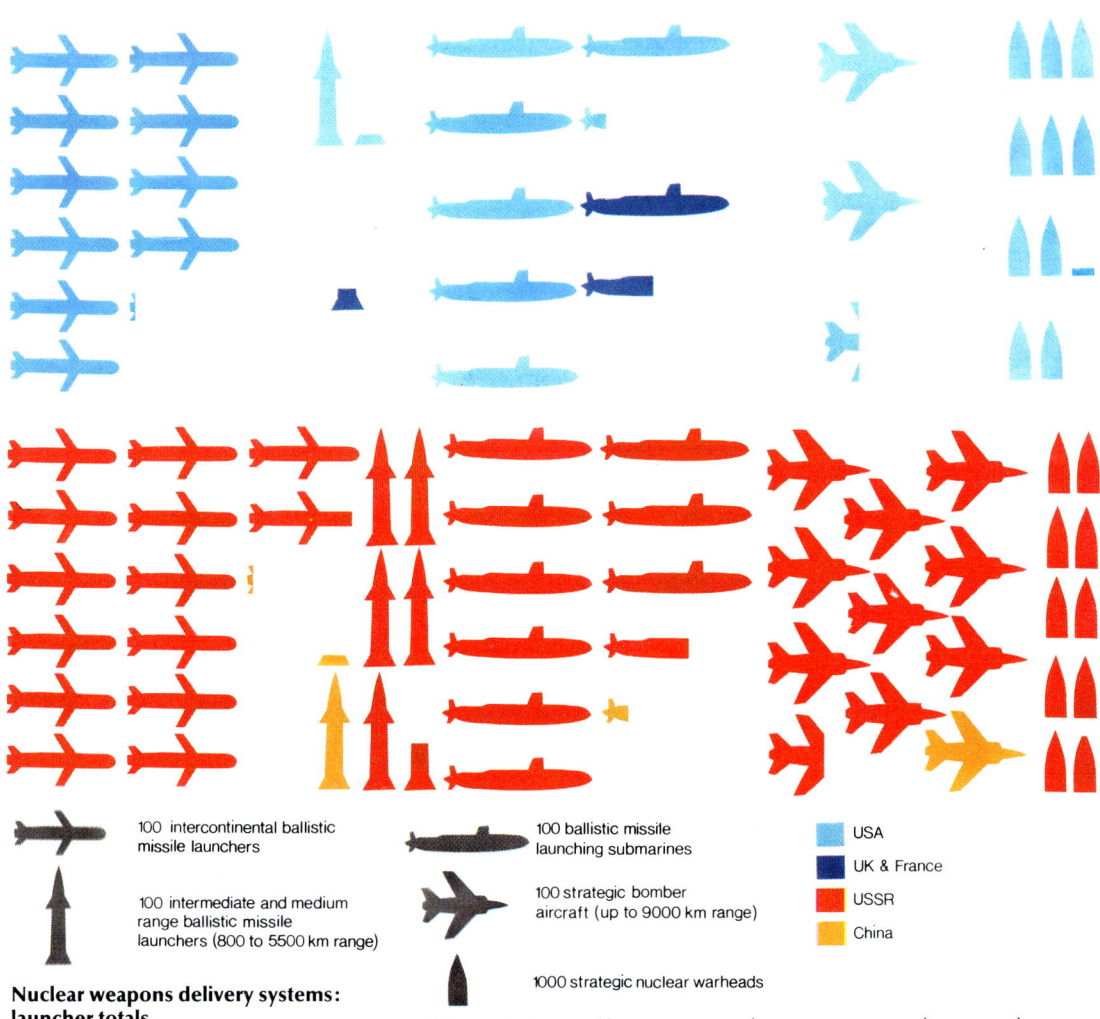

Nuclear weapons delivery systems: launcher totals

- 100 intercontinental ballistic missile launchers
- 100 intermediate and medium range ballistic missile launchers (800 to 5500 km range)
- 100 ballistic missile launching submarines
- 100 strategic bomber aircraft (up to 9000 km range)
- 1000 strategic nuclear warheads

- USA
- UK & France
- USSR
- China

The main types of long-range nuclear weapons are shown on the map. Aircraft-launched, Intermediate and Medium Range missiles are shown above. The possible future role of space satellites cannot yet be estimated; at present their capacity to detect what is going on has a valuable deterrent effect.

Deterrence has worked so far, since 1945, notwithstanding world leaders who publicly parade their countries' might, and although wars are frequent, they have so far been fought by "conventional" forces. The map shows the proportion of the population employed in the armed forces for virtually every country and gives the actual numbers of military personnel for the majority.

SOURCES

Nations of the World
Map & Diagrams: *Whitaker's Almanack* (1986). World Bank. United Nations

Shape of the Land
Map: Engineering Surveys Reproduction Limited
Diagrams: Kurian, G.T. *World Data*, World Almanac Publications (1983)

World Vegetation
Map: Engineering Surveys Reproduction Limited
Diagrams: FAO & UNESCO Desertification Map of the World (1977) UNEP General Assessment of Progress in the Implementation of the Plan of Action to Combat Desertification (1984). Goudie, A.S. *The Human Impact*, Basil Blackwell (1986)

World Climate
Maps: Engineering Surveys Reproduction Limited
Diagrams: *World Survey of Climatology*, Elsevier (various volumes)

Environment
Map: World Wildlife Fund. Wildlife Trade Monitoring Unit of the International Union for Conservation of Nature and Natural Resources.
Diagrams: World Wildlife Fund. International Maritime Organisation. Goudie, A.S. *The Human Impact*, Basil Blackwell (1986). Gribbin, J. *Climatic Change*, CUP (1978)

Population Density
Map: UN population division of Department of International Economic and Social Affairs.
Diagrams: *World Bank Atlas* (1986. *UN World Statistics in Brief* (1985). UN demographic estimates and projections assessed in 1982

World Population Growth
Map: UN population division of Department of International Economic and Social Affairs. UN High Commissioner for Refugees
Diagrams: *UN Population and Vital Statistics Report* (1985). *UN Demographic Yearbook* (1983)

Gross National Product
Map: *World Bank Atlas* (1986). *UNESCO Statistical Digest* (1985)
Diagram: *World Bank Atlas* (1986

GNP Growth Rate
Map: *World Bank Atlas* (1986
Diagram: *World Bank Atlas* (1986)

Religions of the World
Map: *The Europa Year Book* (1980)
Diagrams: *Information Please Almanac*, Houghton Mifflin (1986). Ministry of Labour, *Atlas of Israel*, Elsevier (1970)

Languages of the World
Map: *The Europa Year Book* (1980)
Diagram: *Guinness Book of Answers* (1985)

World Food Production
Map: *Whitaker's Almanack* (1986). *Philips' Certificate Atlas* (1984)
Diagrams: *The State of Food and Agriculture*, FAO (1984)

World Grain Trade
Map: *FAO Production Yearbook* (1984)
Diagrams: *FAO Trade Yearbooks* (1974 and 1984). *FAO Production Yearbook* (1984)

World Food Consumption
Map: *FAO Production Yearbook* (1985). *The State of Food and Agriculture*, FAO (1985)
Diagrams: N. Middleton and N. Grant. *The State of Food and Agriculture*, FAO (1985)

World Health
Map: *UN World Statistics in Brief* (1985)
Diagrams: *UN World Statistics in Brief* (1985). UN Statistical Yearbook (1982)

World Disease
Maps: Howe, G.M. (ed) *A World Geography of Human Diseases*, Academic Press (1977). *Monthly Index of Medical Specialities* (June 1986). *The Geographical Magazine* (October 1986). Warren, K.S. & Mahmoud, A.A.F. (eds) *Tropical and Geographical Medicine*, McGraw-Hill (1984)
Diagrams: *WHO World Health Statistics* (1985). Worldwatch Paper 59 (1984) WHO International AIDS Conference, Paris (June 1986). House of Lords debate (14 October 1986) *The Times* (27 October 1986)

Foreign Aid
Map: *The World in Figures*, The Economist (1984). *Twenty-five years of Development Co-operation, a review*, OECD (1985)
Diagrams: *Twenty-five years of Development Co-operation, a review*, OECD (1985). OECD Press Release (18 June 1986)

Mineral Wealth
Map: US Bureau of Mines
Diagrams: *Minerals Yearbook* (1984). *The World in Figures*, The Economist (1984)

World Tourism
Map: *UN World Statistics in Brief* (1985). *The World in Figures*, The Economist (1984)
Diagrams: *Tourism Policy and International Tourism*, OECD (1985)

World Energy Production
Map: *UN World Energy Statistics Yearbook* (1983)
Diagrams: *UN World Energy Statistics Yearbook* (1983)

World Energy Consumption
Map: *UN World Energy Statistics Yearbook* (1983)
Diagrams: *UN World Energy Statistics Yearbooks* (1970–83)

World Manufacturing
Map: *UN World Statistics in Brief* (1985). *UN Industrial Statistics Yearbook* (1983). *UN Monthly Bulletin of Statistics*. *NIESR Quarterly Bulletin*.
Diagrams: *UN Monthly Bulletin of Statistics* (June 1986). *Fortune Magazine* (4 August 1986).

International Trade
Map: *UN World Statistics in Brief* (1985). *UNCTAD Handbook of International Trade and Development Statistics* (1983).
Diagrams: *Statistical Abstract of the United States*, US Bureau of Census (1985). *Fortune Magazine* (4 August 1986).

Foreign Investment
Map: *International Financial Statistics* (May 1986). World Bank (1986). *Fortune Magazine* (4 August 1986).
Diagrams: World Bank (1986). *World Bank Atlas* (1986). *Fortune Magazine* (4 August 1986).

Exchange Rates
Map: *UN Monthly Bulletin of Statistics* (March 1985)
Diagrams: *World Outlook 1986*, Economist Intelligence Unit. *International Financial Statistics* (1986)

World Road and Rail Transport
Map: *UN World Statistics in Brief* (1985). *The World in Figures*, The Economist (1984).
Diagrams: *UN Monthly Bulletin of Statistics* (1985)

World Air and Sea Transport
Map: *Annual Report of the International Civil Aviation Organisation* (1985). *Statistical Abstract of the United States*, US Bureau of Census (1985). *The World in Figures*, The Economist (1984).
Diagrams: *Statistical Abstract of the United States*, US Bureau of Census (1985)

World Communications
Map: *UN World Statistics in Brief* (1985). *UNESCO Statistical Digest* (1985).
Diagrams: *UN World Statistics in Brief* (1985). *Guinness Book of Answers* (1986).

Literacy and Learning
Map: *UNESCO Statistical Digest* (1985)
Diagrams: *UNESCO Statistical Digest* (1985)

World Development
Map: *UN World Statistics in Brief* (1985). UNESCO (1985).
Diagrams: *UN World Statistics in Brief* (1985)

Governments in Power
Map: N. Grant. *Whitaker's Almanack* (1986). *Keesing's Contemporary Archives* (1976–86).
Diagram: Amnesty International

Alliances and Associations
Map: *Whitaker's Almanack* (1986)
Diagram: United Nations

Nations in Turmoil
Map: Imperial War Museum. *Wars and Revolutions: a comprehensive list of conflicts, part 2,* Hoover Institution on War, Revolution and Peace. Carver, M. *War Since 1945*, Weidenfield & Nicholson (1980). Mydans, C. & Mydans, S. *The Violent Peace,* Atheneum. Leger Sivard, R. *World Military and Social Expenditures* (1983). *Keesing's Contemporary Archives* (1976–86). Press reports.
Diagrams: Verrier, A. *International Peacekeeping,* Penguin (1981). *Keesing's Contemporary Archives* (1980–86). Press reports.

Military Expenditure
Map: *The Military Balance 1986–87,* International Institute for Strategic Studies (1986).
Diagrams: *The Military Balance 1985–86,* International Institute for Strategic Studies (1985).

Military Might
Map: *The Military Balance 1986–87,* International Institute for Strategic Studies (1986).
Diagrams: *The Military Balance 1985–86,* International Institute for Strategic Studies (1985)

INDEX

acid rain, 18, 19, 33
Africa: food shortages, 69
African epidemic, 77
agriculture, 60; map, 58–9
    exports, map 58–9
aid, economic, 80–1; map, 78–9
AIDS, 77
air transport, 120; map, 118–9
    cargo, 120–1; map, 118–9
    passengers, 120; map, 118–9
alliances and associations, 140–1; map, 138–9
arms, importers and exporters, 148–9

balance of payments, 105, 113; map, 102–3
birth control policy, 41
birth rates, 40–1
border disputes, map, 142–3
borrowers, 108
    countries in debt, 108; map, 106–7

cars, 116, 132–3
casualties from wars, map, 142–3
cereals: aid to Africa, 69
    production, map, 62–3
    stocks, 60
    yields, 64
cities, 132
    ranked by population, 36
civil wars, map, 142–3
climate, 28–9; maps, 20–7
    rainfall, 29; map 26–7
    temperatures, 28–9; maps, 22–5
    zones, 28–9; map, 20–1
coal, 92
    consumption, 96–7
    exporters and importers, 93
coldest places, 29
communications, 124–5; map 122–3
coniferous forests, 18
consumer price inflation rates, 112
continental drift, 14
countries: at war, map, 142–3
    in debt, 108; map, 106–7
    occupied by foreign military, map, 142–3
    ranked by GNP, 45
    ranked by population, 37
    under military rule, map, 134–5
currency: exchange rates, 112–3; map, 110–1
    movements, map, 110–1
cyclones, 29; maps, 22–3, 24–5

deaths: causes, 76–7
    infants, 72–3; map, 70–1
    rates, 40–1
defence expenditure, 148–9
desertified land, 18–19

developing countries, aid, 81
dietary requirements, 68–9; map, 66–7
disease, 76–7; map, 74–5
    infectious and parasitic diseases, 76; map, 74–5
disasters, natural, 15

earth's crust, 14
earthquakes, 14, 15; map, 12–13
economic aid, 80–1; map, 78–9
economic development, 132
education, 128–9; map 126–7
    expenditure, 129; map 126–7
    primary, 128; map, 126–7
endangered species, 32; map, 30–1
energy, 92–3, 96–7; maps, 90–1; 94–5
    consumption, 96–7; map, 94–5
    crisis, 92, 97
    production 92–3; map, 90–1
environment, 32–3; map, 30–1
European Economic Community, 140
European tourism, 88
exchange rates, 112–3; map, 110–1
exports, 104–5; map, 102–3
    agriculture, map, 58–9
    arms, 148–9
    coal, 93
    gas, 93
    grain, 65
    manufactured goods, 100
    oil, 93

famine, 69
fertilizers, consumption and imports, 60
fish: catch, 61
    grounds, 58–9
    production, 61
food: avoidance, 68
    consumption, 68–9; map, 66–7
    production, 60–1; map, 58–9
    shortages, 69
foreign aid, 80–1; map, 78–9
foreign investment, 108–9; map, 106–7
foreign visitors, 88–9
forests, 18–19
    coniferous, 18
    depletion rates, 19
    tropical, 18–19
freedom fighters/revolutionaries, map, 142–3

gas, 92
    consumption, 96–7
    exporters and importers, 93
geological changes, 14
gold, 85
    gold standard, 112
    price, 113
    producers, 84

governments in power, 136–7; map, 134–5
grain trade, 64–5; map, 62–3
    exports, 64–5; map, 62–3
    imports, 64–5; map, 62–3
greenhouse effect, 33
Gross Domestic Product, 132–3
Gross National Product, 44–5, 97; map, 42–3
    growth rate, 48–9; map 46–7

health, 72–3; map, 70–1
hijacks, 145
hottest places, 29
human rights violations, 137
hurricanes, 29

illiteracy, 128–9; map, 126–7
immigrant workers, 41
imports, 104–5; map, 102–3
    arms, 148–9
    coal, 93
    gas, 93
    grain, 65
    oil, 93
industry
    corporations, map, 106–7
    productivity, 97, map, 98–9
infant mortality rate, 72–3; map, 70–1
International Monetary Fund, 108, 113; map, 106–7
International trade, 104–5; map, 102–3
iron ore producers, 85
Islam, 53

Jews, 53; distribution, 53

labour costs, 100
land, 14–15; map, 12–13
    desertification, 18–19
    highest mountains, 14
    longest rivers, 15
    under cultivation, 60
    worst natural disasters, 15
languages, 56–7; map, 54–5
lenders, 108
life expectancy, 41, 72–3
literacy and learning *see* education

manufacturing, 100–1; map, 98–9
    goods exports, 100
    production growth rate, map, 98–9
    value, map, 98–9
Marxism, 53
Mediterranean, pollution of, 32, 33
merchant shipping fleets, 121

military: expenditure, 148–9; map, 146–7
    manpower, 152
    might, 152–3; map 150–1
    personnel, 153; map, 150–1
mineral wealth, 84–5; map, 82–3
    fossil fuels, 92–3; map, 90–1
    reserves, 85
monetary reserves, 108; map, 106–7
mountains, highest, 14

nations: map, 8–9
    capitals, 10–11
    dates of independence, map, 8–9
    in turmoil, 144–5; map, 142–3
    land area, 10–11
    population, 10–11
    trading blocks, map, 62–3
NATO v. Warsaw Pact
    conventional forces, 152
    military expenditure, 148
natural disasters, 15
newspapers, 125; map, 122–3
nuclear reactors, map, 90–1
nuclear weapons, 152–3; map, 150–1

OECD aid, 80–1
    currencies, 113
OPEC, 141
    aid, 81
    member countries, 141
    oil crisis, 92, 97
    oil production, 93
oil, 92–3
    consumption, 96–7
    crisis, 92, 97
    exporters and importers, 93
    major routes, map, 30–1
    pollution, 33
    tanker disasters, map, 30–1
overseas development aid, 80–1; map, 78–9

Pangaea, 14
plant life, 18
plates of the earth's crust, 14–15; map, 12–13
pollution in the Mediterranean, 32, 33
poorest countries, 45
population, map, 130–1
    by continent, 41
    by language, 56–7
    by religion, 52
    density, 36–7, map, 34–5
    growth, 40–1, map, 38–9
    rate of increase, 40–1; map, 38–9
printing and writing paper, 124
publishing, 128–9

radio broadcasting, 125
   sets, 125–6; map, 122–3
rail transport, 117; map, 114–5
   cargo, 116; 114–5
   passengers, 116; map, 114–5
rain forests, depletion rate, 19, 32
rainfall, 29; map, 26–27
refugees, 41; map, 38–9
religions, 52–3; map, 50–1
richest countries, 45
rivers, longest, 15
road transport, 116
   passenger vehicles in use, 116; map, 114–5

San Andreas fault, 14
sea transport, 120–1; map, 118–9
   cargo, 120–1; map, 118–9
steel producers, 101
sulphur emission, 33

telephones, 124–5, 132–3
television receivers, 124; map, 122–3
temperatures, 28–9; maps, 22–5
terrorism, 145
Third World, 132
   deaths, 77
   economic aid, 80
   food aid, 69
   manufacturing, 100
   military expenditure, 149
   minerals, 84
threatened species, 32; map, 30–1
tourism, 88–9; map, 86–7
   accommodation, 88
   spending, 89
trade, 104–5; map, 102–3
transport *see* air transport; rail transport; road transport; sea transport
tropical forests,
   depletion rate, 18–19

United Nations, 140
   peace-keeping forces, 144–5
uranium producers, 92
urban population, 37; map, 130–1

vegetation, 18–19; map, 16–17
   at risk, 18–19
volcanoes 14, 15; map, 12–13

wars, 144; map, 142–3
water supplies, 76
wildlife, threatened species, 32; map, 30–1

wind patterns, 29
   January, map, 22–23
   July, map, 24–25
World Bank, 108
world development, 132–3; map, 130–1